Churchill, Whitehall and the Soviet Union, 1940–45

Cold War History Series

General Editor: **Saki Dockrill**, Senior Lecturer in War Studies, King's College, London

The new Cold War History Series aims to make available to scholars and students the results of advanced research on the origins and the development of the Cold War and its impact on nations, alliances and regions at various levels of statecraft, and in areas such as diplomacy, security, economy, the military and society. Volumes in the series range from detailed and original specialised studies, proceedings of conferences, to broader and more comprehensive accounts. Each work deals with individual themes and periods of the Cold War and each author or editor approaches the Cold War with a variety of narrative, analysis, explanation, interpretation and reassessments of recent scholarship. These studies are designed to encourage investigation and debate on important themes and events in the Cold War, as seen from both East and West, in an effort to deepen our understanding of this phenomenon and place it in its context in world history.

Titles include:

Günter Bischof
AUSTRIA IN THE FIRST COLD WAR, 1945–55
The Leverage of the Weak

Martin H. Folly
CHURCHILL, WHITEHALL AND THE SOVIET UNION, 1940–45

Saul Kelly
COLD WAR IN THE DESERT
Britain, the United States and the Italian Colonies, 1945–52

Donette Murray
KENNEDY, MACMILLAN AND NUCLEAR WEAPONS

Cold War History
Series Standing Order ISBN 0–333–79482–6
(*outside North America only*)

You can receive future titles in this series as they are published by placing a standing order. Please contact your bookseller or, in case of difficulty, write to us at the address below with your name and address, the title of the series and the ISBN quoted above.

Customer Services Department, Macmillan Distribution Ltd, Houndmills, Basingstoke, Hampshire RG21 6XS, England

Churchill, Whitehall and the Soviet Union, 1940–45

Martin H. Folly
Lecturer in the Department of American Studies and History
Brunel University
London

First published in Great Britain 2000 by
MACMILLAN PRESS LTD
Houndmills, Basingstoke, Hampshire RG21 6XS and London
Companies and representatives throughout the world

A catalogue record for this book is available from the British Library.

ISBN 0–333–75446–8 hardcover

First published in the United States of America 2000 by
ST. MARTIN'S PRESS, INC.,
Scholarly and Reference Division,
175 Fifth Avenue, New York, N.Y. 10010

ISBN 0–312–23114–8

Library of Congress Cataloging-in-Publication Data
Folly, Martin H., 1957–
Churchill, Whitehall, and the Soviet Union, 1940–45 / Martin H. Folly.
p.   cm. — (Cold war history series)
Includes bibliographical references and index.
ISBN 0–312–23114–8 (cloth)
1. Great Britain—Foreign relations—Soviet Union. 2. Churchill, Winston, Sir,
1874–1965—Views on Soviet Union. 3. Soviet Union—Foreign relations—Great
Britain. 4. Great Britain—Foreign Relations—1936–1945. 5. Soviet Union—
Foreign relations—1917–1945. 6. Great Britain. Foreign Office. I. Cold war
history
DA47.65 .F65   2000
327.41047—dc21   99–055576

This book is printed on paper suitable for recycling and made from fully managed and sustained
forest sources.

10   9   8   7   6   5   4   3   2   1
09   08   07   06   05   04   03   02   01   00

Printed and bound in Great Britain by
Antony Rowe Ltd, Chippenham, Wiltshire

For Alan and Marjorie

Contents

Preface

This book arose originally out of an interest in explaining apparent British 'appeasement' of the Soviet Union at the end of the Second World War, and to reconcile it with the popular image of Churchillian 'toughness'. From this beginning grew a desire to understand how British foreign policy-makers encountered and conceptualised the Soviet Union throughout the period of the wartime alliance. Too often the events that followed the end of the war have overshadowed our understanding of the thought-processes of the war years, but now the distance of time and changing geopolitics can allow them to be assessed on their own terms. I found on examination that very little study had been done of what was known, or believed to be known, by British policy-makers about what was going on in the Soviet Union, and how that shaped their approaches. This book attempts to rectify that situation.

Undertaking a work of this kind incurs many debts. It is fitting that for my first book I should look back with gratitude to those who sparked my interest, particularly the history staff of Minchenden School, Southgate – now sadly defunct – and notably Richard Grunberger. Working in an interdisciplinary team has brought me fresh insights and perspectives and my thanks go to my past and present colleagues in American Studies at Brunel University and the old West London Institute, especially Inderjeet Parmar, Niall Palmer and Stephen Want. The thesis on which this book is based would never have been completed without the input of my supervisors at the LSE, Donald Cameron Watt and Antony Best. The staff at all the archives I have worked in have been uniformly courteous and helpful. Crown copyright material in the Public Record Office is reproduced by permission of the Controller of Her Majesty's Stationery Office. Finally, no long-term project can be finished without the support and encouragement of friends and family. Thank you then to Corinne and Sharon, to Pete and Liz, and of course to my parents, to whom this book is dedicated.

List of Abbreviations

The full name is given on first reference, abbreviations thereafter. They are all listed together here for convenience.

AI	Air Intelligence
APWC	Cabinet Armistice and Post-war Committee
BBK	Beaverbrook papers
BNLO	British Naval Liaison Officer
BoT	Board of Trade
CA	Confidential Annexe
CAS	Chief of the Air Staff
CCS	Combined Chiefs of Staff (US/UK)
CIGS	Chief of the Imperial General Staff
COS	Chiefs of Staff Committee
DEA	Department of European Affairs, US State Department
DMI	Director of Military Intelligence
DDMI	Deputy Director of Military Intelligence
DNI	Director of Naval Intelligence
DO	Dominions Office
DoP	Director of Plans
EAM	Greek Communist Movement
FO	Foreign Office
FORD	Foreign Office Research Department
FRPS	Foreign Research and Press Service
GKO	Soviet State Defence Council
HMRR	His Majesty's Representatives Abroad
HPC	Home Policy Committee, Ministry of Information
JCS	Joint Chiefs of Staff (US)
JIC	Joint Intelligence Sub-committee of COS
JPS	Joint Planning Staff
JSM	British Joint Staff Mission (Washington)
MEW	Ministry of Economic Warfare
MI	Military Intelligence
MSC	Military Sub-committee of the Ministerial Committee on Reconstruction Problems (Jowitt Committee)

Narkomindel	Soviet People's Commissariat for Foreign Affairs
NKVD	Soviet People's Commissariat for Internal Affairs
NI	Naval Intelligence
OSS	US Office of Strategic Services
PHPS	Post Hostilities Planning Staff
PHPS/c	Post Hostilities Planning Sub-committee
PID	FO Political Intelligence Department
PWE	Political Warfare Executive
SBNO	Senior British Naval Officer
UPP	Union of Polish Patriots
VCIGS	Vice-Chief of the Imperial General Staff
WO	War Office
WOID	War Office Intelligence Directorate

1
Introduction

The end of the Cold War has offered opportunities to rewrite the history of the Second World War: not just the Soviet side of the war, but also the Allied side of the Grand Alliance. For years the history of the diplomacy of the war years has been dominated by the search for Cold War origins, and hindsight concerning the 'lost peace' has affected our approach to this period. It is now possible to view this era in its own right – in particular to study attempts to develop inter-Allied cooperation free from an overriding concern to show that it was a doomed venture. It has become something of an historical truism that the so-called Grand Alliance of Britain, the USSR and the United States was a marriage of convenience which was united only by shared enmity towards Nazi Germany, and that consequently its dissolution was inevitable after the enemy was defeated. Official British policy during the war was based, however, on a different assumption. It was stated by Anthony Eden, the Foreign Secretary, that the alliance with the USSR would be the centre of Britain's European policy, providing the overarching element to link eastern and western Europe and therefore serve Britain's aim of preventing a resurgence of German dominance of the Continent and at the same time ensure some British influence in events throughout Europe. Moreover, in a paper approved by the War Cabinet in August 1944, it was strongly asserted that as far as the policy of the Soviets was concerned, cooperation with Britain and the United States was by far the most likely choice of all their policy options.[1] The key question is, beneath the official pronouncements, was there a genuine thesis of a *cooperative* USSR – not just for wartime, but for 20 years after the war, as the Anglo-Soviet Treaty declared?

1

To plan on the basis of friendly relations, let alone close collaboration, was a radical departure for British policy. Historians have tended to be either sceptical about the sincerity of the assertion that cooperation was really possible, or to explain it by reference either to the short-term needs of the wartime situation or to the activities of Soviet sympathisers who attained positions of influence during the war. The basic historical approach to the broad issues of Britain's wartime policy to the USSR for a long time followed the lead set by Churchill in his war memoirs. British policy was pragmatic and unideological: the British did their best to forge good relations, but were never deluded about the chances.[2] Soviet uncooperativeness made it ultimately impossible. Until some while after the release of British official documents in 1971, there was no significant British revisionism such as took place in the USA. It was not until the mid-1980s that the revisionist theme that cooperation was never really feasible because of Anglo-American hostility to the Left was picked up by some writers on British policy, notably Gabriel Gorodetsky.[3]

Three broad tendencies are now evident in British writing on the subject. Two are sharply critical of British policy from opposite angles. Neo-revisionists find British policy dominated by political concepts that meant that Whitehall never seriously attempted to gain cooperation or believed that it was possible or desirable.[4] Subversion theorists claim the opposite: that Britain appeased the Soviets, making large concessions to them, principally because of the influence of Soviet agents and fellow-travellers and of those taken in by Stalin, such as Beaverbrook and Eden.[5] British policy, it has been claimed, was not based upon a serious assessment of Soviet objectives; they were dupes of their own 'wishful thinking'.[6]

The third tendency comprises the majority of writers in the field and is less critical. This school has tended to focus on the minutiae of policy-making, using the vast amount of detail available in the archives of Britain and the United States. It does not seek to criticise British policy in the same way. Instead, it finds it to be 'pragmatic' – essentially echoing Churchill that the British did the best they could. This argument builds on the commonplace that the alliance was bound to fall apart after the war because of the fundamental difference in outlook and interests of the Soviets and the British, and the principal concern of British policy-makers was to keep it together at least until victory was assured. They had to work with the Soviets to that end, and so made the best of it. The driving force is seen as Britain's imperatives – Britain needed the Soviets for the purposes of victory over Germany and to participate in the postwar policing of Germany. In order to keep the alliance going, bad thoughts were eschewed, though with little conviction, given the social and political background of most of the individuals concerned and the institutional traditions of the Foreign Office (FO), military and other parts of the Government. Statements about long-term collaboration were merely expedient.[7] Thus, in answer to the subversion argument, Robert Cecil asserted that the members of the British Government were never really convinced the USSR would be cooperative, and did not build their policy on that assumption; they hoped for it but did not expect it. Nobody was deluded – though strangely many of these writers refer to 'disillusionment' after Yalta, which implies some internalisation of the idea that the USSR could genuinely be a collaborative partner.[8]

These three approaches have one point in common. They judge British actions in terms of the subsequent course of Anglo-Soviet relations, and cannot resist making judgements in relation to the issue of the blame for the Cold War. Those studies which concentrate most specifically on Anglo-Soviet relations in the war as a topic in itself, when they go beyond narrative, do not attempt to assess British policy in terms of the way the USSR was perceived. The possibility that the commitment to the cooperative idea was real is not addressed. A contemporary of Cecil, Gladwyn Jebb, recollected differently: that many in the FO sincerely believed in 1944 that the USSR would try collaboration, and could be cooperated with.[9] However, historians have tended to disparage or discount many of the ideas expressed during the war in the British Government about the USSR, often on the basis of a subsequent image of Stalin that saw him as set, even in 1941, on clear-cut and detailed objectives, which he then consistently followed. Thus ideas about a Soviet inferiority complex, sensitivity to other states' actions, of different schools of thought among Soviet leaders affecting their actions, or of Soviet changeability are passed over as odd or 'diverting', with no attempt to assess their origins or indeed their relevance.[10]

There is plenty of documentary evidence to show the process by which such theories were formulated. British 'pragmatism' can be placed in the context of what was known or assumed – of what the image of the USSR actually was in the British Government. Even if British policy-makers conceived a strong imperative to maintain cooperation with the USSR, to base policy upon this required estimates of the possibility of achieving it. The Cold War assumption that the Soviets were not cooperative, and consequently that any assumption that they were cooperative was either a plant, a delusion or a glossing over of the facts for the needs of the moment, is simply not adequate. Exploration must be conducted to see what was actually assumed about the USSR, and on what evidence and under whose influence.

In order to explore the development of the thesis of a cooperative USSR, analysis will commence at the point when the idea was introduced into the British Government and serious discussion of it began: the appointment of Sir Stafford Cripps as Ambassador to the Soviet Union. This was done soon after Churchill became Prime Minister, in May 1940. In terms of the individuals involved, it also makes sense to begin with the establishment of the Churchill Coalition, rather than is conventional, with the German invasion of the USSR, Operation BARBAROSSA. Some of the key perceptions that made up the thesis of the cooperative USSR were in place before the co-belligerency period. This point is significant in view of the tendency to deal with the question either in terms of the situation in 1941–45, or of personnel introduced during that period.

The focus will be on individuals who had influence in some way within the Government on the formulation of policy decisions regarding the USSR, in particular those who can be identified as contributing to the cooperative image. Within the Government, there were two avenues of influence, the formal and the informal. The formal were the official Government institutions. Here, fairly junior-ranking and apparently unimportant individuals were required to evaluate the raw material on the Soviet Union – in Military Intelligence (MI), in the FO political departments, in the Moscow (or Kuibyshev) Embassy and the Russian Section of the Ministry of Economic Warfare (MEW). These assessments would be approved or revised as they passed up the institution or laterally to other interested departments, until they reached a level at which a decision could be made. Thus many issues of Anglo-Soviet relations never went beyond Deputy Under-Secretary level in the FO or the Director of Military Intelligence (DMI) in the War Office (WO). Senior officials certainly did not simply endorse the views of their subordinates – but these views often provided the starting-point for debate, and in more arcane areas carried the weight of their authors' supposed expertise. Indeed, the nature of the FO was such that its experts were usually of fairly junior rank; the senior officials were by contrast 'all-rounders'. This was true even for heads of the political departments; Christopher Warner, Head of the Northern Department, 1941–46, often prefaced a comment with 'as those who know Russia tell me' – a strange admission for someone who was in charge of the department that dealt with the USSR and who should, one would think, have had such specialist knowledge himself.[11] The lack of extensive and unambiguous material on Soviet policy-making meant that politicians and senior officials tended to lean more on 'specialists' than they did for other countries where they felt more able to reach conclusions unaided. This raised the importance of more junior officials like Fitzroy Maclean, Geoffrey Wilson and Armine Dew in the Northern Department or others regarded as experts, like Sir Robert Bruce Lockhart. While senior figures formed impressions from direct contacts (messages and meetings), these still left plenty of uncertainties requiring contributions from those regarded as experts. Focus on fairly junior clerks, who provided extensive interpretations of fragmentary and confusing Soviet evidence, is therefore essential. Conversely, at the highest level, Churchill dealt with some issues without reference to the bureaucracy, relying upon his informal advisers, War Cabinet ministers and the military for advice, depending on the matter at hand. Decision-making in the Coalition was fragmented, with distinct centres in the FO, 10 Downing Street and the Chiefs of Staff (COS) organisation rather than a unitary pyramid structure.[12]

Each senior figure, moreover, had other sources which they regarded as authoritative. These informal advisers could be far more influential than those formally charged with giving advice. Bruce Lockhart, for instance, was called upon frequently as a Soviet expert, though this was not his official status. His influence is clear from his excellent diary, an under-used source, and also papers in the public records and the Beaverbrook papers. Other informal influence is less easy to detect. The social context for debate is difficult to trace except in a fragmentary way, though it was a factor in the spreading of assumptions within what was a fairly small and socially cohesive elite (even allowing for wartime inductees).

British politicians and officials did not, of course, operate in a vacuum, isolated from political pressures and movements in public opinion. There will, however, be little discussion of these in this book. On the subject of the USSR, public opinion provided little more than a background noise. Policy-makers were more concerned about the impact that Soviet perceptions of British opinion would have on Soviet policy than they were influenced in their own assumptions or indeed policy formulations by the public mood or the views of House of Commons backbenchers, both of which could be managed. Public opinion on the USSR in the war is a significant subject in its own right, and has been covered elsewhere. For the purposes of this study, its influence on views within the Government was small: its significance for the Government lay in fears about the impact of Soviet successes on the popularity of British Communists.[13]

Instead of following the conventional approach of outlining policy in a chronological or country-based framework, this study will analyse the central aspects of the image of the USSR. It will argue that the thesis of a cooperative Soviet Union was based on perceptions of that state, its policy and its leader, and was not just an empty set of phrases designed to sustain the temporary wartime relationship. These perceptions could be described as the British equivalent of what Daniel Yergin called the US 'Yalta Axioms'.[14] Certain key concepts can be identified which made up the thesis of a cooperative USSR. The main ones were Stalin's sagacious realism, Soviet fear of Germany and concern to prevent postwar German resurgence, the centrality of the security motivation, Soviet suspiciousness and Soviet reconstruction needs, which reinforced the longer-standing desire to achieve security in order to focus on internal development. The development of these ideas within the British Government between 1940 and 1945 and their implications for policy-making are the subjects of this book.

It should perhaps be made clear here that a basic assumption of this study is that attitudes of policy-makers matter. While the structure of international politics sets the environment in which decisions are made and limits the range of choices that policy-makers can make, these choices are not always predetermined. Specific policy decisions and broad strategy are the product of the way that actors in international relations perceive this environment, and of their assumptions and expectations of the policies of other states and actors. This study makes no claim to describe fully and explain all aspects of Britain's wartime policy towards the USSR, but is an examination of the images of the USSR and the debates upon them that were significant influences on the reactions of policy-makers to the environment of international events.

2
'Let us expect nothing good from the Soviet'

Prior to the start of the Second World War there had been some discussion in British Government circles of the possibilities of Anglo-Soviet cooperation. The Nazi–Soviet Pact, followed by the Soviet invasion of Finland and evidence of Soviet supply of war materials to Germany, brought all this to an end. It had anyway never been believed within the policy-making elite that such cooperation was very important for British interests, even if the vast gulf of ideology and diplomatic methods could be bridged.[1] The events of 1939–40 reinforced this. The rapidly changing war situation, however, was to alter the context in which the Soviet Union was viewed. Moreover, Soviet policy itself had to adapt to the changed international environment.

Perceptions of the USSR, 1940–41

Within the FO, primary analysis of the USSR was conducted by the Northern Department, headed since 1933 by Sir Laurence Collier. The official responsible for the USSR under Collier was Fitzroy Maclean, who had served in Moscow during the show-trials.[2] The Department's viewpoints were channelled through Deputy Under-Secretary, Sir Orme Sargent, to the Permanent Under-Secretary, Sir Alexander Cadogan, and from thence to the Foreign Secretary, Lord Halifax.[3] In early 1940 the major issue of debate was the Soviet relationship to Germany and the underlying motivations that shaped it. Prior to the Russo-Finnish War many, including Churchill, had thought that German and Soviet interests would easily clash.[4] The Northern Department now, in January 1940, asserted that the USSR was Germany's ally. Maclean strongly argued that the alignment with Germany was a natural consequence of the affinity of the two regimes and of their shared enmity towards Britain. The USSR, however, looked like the weak link, and it was claimed that Germany could be defeated by striking at the fragile Soviet economy. The attraction of this was twofold: apart from indulging feelings of hostility to the Soviet Union, it offered an easy path to victory without directly confronting Germany on the Western Front.[5]

By no means everyone accepted this theory, and once the Russo-Finnish War ended, there was less pretext for striking at the USSR. Opinion swung behind another interpretation. Already Sargent, Churchill and to a degree Collier, felt that Soviet–German collaboration was unnatural and likely to be of short duration.[6] By the end of the 1930s, Soviet policy had come to be characterised as driven by motives of self-preservation, not Marxist ideology – though there were residual effects of the latter in their amorality, their untrustworthiness and the underhanded, subversive methods they were prepared to employ. This produced an essentially opportunistic policy.[7] By April 1940 the most common explanation for Soviet policy was the 'mutual exhaustion' theory. Stalin was believed to be aiming to avoid hostilities with a Great Power while at the same time working to prolong the war in order to weaken both sides. The resulting exhaustion of both belligerents would ensure Soviet survival as well as provide ideal conditions for the Soviets to extend their influence into a disordered and weakened Europe. As an explanation for Soviet support of Germany, this theory depended on the assumption that the Soviets saw Germany as the weaker power, and were supplying aid to ensure the war lasted.[8]

The belief that ultimately they wished for the defeat of both Germany and the Allies meant that there would be limits on the extent and permanence of their cooperation with Germany.[9] While Maclean, and some others, thought otherwise, the general inclination was that Hitler and Stalin were uncomfortable bed-fellows, brought into such a position by a temporary coincidence of interests, not political affinities. When German successes in the west made it hard to assert that the Soviets were supporting Germany as the *weaker* power, therefore, the widespread interpretation was that fear of Germany now impelled Stalin to continue cooperation. He would be pleased by the collapse of the British Empire, but this would not completely outweigh the dangers of a victorious and powerful Germany. Sargent summarised departmental views in July 1940. The USSR was seen to have both defensive and expansive motivations.

Stalin was upset by the fall of France and was frightened of German expansion, but would also himself seize the opportunity to expand. Stalin intended to keep on good terms with Hitler because he could not stop him. Germany and the USSR had a common interest in not fighting each other and in the Soviets staying out of the war. However, there were clearly tensions amid the continuing collaboration.[10] Thus, when Stalin annexed the Baltic states, these moves were seen as defensive – and that could only be against Germany.[11] The FO believed he would want to keep on good terms with the German victor, hoping that Germany might not be entirely stable with so much territory to assimilate and that Hitler would not attack the USSR while gaining economic advantages from the existing relationship.[12]

Through the rest of 1940, the sense that Soviet policy was principally designed to avoid a clash with Germany strengthened. Stalin was depicted as an 'appeaser' – now a term of derision in British Government circles – and by the last months of 1940, seemed to be getting into the kind of mess that appeasement produces. He was still seeking to buy time, but the spread of German influence and control in countries like Bulgaria and Romania was impinging into areas of traditional Russian/Soviet interest. The FO Southern Department had long perceived Soviet ambitions in these areas; at least partly these were defensive, in that the Soviets were concerned that no other power should be in control there.[13]

After Molotov met Hitler in Berlin in November 1940, it was initially assumed that agreement had been reached on dividing up the Near and Middle East.[14] Further information, however, suggested that in fact Soviet–German relations were becoming more difficult and that the predicted clash of interests was developing. Collier remarked that the Soviet position on the fence was becoming increasingly uncomfortable, and their long-cherished freedom of manoeuvre was being compromised. Comments reveal a certain sense of poetic justice about this: Churchill remarked that their position was 'unenviable'.[15]

By early 1941, the Soviets were clearly seen to be in a serious position. Their policy was believed to be driven principally by a desire to stay out of the war – which by now meant avoiding provoking the Germans. This involved continued, indeed increased, economic aid and keeping the British at arm's length so that the Germans would not become suspicious. Fear for Soviet security, directly threatened by Germany, was the principal motivation. Thus

Soviet appeasement of Germany, right up to the moment of the attack, was perceived by most in the Government – especially once Maclean left the FO in March 1941 – to be a consequence of Soviet fear, and this perception was not shaped by a political concept of Nazi–Soviet affinities.[16]

While there was no sympathy with such appeasement, the driving force for it on Stalin's part was seen to be his own realism about Soviet weakness. The British wished the Soviets, as Collier wrote, to 'take courage' (largely because it was in Britain's interest), but they also believed Stalin had very good reasons for wanting to avoid a fight. Probably the most important fundamental assumption about the USSR was of Soviet weakness. The Soviet Union was characterised throughout the elite as incompetent, inefficient and corrupt. Communism had sapped initiative and patriotism. The purges and collectivisation had created such chaos that the Soviet economic infrastructure was expected to collapse very quickly if mobilisation for war was attempted. Moreover, the regime's hold on its own people was tenuous, only having any strength at all in the cities, and even there Stalin and his terror regime were believed to be unpopular.[17]

The British military concurred entirely with this assessment. Early in the 1930s, British services opinion was that Soviet forces, whose quality had previously been regarded as low, were improving. It was felt that the Soviets were making great strides in equipment and training, especially of armoured and parachute divisions. When air and military attachés were appointed for the first time in 1934, they were able to attend manoeuvres and gain first-hand knowledge. They found Soviet officers reasonably good, but tactics disorganised and primitive; morale was very high and overall the forces seemed more resilient than those of 1914. Even if not effective in attack, the WO concluded that it would 'be a risky matter for any . . . Power to attempt a war of aggression against the Soviet Union'. Observers at the manoeuvres at Minsk in 1936, who included Wavell and Martel (both to revisit the USSR in the war), reported that the use and development of mechanised and parachute forces were good, though staffwork and coordination were somewhat suspect.[18]

It was just these aspects that were believed to have suffered in the subsequent purges of officers. The 1937 manoeuvres, at which no foreign observers were allowed, were rumoured to have been a shambles. In view of poor Soviet administration and the appalling state that communications were believed to be in, the COS concluded in 1939 that the Red Army was an unreliable, uncertain quantity, and that within two or three weeks of hostilities the USSR would be forced to suspend mobilisation to avoid a complete breakdown in industry and national life. They were prepared to concede that the Soviet forces would probably fight reasonably well when defending their own soil. They had no enthusiasm for cooperation with the Soviets; many senior officers had been involved in the Intervention against the Bolshevik Revolution in 1919, and in planning for the defence of India against a potential Russian enemy.[19]

Soviet performances in Poland in September 1939 were reported to be unimpressive, with a lack of discipline (believed to be partly the result of the system of political commissars), poor reserves and widespread breakdowns in transport, all of which served to confirm expectations based on the latest reports of the attachés in Moscow. Little notice was taken of the more creditable performance against the Japanese in August 1939. These perceptions received further confirmation in the first month of the war with Finland. Once again, Soviet tactics were seen as unsophisticated in the extreme and their inter-service cooperation poor.[20]

In November 1940, MI2b, the section of MI that dealt with Soviet matters at that time, noted that attempts had been made to improve the Red Army after the Finnish fiasco, chiefly by decreasing political control within military units.[21] However, at the turn of the year, MI were strongly of the opinion that the Soviet leadership would give in to the Germans and would not resist an advance into the Ukraine. The DMI thought they would fight, but deferred to MI2b's 'judgement and up to date knowledge'. When the Military Attaché in Moscow, Colonel Greer, asserted that the Soviet people were being prepared for war against Germany and that any form of occupation of the Soviet territory would be resisted, indeed that dissatisfied elements would unite behind the Soviet Government, MI2 were sceptical. They dismissed the idea, originating with Cripps, that the Red Army was developing an anti-German attitude, or any kind of view of its own.[22] Major Tamplin of MI2b thought such an idea to be the result of a dangerous wishful thinking. It is clear that the department the British military relied upon for interpretation of the Soviet situation was of the opinion that the Soviet Union counted for little, that its regime would do anything to secure its own survival, and that the Soviets were looking to the mutual exhaustion of the belligerents, partly for the opportunistic gains that might result, but also in the hopes of avoiding attack. A Soviet–German clash was quite possible eventually, but not while the Germans had the British as their main enemy, and while the Soviets were too weak to follow any policy other than submission. MI assumed the latest territorial acquisitions added nothing to Soviet defences; the Lithuania-East Poland line was indefensible, where the pre-war frontiers had presumably been strongly fortified. Soviet troops were now deployed *ahead* of those fortifications in the new (and politically unreliable) territories.[23]

Nothing was to alter the services' low opinion of the Soviet forces up to the time of the German invasion. The reforms made by Marshal Timoshenko were not considered to have brought Soviet forces to a level where they could face the *Wehrmacht* on anything like equal terms. The earlier caveat about Soviet defensive capabilities was no longer certain, given the effect of the purges on the one hand, and the offensive abilities of the Germans on the other. The Joint Planning Staff (JPS) found the Soviet Air Force to be inefficient and its equipment obsolescent. Soviet tanks were technically better, but like the aircraft suffered from poor maintenance. These forces were certainly large, but their fighting value, the Joint Intelligence Committee (JIC) asserted, was low, even taking into account that they were best in defence and that they had vast territories to fall back on. The weakest points were tactical and logistical organisation, supply and maintenance. After major operations strategic retreat would be found impossible as organisation of formations would break down. The Soviet General Staff was no match for the German. MI2 thought that traditional Russian patriotism and fighting spirit had been eroded by the years of Communist rule and were not counting on protracted irregular resistance.[24]

While these attitudes reproduced many of those held by the FO, it would be incorrect to say that the FO had forced them on the military. They sprang from MI's own analysis, founded on perceptions of Soviet policy and military weakness.

It was this fundamental weakness that brought most to see fear of Germany – and anxieties about future security – to be the driving Soviet motivation. Stalin's concern for self-preservation made him obsessed with security, and given his vulnerability it was expected in May–June 1941 that he would give up a great deal, including territory, in order to avoid a war that could only mean total defeat and the end of himself and his regime. This also guided British policy, for it offered little incentive to chase the Soviets or offer them inducements such as recognition of their annexations of Bessarabia, Northern Bukovina and the Baltic states, in order to buy their neutrality or support. Few in the FO, military or War Cabinet would have disagreed with Cadogan's warning, 'Let us expect nothing good from the Soviet.'[25]

Alternative Views

There was not, however, complete consensus. When he became Prime Minister in May 1940, Churchill agreed with the FO that the fall of France should be causing agonising reappraisals in the Kremlin of the wisdom of supporting Germany, since doing so was shortening, not prolonging the war. A long-standing Soviet request for trade talks was taken up, though the aim of the British mission was political – to discover if Soviet attitudes were, at this moment, amenable to change. The man sent to Moscow was Sir Stafford Cripps. Cripps was a prominent left-winger, though also, as a baronet and KC, a member of the elite. He had been expelled from the Labour Party for advocating a popular front with Communists against Fascism. He had already opened contacts with the USSR, having visited there early in 1940 (accompanied by Geoffrey Wilson, later to be a clerk in the Northern Department). He more or less pushed himself forward for the post. Churchill was willing to indulge him, partly because few people were interested in going to Moscow, partly hoping that 'left would speak to left', and partly for political reasons: it would balance the despatch of Samuel Hoare to Madrid. It would also remove a potential critic, though this could not have been a major reason, for Cripps' mission was intended to be a short one. Neither the FO nor the MEW trusted him to represent their views, but the Soviets insisted they could only receive a permanent Ambassador, not a special envoy, so as not to raise German suspicions. So the installation of Cripps in Moscow did not represent a new direction in British policy, but it did force a continued debate on Soviet policy in the FO and Cabinet, for Cripps energetically expressed his dissent from the prevailing consensus in Whitehall.[26]

Cripps' attitudes, as shown in his writings in *Tribune*, were almost completely unaffected by the Nazi–Soviet Pact, which had disillusioned so many on the Left. He believed that the Soviets were essentially peace-loving, and that they in no sense threatened British interests. He believed that British policy before the war, including that of his own party leaders, had been misguided. The genuine Soviet commitment to collective security had been ignored; instead the Fascists had been appeased, which had resulted in war and driven the Soviets to look to their own security. Cripps believed the Soviets were forced into the pact with Germany and their later actions in Finland and the Baltic states because their previous and preferred policy had depended on cooperation with Britain and France, which they had been unable to achieve.[27] He was not blind to the nature of the Soviet regime, but saw it to be quite different to Nazism. This set of basic perceptions brought him to radically different conclusions from those of the FO.

Cripps' central thesis in June 1940 was that the Soviets were potentially friendly and that a cooperative relationship was possible and desirable both for the purposes of the war and the longer term. He saw the German–Soviet *entente* as neither permanent nor unbreakable, and since he retained his view that the Soviets had been forced into it by maladroit Anglo-French diplomacy it could therefore be broken by renewed British efforts.[28] To him, Soviet policy was 'fundamentally against the Axis and Japan' and they desired an Allied victory. He did not accept the mutual exhaustion theory. Soviet close relations with Germany were *realpolitik* to buy time to improve their strategic position in preparation for the inevitable conflict.[29] This gave some community of purpose with Britain. It had yet to be drawn out from behind the barrier of 20 years of British anti-Soviet policy.[30] After France collapsed, he believed this had become harder to achieve. It removed any chance of a Soviet–German rupture for as long as a rapid German victory seemed likely, as the Soviets were not ready to repel an attack. They also believed that no action of theirs would influence Britain's resistance, so although they wanted friendly relations with Britain as insurance for the future, they would not do anything to provoke Germany. At the same time they would seek to strengthen their defensive position. Soviet moves in the Baltic states were part of this policy: 'actively opportunist' with the aim of protection from a German attack.[31]

Cripps believed the Soviets (except Molotov) had not lost their fundamental enmity towards Nazi Germany.[32] The predominant Soviet aim was to ensure the survival of the Soviet state and system, and Soviet policy was guided by a realistic assessment of the threats to it, against the background of the experience of the past 20 years. Their attitude to Britain was thus not ideological, but was shaped by their perception of the British attitude. Cripps credited the Soviets with a sensitivity that affected this assessment of interest, while others assumed a largely internal dynamic for Soviet policy-making, independent of the attitudes of other states. He maintained the Soviets were sensitive on two counts and because of this could be affected by what he called a 'psychological improvement' in the atmosphere.

First, he believed the Soviets were sensitive about British policy and suspicious of its motives (with some justice, Cripps thought). They believed Britain sought to embroil the USSR with Germany and play *tertius gaudens*. This factor was aggravated by what he saw as the clumsy manner of handling that policy by the FO, in the continual leakages (which he refused to acknowledge came from the Soviet Embassy), and 'wishful thinking' in the press about a Soviet–German break. There was a fear that a victorious Britain would lead a postwar anti-Soviet coalition. Cripps felt that a removal of this fear should be a target for British policy, for doing so might alter Soviet policy towards Germany.[33]

Second, he believed they were concerned about their international status. Cripps asserted that the Soviets, as a newly established regime, were anxious to be accepted as the legitimate rulers of a powerful nation, both for internal and for international reasons. They felt that they had been treated as inferiors and outsiders, especially at Munich in 1938. If they were now treated as equals, then progress could be made in improving relations.[34] Cripps was assuming the Soviets took the same view of British pre-war policy as he did. It was what he called the 'old diplomacy' that had caused the coolness in relations. He took Stalin's comments about a 'new equilibrium' in their first interview to be confirmation of this. Cripps recommended that the Government go 'all out' for better relations to divorce the Soviet Union gradually from Germany, with a thoroughness equal to that of the Germans, and a preparedness to 'make some sacrifice':

> I believe that given adequate encouragement such an evolution might be gradually brought about from the moment when Great Britain shows herself capable of resisting German attack, but ground must be prepared in advance.[35]

These arguments made little impression on the established view in Whitehall, where Stalin's 'authoritative and discouraging statement' had been interpreted differently.[36] When Cripps asserted that the Soviets were sensitive about the European status of the USSR and had the Orientals' concern for 'face', Maclean answered that they possessed the equally Oriental trait of assessing their own interests very cold-bloodedly, disregarding past policies or agreements if necessary. If they liked to bargain, they equally appreciated displays of strength and firmness of will. They looked for motives of self-interest in others and preferred them to be openly displayed. These characteristics implied the Soviets had little time for purely ideological considerations either; though their attitude to Britain had an ideological aspect, their basic motivations were of an older vintage. While stressing the Georgian and Jewish origins of the Soviet ruling clique (Georgians and Jews being classed as 'Asiatic'), Stalin was at the same time characterised as a traditional-style Great Russian nationalist.[37]

The fundamental divergence of viewpoints between Cripps and the FO was in no sense reproduced in the War Cabinet. Soviet Ambassador Maisky frequently voiced his disappointment with the Labour members of the Coalition, whom he had assiduously courted when they were in opposition. Notwithstanding the Labour Party's traditional regard for the Soviet Union and the continued enthusiasm for that state on the part of the rank-and-file and the intellectuals of the Left, Attlee, Bevin and Greenwood made no attempt to propose an alternative policy to that of Halifax and the FO. To them, Stalin's policy appeared selfish, short-sighted and opportunistic. After the Soviet attack on Finland, the *Daily Herald*, the vehicle for the views of the leadership, proclaimed that the socialist USSR was dead, having been replaced by Stalin's new imperialist Russia. However, they were less interested in attacking the USSR than using the opportunity to rout their own left-wingers, who were in considerable disarray.[38]

There was support for Cripps' interpretation from the Ministry of Economic Warfare. The dons and businessmen called into service there, and the Minister, Labour's Hugh Dalton, found FO methods infuriating and their conduct of diplomacy inapplicable to the circumstances of the war.[39] The MEW's Soviet expert, Michael Postan, argued for a radically different interpretation of the USSR from that of the FO. Postan was by no means pro-Soviet, but his attitude was typical of the academic or commercial detachment towards the USSR of the Ministry experts. Postan and his associates founded their arguments on a belief that British policy should be framed in the context of the immediate needs of the war with Germany, and they saw cooperation with the Soviet Union to be more feasible than did Collier or Maclean.[40] The key divergence in perceptions was a higher estimate of the likelihood of a Soviet–German clash of interests. Greater hope was derived from Soviet opportunism and the interest-based nature of their policy, and there was no emphasis on innate Soviet hostility towards Britain, apart from justifiable caution on the Soviets' part.[41] The MEW argued that the FO view of the response of the Soviets to external stimuli was unduly pessimistic, and that concessions could indeed be effective.[42]

Postan stated that whatever Soviet policy was now, a future *entente* was not inconceivable. He argued that Soviet policy since July 1938 could be explained without reference to such 'ill-defined conceptions as "imperialist tradition" or "communist ideology"'. If Stalin was mainly driven by hostility to the British Empire, why, Postan asked, were his advances in the Baltic states, not Persia or Afghanistan? All Soviet actions could be explained by reference to fear of future German designs on the USSR, tempered by a fear of present German power. It was this that made Stalin reluctant to improve relations with Britain.[43]

The Policy of 'Reserve'

However, in 1940–41 policy to the Soviet Union largely lay in the hands of the Foreign Office. Churchill made occasional interventions, and important decisions were approved by War Cabinet, but until June 1941 policy essentially followed lines formulated in the FO. Cripps and the MEW proposed alternatives, based on their different views of the Soviet Union, but with little impact on policy.

The policy of 'passive hostility' followed during the Russo-Finnish War had been replaced by the time Churchill became Prime Minister by a policy best described as 'reserve'.[44] This was to be the fundamental British policy down to June 1941, and indeed a little way beyond: though on a number of occasions short-lived attempts were made to find a more active policy. The basic logic for the reserve policy could be found in Cadogan's statement:

> I personally attach no importance whatever to Russia. Russia is in no event going to do us any good: and I am optimistic enough to think she won't do us much harm.[45]

This was possible because for most policy-makers, the USSR was a weak power and one on the periphery as far as significant British interests were concerned. Moreover, Soviet policy was believed to be outside British influence – at least until the threat to bomb Soviet oil-wells in the Caucasus became plausible again.[46] The Soviets, it was believed, would only respond to force: 'the only language the Kremlin understands.'[47] Gestures made to gain goodwill would be futile – or indeed counter-productive, for the Soviets would see them as signs of weakness.[48] Stalin was seen to assess his interests cold-bloodedly and be difficult to influence through normal diplomacy. It was better, as Eden put it after he became Foreign Secretary at the start of 1941, to 'possess our souls in patience'.[49]

There were those who attempted counter-arguments. R.A. Butler, Parliamentary Under-Secretary at the FO in 1940, asserted that the USSR, or Russia, had always counted in the balance of power, and might well be needed to complete the encirclement of Germany and to free Poland and Czechoslovakia from German domination.[50] Cripps took such arguments much further. He clearly felt that a close relationship with the Soviets was possible and desirable, and that since British policy was responsible for Soviet suspicions of British long-term intentions, it was up to Britain to take action to improve relations. A concession on the Baltic would show the Soviets British goodwill, and in particular show that the British agreed that the Soviets had a right to security.[51] He was supported by the officials of the MEW. They did not share the view that the USSR did not matter, since in their field of interest, Soviet economic aid to Germany was clearly of great significance as it was a loophole in the blockade. Like Cripps, they argued against the idea that nothing could be done. They felt Britain could not afford not to try – and perceived the USSR in such a way that action could succeed.[52]

These arguments made little impression in the FO. Halifax, in fact, was ready to consider a concession on the Baltic states if it would work, but no one in the FO thought that it would.[53] Cripps himself by the end of 1940 had become a strong advocate of a 'firm and dignified attitude of reserve'.[54] Indeed, he interpreted the policy in a much sterner way than did Sargent or Collier, and called for a 'firm, negative attitude'.[55] Cripps still believed that British actions mattered to the Soviets (where the FO did not) and that Britain could use threats and rewards to change their policy. He therefore advocated that 'reserve' be quite aggressive; the aim was clearly to move Soviet policy, not simply to wait on events while being 'suave and uncontentious' as Sargent argued.[56] So Cripps, while pressing for 'aloofness', continued to argue that a concession on the Baltic states would also bring about a movement in Soviet policy.[57] The FO rejected this idea in January and February 1941: instead, Sargent advocated a 'distant amiability', allowing Soviet–German rivalry to develop naturally.[58]

However, by early 1941, FO attitudes were based firmly on the idea that the Soviets were anxious about the steady advance of the Germans, especially into the Balkans. When the anti-Nazi coup took place in Belgrade in March 1941, it looked for a short time as if the Soviets were going to 'take courage' and openly support the opponents of the Germans. This prompted a departure from the reserve policy. This had been tried twice before, though both attempts were short-lived.

The first occasion was immediately after Churchill became Prime Minister. Churchill's first message to Stalin laid out in fairly basic terms what the impact of German victories in the west should mean to Soviet interests.[59] Stalin had interpreted it to mean Churchill was trying to enlist the Soviets to defend the *status quo* in Europe.[60] Since Stalin was supposed to be a hard-headed realist, it had been thought possible he might respond differently, but expectations had been low, except on the part of Cripps, and the effect was to confirm the policy of reserve.

Cripps continued to argue for concessions, and once again, in October 1940, the Cabinet was prepared to allow an approach, to see if events had yet had an impact on the Soviet attitude to cooperation with Germany. Although the Americans suspected the British of concocting an appeasement deal, in fact Cripps was left to design the approach himself. The result was some ill-judged wording regarding 'the former Polish state', but no response from Vyshinsky. Molotov did not even bother to see Cripps. As in July, the British reaction was to become more 'reserved', this time mainly on the part of Cripps.[61] He took his rebuff hard, and took a pessimistic view of Molotov's trip to Berlin.[62] The third time when reserve was temporarily dropped also produced such a response, and one that spilled over into reactions to BARBAROSSA. When the Soviets reacted positively to the Belgrade coup (it was noted that oil supplies to Germany were reduced), Eden was in the eastern Mediterranean, and had just conferred with Cripps.[63] Away from his advisers, Eden, who saw himself as having a good reputation in relations with the Soviets and was eager for an active diplomacy towards them, took Cripps' ideas on board.[64] The FO despatched a very long telegram to him, reiterating the grounds for reserve, but Eden began to move forward.[65] On his return to London, he and Sargent explored ways to exploit Soviet anxieties about developments in the Balkans. Sargent argued that Britain could no longer afford to take the line she had in the 1939 Moscow negotiations.[66] After discussion in Cabinet, it was hinted to both Maisky and the Americans (through Halifax, now Ambassador in Washington), that a concession regarding recognition of the Soviet annexations of the Baltic states was a worthwhile exchange for a movement to Soviet neutrality, a cessation of Soviet supplies to Germany and the closure of the loophole in the blockade. Collier and Cadogan were doubtful, but even when coining the strongest statements of 'reserve', Sargent had always conceded the likelihood of a Soviet–German clash of interests.

The breach in reserve was actually threefold, for in addition Churchill and Cripps attempted to seize the moment. Independently, Churchill had decided on his own departure from the policy. He had supported reserve, but did not exclude the possibility of the Soviets and Germans falling out.[67] As he had in June 1940, he felt that a simple setting out of the facts might impress a realist like Stalin. This time, his message to Stalin described German troop movements, based on material gained through the decryption of German signals traffic (though Stalin was told it came from an agent).[68] The aim was to show Stalin that his appeasement policy was not working, for the Germans had been preparing an invasion anyway, only to be delayed by the problem in Belgrade. Churchill let the facts speak for themselves and suggested no threat or reward. The message, however, was sent to Cripps accompanied by a 'line' from the FO on which he was to speak, which tended to reflect the continued pessimism of most of the FO and minimised the significance of the message.[69] Cripps instead made his own approach, believing that Eden had given him the go-ahead.[70] This was a much more complicated démarche, involving hints of threats. Churchill was later furious with Cripps for delaying his message, and the FO blamed Cripps for 'spiking' Eden's approach by moving too quickly for the cautious Soviets, though in fact the rapid deterioration in events in the Balkans meant that the Soviets would always have done what they did, and swung back into full-blooded appeasement.[71] The significance of this short phase was not, however, Cripps' handling of Churchill's message, though historians' focus has tended to follow Churchill on that. More important was that it emphasises that Eden, Churchill and some in the FO, such as Sargent, did not see the Soviets and Germans as in any way natural partners and were prepared to act on that perception. After the attempt came to nothing, once again the inclination to reserve was reinforced. Churchill, who had characterised the Soviet attitude in the Balkans as 'loyal and friendly', told Eden that it was wiser to let the force of events work further rather than to make

> ... frantic efforts to assure them of your love. This only looks like weakness and encourages them to believe they are stronger than they are. Now is the time for a sombre restraint on our part, and let them do the worrying.[72]

This mood continued through June 1941. No political offers were considered then, when a German attack seemed imminent, only rather vague military assistance. What had been confirmed in April was the determination of Stalin to avoid war at all costs. This reinforced the impression of chronic Soviet weakness and was to shape initial reactions to the prospect of alliance by establishing the expectation of precipitate collapse.

Facing the Prospect of a German Attack on the USSR: Could the Soviets be Allies?

As information and rumours of German pressure on the Soviets increased, the new Head of the Northern Department, Christopher Warner, summarised the position as it looked from Whitehall. Much as the Government might wish to influence the Soviets in favour of the Allies, he wrote on 14 May, Stalin's policy was governed by his fear of Germany and his estimate of the concessions he could make without bringing the collapse of his regime. It was assumed that negotiations were 'almost certainly proceeding'. Stalin's assumption of the Presidency of the Council of People's Commissars was believed to indicate serious decisions were at hand. There was little doubt Stalin would go to great lengths to avoid war. On this issue Cripps' reports from Moscow matched views in Whitehall.[73]

The US Government was apprehensive that the British were again contemplating concessions on the Baltic states and other issues. In contrast to his stance in April, Eden assured Halifax that the Government had no intention of giving in to the Soviet Union and was only exploring what course to follow if war came. No political moves were thought worthwhile. As Butler put it, a move in the direction of the Soviets would recognise that they could be a 'great makeweight in the balance of power', but on the other hand a continuance of the policy of negation meant that 'we have no bargain with the devil and can become his adversary later with a clear record'. Halifax was told the FO had good reason to believe Hitler wished to put an end to the USSR as a potential menace and intended to force the issue immediately. The planned British response was:

> while we should not become the allies of the Soviet Union, we should have a common enemy and a common interest – i.e. to do Germany all the harm we can. Our present approach has this situation only in view.[74]

On the eve of BARBAROSSA all the FO were thinking of in this connection was a rather distant co-belligerency. In the fairly likely event of a German attack, closer relations were desirable, but '[t]hat we should not welcome or hug the Soviet as an ally also seems desirable'.[75] Perceptions of the Soviets suggested two possible outcomes; Soviet acquiescence to German demands, or, if Germany attacked, rapid Soviet defeat. The question of long-term relations seemed academic, since prolonged Soviet resistance was not expected and the unpleasant implications of close cooperation did not have to be faced. The general inclination of the Government was towards a limited response; in effect fighting separate but parallel wars and continuing to a certain degree the policy of reserve until matters were clarified by Soviet collapse.[76]

The JPS concluded that if the USSR was attacked, there would be little material assistance Britain could give, if only for geographic reasons. They informed the FO that they saw no reason to refuse collaboration if the Soviets asked for it. They would be told, however, that Britain was already doing all she could against the common foe, and would continue to do so. Air Chief Marshal Portal, the new Chief of the Air Staff (CAS), made it clear that strategic discussions could only take place once the Soviets had revised their policy and decided to fight the Germans instead of appease them.[77] The COS concurred in Eden's offer to Maisky of increased air activity in the west and a military mission should the Germans attack. However, the military were none too enamoured of the idea of an alliance with the Soviets, notwithstanding the fact that they had advanced it in 1939 on strategic grounds. Whatever the advantages to Britain of even the momentary respite afforded, they disliked the prospect of the extra military commitments that might be found necessary, the possibility of sharing US material aid, and of joint planning with the Soviets. They also found it distasteful. The CIGS, General Dill, thought the idea was 'foul', and the VCIGS, General Pownall, wrote in his diary:

> I avoid the expression 'Allies' for the Russians are a dirty lot of murdering thieves themselves and double crossers of the deepest dye. It is good to see the two biggest cut-throats in Europe, Hitler and Stalin, going for each other.

From a personal point of view, like many other members of the elite, most high-ranking servicemen would have been happy to watch the Soviets and the Nazis mutually exhaust themselves. However, it was feared that the Germans would win all too quickly, so they found themselves placing their hopes in the unlikely direction of the Soviet leader. Pownall's comment continued:

> I only hope Stalin will make a deep gash in Hitler's throat. With a bit of luck he will. It's impossible to say how long Russian resistance will last – three weeks or three months? The main thing is that even when they find themselves forced to pack up that they still maintain a front somewhere – even in the Urals.[78]

However, prolonged resistance seemed unlikely. The JIC and JPS had, by 9 June, come to expect either agreement or war by the end of the month and believed that if war came the Soviets would hold out for 4–6 weeks. Edward Grigg, Parliamentary Under-Secretary at the WO, however, told Harold Nicolson that 80 per cent of the WO gave the Soviets only ten days. Dill said the Germans would go through them like 'a knife through butter', and gave them odds of 5–4 on.[79]

Initial Reactions: Churchill Favours an End to Reserve

The unexpected fact of Soviet survival thus inevitably forced certain changes in views of the USSR – moreover that survival left it aligned with Britain and an important part of the Allied war effort. An exception was Churchill, for his approach was changed by the simple fact that the Soviets were now co-belligerents. He wanted a more active response than a continuation of reserve. Days before the event, he had told Roosevelt that he would try to help the

Soviet Union should it become Germany's enemy. This did not signify a change in Churchill's view of the USSR. His attitude was governed by his pursuit of defeat of Germany.[80]

Churchill believed the British people shared his views of the primacy of the struggle against Hitler and would respond unequivocally to an appeal expressed in such terms. He took the view that 'Russia was now at war: innocent peasants were being slaughtered and we should forget about Soviet systems or the Comintern and extend our hand to fellow-human beings in distress.'[81] Hitler was counting on stirring up class divisions, he said, and this was all the more reason to 'to go all out to help Russia'. Eden, Cranborne and Duff Cooper, who were by no means Chamberlainites, were not so certain. Eden and Cranborne said that if there was to be a Commons debate it should be confined to the purely military aspect as, politically, the USSR was as bad as Germany and half the country would object to being associated with it too closely. Duff Cooper also (wrongly) expected resistance amongst the public to the idea of a close association with the Soviet Union.[82]

Churchill's attitude was born of his firm belief that Britain was Hitler's ultimate target. If the USSR was holding up his plans for invasion and exhausting his military resources, then it should be helped. If the Germans were to be prevented from returning to the attack in the west that autumn, this help had to be immediate. In this context, the Soviet system was irrelevant; 'Russia' was fighting in her national interest, not Communist interest, and that was all that was important to Britain at that time.[83] If this reflected the nature of his interest in the USSR as a partner-in-arms against Germany, it also reflected his perception of Soviet policy as it had developed under Stalin. It was realist and self-interested; nationalistic and not revolutionary, more 'Russian' than 'Soviet'. This is not to say he was not alive to the domestic angle: even before any Soviet victories, he was worried about the effect close association with the Soviet Union would have in increasing the credibility of British Communists. The issue was immediately put to Attlee and Herbert Morrison, who shared his anxiety.[84]

Churchill's rejection of the policy of reserve did not derive from a firm belief in Soviet victory – but a lesser hope that the Soviet peoples would put up a stern fight in defence of their homeland. It was not based on a different perception of Soviet capabilities from that of his colleagues and advisers. John Colville later claimed that Churchill believed the Soviets would fight well and perhaps win, but at the time he noted that Churchill believed the USSR 'would certainly be defeated'.[85] He agreed it was just a breathing space, but one that Britain should exert herself to extend. On 23 June, he exhorted the COS to 'make hell while the sun shines'. He spurred others into action which they themselves considered would be wasted by an early Soviet collapse. The COS attitude was that this was the time to build British strength, instead of squandering it on a cause they could not help. They were cold to Soviet demands for help, telling Lieutenant-General Mason-Macfarlane, the Head of the new Military Mission to Moscow (30 Mission), they 'must save themselves just as we saved ourselves in the Battle of Britain and in the Atlantic'.[86] Macfarlane was instructed to encourage the Soviets to resist as long as possible, retreating if necessary into Siberia, ensuring they destroyed important oil installations before the Germans overran them, and then himself to escape to safety over the Pamir mountains.[87]

Likewise, the first reaction to BARBAROSSA in the FO was to maintain the policy of reserve. Cripps initially agreed. Harold Nicolson's impression that the FO would welcome a full alliance was incorrect.[88] This shaped Cripps' preference that the first formal agreement with the Soviets would merely be concerned with mutual assistance: to make a political agreement, he said, should wait until confidence had grown, though he also felt an agreement of some sort was advisable to remove mistrust. It would give the Soviet leaders international respect and make them 'entirely manageable' at the peace conference. To most, the anticipated Soviet defeat meant a potentially embarrassing political agreement was unnecessary. Eden took a similar line to Cripps in discussions with Maisky, though he favoured active measures in the military and economic spheres. The FO attitude was characterised by caution and a reluctance to make commitments ahead of events. This was to change as Soviet resistance failed to crumble; the longer they survived, the more anxiety there was that they would continue to fight, and to cast around for methods by which Britain could exert influence to this effect.[89] The preconditions that supported the reserve policy began to change as the Soviets survived; this was a more important development than the actual German invasion in changing British attitudes towards the Soviet Union, including some individuals' fundamental perceptions.

Beaverbrook

Strident Soviet complaints about British actions – or the lack of them – from September 1941 reopened the debate on how far Soviet policy was influenced by such external factors as British policies. The individual who more than anyone brought this question into prominence in the agencies where policy was made, when many in the Cabinet and FO preferred to ignore it in expectation of a German victory, was Beaverbrook. The military situation and the repercussions of the lack of British victories on the Government's domestic political position rendered Beaverbrook's stress on the prominence of Soviet morale and susceptibilities highly pertinent, with profound implications for the development of attitudes and policies during the rest of the war in Europe.

Beaverbrook has been marginalised in accounts of the course of British policy to the Soviet Union during the Churchill Coalition. Studies of Beaverbrook have tended to view his support of aid to the USSR in 1941–42 in terms of his personal ambitions, and give the impression that this was merely a piece of political calculation. This is unfortunate, for Beaverbrook's attitude was important for British policy and by no means was it purely a function of domestic politics.

Oliver Harvey, Eden's Private Secretary at this time, found Beaverbrook obsessed with Russia.[90] Beaverbrook's earlier attitude had not suggested any such obsession. His guiding principle in foreign affairs was the continued survival and integrity of the Empire. His concept of the Empire centred on the English-speaking Dominions; he cared nothing for Asia, so his imperialism carried with it no in-built hostility to the USSR deriving from concern about India. From the perspective of an isolationist, he could see no area where British and Soviet vital interests clashed, which was not the case, he felt, with Britain's other major ally, the United States. Beaverbrook had opposed intervention after the October Revolution, and accepted Bruce Lockhart's line that the Bolshevik state should be regarded as an accomplished fact on the international scene.[91] This did not mean Beaverbrook cherished any enthusiasm for, or indeed interest in, the USSR before the end of the 1930s. He visited the country briefly in 1929 and was not impressed. The key fact was that the USSR, eastern Europe, indeed Europe as a whole, were peripheral in his world-view.[92]

For Beaverbrook in 1939–40, the Soviet Union moved slightly

nearer the centre of his mental map, as a potential ally to deter Germany in 1939 or to fight them in 1940. Beaverbrook seems to have been largely unaffected by the Finnish War. His newspapers argued strongly for a rapprochement with the USSR after the Finnish War ended, and the London *Evening Standard*, in particular, consistently put the best construction on Soviet actions, under the prompting of Michael Foot.[93] Beaverbrook also, however, saw the Soviet Union as a useful partner in the war, which he believed needed to be won as quickly as possible in Britain's own interest.

While Beaverbrook's approach may have been influenced by the left-wing journalists who were his protégés – Foot, Tom Driberg and others – a stronger influence was probably Bruce Lockhart, a close associate. Lockhart had long held that the Bolshevik state should not be treated as a pariah nation, but at the same time was not as uncritical as individuals on the Left, and did not have such a high opinion of Soviet military power. Thus while Beaverbrook favoured improving relations, he did not hold the USSR to be of great account. Despite his own subsequent claims to the contrary, he did not have high expectations of Soviet resistance when they were attacked by Germany, and it is unlikely that his influence was at all significant on Churchill's broadcast of 22 June aligning Britain with the Soviet struggle. His 'obsession' with the USSR only became evident once they had survived the first six weeks, possibly influenced by the conclusions drawn by Roosevelt's first envoy to Moscow, Harry Hopkins, whom he met in August 1941.[94] Beaverbrook's strong desire was like Churchill and the COS to make the most of the respite provided by the failure of the Germans to do as expected and destroy the Soviet Union in the first six weeks of the campaign. Like Churchill, he sought an active policy. Unlike Churchill, Beaverbrook did not change his attitude once it became impossible for the Germans to turn to the west to invade Britain that year.

Beaverbrook was also among Maisky's wide circle of acquaintances. He voiced a critique of British policy reminiscent of the Ambassador, and he found Maisky's frequent assertions about Soviet sensitivity persuasive.[95] However, for Beaverbrook, the point about sensitivity gained its strength from a line that Maisky certainly did not argue. Beaverbrook cared about Soviet morale because he believed the USSR to be decrepit; it was the will to resist of the populace and its leadership that was in need of bolstering. His demands for increased supply for the Soviets, accepting Stalin's statement of his needs without question, was as much to keep the Soviets resisting spiritually as to supply them with the means to do so physically. It is this essentially critical basis of Beaverbrook's concessionary policy that distinguishes it from Maisky and the British Left. The 'soft' or concessionary approach to the Soviets was thus based in the beginning on the assumption of Soviet weakness, and was hardly appeasement of a strong potential enemy.

Beaverbrook's assertions about Soviet morale before his trip to Moscow were largely based on pre-existing perceptions of the USSR, strengthened by his own concern, as Minister of Supply, to be at the centre of events. The larger the role that could be claimed for supply on grounds of encouraging Soviet resistance, the more important became Beaverbrook's own position vis-à-vis his rivals. 'Stalin must be sustained' proclaimed the poster for 'Tanks for Russia', but the prominent figure on it was Beaverbrook.[96] His stance, however, was not entirely cynical, for he undoubtedly grasped quicker than others that BARBAROSSA changed the whole nature of the war and that the Germans could only be defeated if the Soviets were victorious. Britain's fate therefore lay in Soviet hands. These were hands in which he placed no reliance. Underneath considerations of his own position were his perceptions of the Soviet Union; a bankrupt and rotten political system unlikely to supply that will to resist that was to be found in Britain and its Dominions. Morale had to be bolstered, for it was this that would defeat Germany. Thus his perceptions meshed with his political ambitions.

Before his Moscow mission, Beaverbrook was arguing for supply to the USSR, because otherwise their resistance would crumble and Britain would have to fight an enemy whose strength had been augmented.[97] However, his attitude from before the war made it easy for him to move on from such considerations, which had earlier guided Churchill, to a policy of political concessions. Without understanding his pre-war attitude, this does appear simply political opportunism, but it is clear that Beaverbrook was being consistent with his own established perceptions of the USSR. By this time, September 1941, Churchill occupied a sort of middle ground; he appointed Beaverbrook, knowing his views, to head the mission to discuss supply with Stalin, and then warned Beaverbrook just before he left that he would not stand for Britain being 'bled white', and that Beaverbrook should not allow himself to be affected by the atmosphere in Moscow. This proved to be a vain hope.[98]

Beaverbrook Steals Cripps' Thunder

Cripps agreed with Beaverbrook on the need for political concession to strengthen Soviet morale and assuage their suspicions. They disagreed on the supply question. Cripps' advocacy of concession derived from his perceptions of sensitivity and suspicion. However, he continued to believe the Soviets appreciated a 'haggle', so he did not believe a tactic of exchanging information for information would damage relations. On the contrary it now offered the opportunity to get those relations on a regular footing based on the coincidence of interest he had long perceived.[99] Cripps was not suggesting bargaining for purposes of establishing goodwill, but argued for it as the best way to achieve a logical distribution of allied resources. The corollary was that the absence of such a hard-headed approach would raise doubts in Soviet minds as to the seriousness of the British in making the offers. Open-handedness would bring no increase in respect and, as a sign of weakness, would induce the Soviets to make increasingly exorbitant demands with little attempt to justify them. He did not apply this dictum to the political sphere, where he saw prestige as a very influential factor.

Cripps had a much less negative view of the Soviet Union than Beaverbrook and was thus less disposed to pamper them now they had been forced into belligerency. The hard-bargaining approach which both he and Macfarlane advocated for the supply mission was anathema to Beaverbrook and he kept them on the sidelines while he was in Moscow. Their arguments that nothing would be gained in return and that the Soviets would see weakness in a failure to bargain were to Beaverbrook irrelevant in the face of his chief aim, which was to show that the British meant business. He was prepared to promise virtually anything the Soviets asked for, and to eschew any haggling such as would give any impression of reluctance. This unusual method of negotiation was the product of his belief that Soviet morale needed supporting, that matériel was their main concern and therefore assurance of supply and of British sincerity would increase their will to resist. He credited Stalin with his own single-minded preoccupation with the war and therefore brushed aside Cripps' demand for talks on postwar reconstruction. Anything that would bring contention should be avoided: a propaganda and morale-boosting coup in six days was his stated aim from the outset. There was therefore little discussion of strategy though General Ismay, Churchill's Chief of Staff, went for this purpose;

Beaverbrook wanted nothing to detract from the main impact of the Protocol or dilute its effect.[100]

These tactics set an important precedent which was subsequently to make it difficult to initiate a firmer approach without aggravating Soviet suspicions. The mission was also important for further developments in Beaverbrook's perceptions. He had seen them in fighting mood and now believed they would survive. He felt his mission did much to lift morale – but he also experienced at first hand the wall of suspicion regarding British policy, which strengthened his belief in the error of that policy. On his return he moved into the political field, believing that the all-important military cooperation could not be achieved unless this situation was rectified. Stalin's negative attitude in their second meeting made a strong impression on Beaverbrook and he now became the champion of political concessions to the Soviet Union in addition to the supply of matériel. His observations convinced him that the British stance on political issues was a test for them of the sincerity of British support. Interested only in the short term, he tended to discount the future effects of concessions beyond the immediate aim of victory. He pressed for compliance with the Soviet request for a declaration of war on Finland, Hungary and Romania, and after Eden's trip to Moscow in December, for acceptance of Stalin's frontier demands.[101]

Beaverbrook had in any case little interest in eastern Europe: the Soviet claims were to him justified by the part they were playing in the war. He thus readily viewed the Baltic annexations as a matter of security. His justification of it outdid even Cripps in *realpolitik* and employed terms he knew would be understood by his political and military colleagues. In depicting the Baltic states as the 'Ireland of Russia' he was putting a purely military (and imperialistic) viewpoint, but one that would strike a chord with those who like Churchill were regretting the loss of the Western Irish ports. This was therefore a clear attempt to play on the preoccupations of Churchill and the COS and to try to get them to see Soviet strategic defence needs in the same light that they viewed their own.[102]

The Military Opposition to Beaverbrook

Beaverbrook's assertion that the nature of the war had changed brought only qualified agreement in the services departments. Their personal antipathy towards Beaverbrook and his irregular methods was strong. They answered Beaverbrook with arguments based on what they considered military practicalities, but the root of the trouble was that they did not accept the assumptions from which their protagonist argued. What to him gave the overriding force and urgency for his ideas, to them were incorrect interpretations of the Soviet situation and character or else irrelevant to a military strategy based on an assessment of resources and strategic priorities that had been laid down prior to BARBAROSSA.

To be sure, the fact of Soviet resistance and the need to sustain it in a material and morale sense brought them to accept the Supply Protocol and to work hard towards its fulfilment (despite Beaverbrook's assertions to the contrary).[103] They saw they had to accept a Protocol that was not based on information as to needs nor assessment of priorities, though with misgivings. They had not, however, assimilated the USSR into their strategic vision of the war, and in this sense Beaverbrook's criticism was close to the mark. Their priorities placed the USSR below other fronts.[104] The Soviet role in British military eyes was as yet only to survive as long as possible – another form of the attrition strategy – and provide a breathing-space for the build-up of British arms. The despatch of arms to the USSR would divert much needed British and American material from the defence of Britain, the Middle East, the bombing campaign and the blockade. If the Soviets were fighting for their own survival then such a quixotic gesture could hardly make them fight any harder.[105] General Brooke, the new CIGS, deeply resented the supply of tanks to the USSR, where he believed they were poorly used and unlikely to make a great difference to the outcome of the campaign.[106]

At a lower level, the WO in particular does not appear to have revised its perceptions from earlier in the year. Warner described the attitudes of MI3c, the new Soviet section of MI, as so 'anti-Russian as to be dangerous'. Cavendish-Bentinck of the FO Services Liaison Department, who chaired the JIC, added:

> Whenever the Russians achieve some success or even succeed in stemming the German advance, these officers become plunged in gloom. A Russian defeat fills them with joy.

However, he felt that even if the officers of the Soviet section had been less prejudiced, MI would still have been anti-Soviet – and added that Sillem and Tamplin, transferred from MI2b, though 'fanatical' in their anti-Soviet views, were at least less stupid than many in MI. In the absence of full papers for the Intelligence sections, it is hard to know how accurate these complaints were. MI3 were certainly pessimistic about the outcome on the Eastern Front. Polish pessimism was endorsed, as was Polish concern that the press were exaggerating the importance of the Soviet Union in the war.[107]

A further point made by Cavendish-Bentinck on the same paper, that the WO regarded Soviet officers as 'not being nice people to associate with', is borne out by other evidence, as is the British military's sense of superiority towards them. This may well have been enhanced by the origin of the WO's Russian-speaking officers, many of whom were born and raised in Tsarist Russia, as sons of expatriate British businessmen or the like, and most had served with the Interventionist forces in 1919.[108] To be fair to the COS, these factors probably only served to predispose them towards strategic decisions they would have made anyway. It must, though, be borne in mind that such decisions always rested on a set of priorities, and military attitudes by the end of 1941 were remarkably unaffected by the alteration in the basic facts of the Anglo-Soviet relationship.

Developments in Foreign Office Perceptions and the Decline of Reserve

There was a greater and more notable shift in FO attitudes led from the top by Eden. Eden sided with Beaverbrook in the Cabinet and Defence Committee. In doing so, he was strongly supporting a line that in the FO was still the subject of lively debate. Cadogan ascribed Eden's attitude to the influence of Harvey, reappointed as his Private Secretary in a voluntary demotion, and some historians have tended to follow suit.[109] Harvey's diary gives vivid testimony to his own views, but his actual influence on Eden is more problematic. Eden's stance was consistent with his long-standing view of Soviet suspiciousness and fitted in with his aspiration towards improving relations. In the FO debate he appears at times to belong to both sides, for the reservations in his attitude had also by no means disappeared.

The Northern Department had not acquired a Soviet specialist to replace Maclean until July 1941, with the appointment of Armine Dew, who had previously succeeded him in both his posts at Paris and Moscow. He was to prove a knowledgeable official on the subject of the USSR. He was by no means a Soviet sympathiser – he was no Crippsite – though he did believe in the need to draw the USSR out of isolation. In autumn 1941 he was arguing like his colleagues and superiors for a cautious but definite movement away from reserve.[110]

By mid-October, FO officials were, like Beaverbrook, finding the reserve policy unsatisfactory.[111] Contrary to expectations, the USSR had survived, but the Germans continued to press forward towards Moscow, Leningrad and the Caucasus. Far from making relations easier, this meant that the postponed consideration of long-term Anglo-Soviet relations not only now had to take place, but did so against the backdrop of continued Soviet demands for assistance. In the last quarter of 1941, there was little study as yet of the likely shape of Soviet foreign policy in the new situation. Crucial developments in the FO image of the USSR were, however, in the process of taking place. Soviet suspicions and sensitivity now began to be acknowledged – and it was not only Cripps and Beaverbrook who found them to have some justification. This was particularly so in the FO for military questions. Soviet suspicions that the British saw their conflict as separate, and hoped for German–Soviet mutual exhaustion were considered to be an important determinant of their actions.[112]

Earlier, the FO had not been interested in a political rapprochement when Cripps had suggested it on 29 July. Military action seemed to be what the Soviets wanted.[113] It was the Beaverbrook mission which first raised a potential political dimension to the question. At the final banquet, discussion between Beaverbrook and Stalin had ranged far and wide, and Stalin suggested an Anglo-Soviet postwar alliance, declaring that all Soviet officials favoured it.[114] Beaverbrook had not immediately taken this idea up on his return; it was Eden who raised the issue with the War Cabinet, on 13 October.[115] He was authorised to discuss it with Maisky, but discussions quickly became bogged down on the issue of the Soviet request that Britain declare war on Finland, Hungary and Romania.[116] This request had been made in September, as a gesture to show solidarity in the absence of military activity. No one in the British Government had been very keen at the time; when the issue was discussed again in Cabinet after Maisky's comments, Beaverbrook and Eden now favoured it, as a substitute for sending troops to the USSR or opening a second front. Churchill and the Labour ministers opposed it, on the grounds that it would simply drive the three countries further into coalition with Hitler. The real difference was that Beaverbrook and Eden felt that Soviet morale was a key factor and needed bolstering, and that Soviet suspicions that the British hoped to play *tertius gaudens* were strong and likely to have an effect on Soviet resistance and might even affect their readiness to make peace with Germany.[117]

Some of Cripps' interpretations now struck a chord within the FO. In particular, he claimed that the Soviets were not being treated on the equal terms that their efforts warranted. Greece and Turkey had been favoured with visits by the CIGS and the Foreign Secretary, every effort was made to meet US susceptibilities, but the USSR, which was fighting the battles on which Britain's survival rested, was fobbed off with lame excuses. At the least they deserved a statement delivered in person by someone in authority as to why no second front or troops to the Eastern Front were possible – something Ismay could have done while in Moscow. Their political requests should be given sympathetic consideration. Cripps did not believe that there was a risk of driving them to make a separate peace, but did believe that it might make the difference in ensuring their morale held through the winter and they continued fighting.[118] In addition, looking ahead, as was his wont, he saw that if postwar collaboration was desired, now was the best time to make a firm arrangement; with success, the Soviets were not likely to be so modest in their requests.[119]

The FO refuted the analogy with Greece and Turkey, but on having the issue put squarely before them, came to the conclusion that they did indeed desire postwar collaboration. That being the case, something clearly had to be done to improve relations. That they were in a parlous state was demonstrated forcefully by a message from Stalin to Churchill on 8 November. Alongside a number of complaints, made in the most brusque tone, Stalin raised once again the question of a postwar arrangement.[120]

To Cripps' telegrams, Stalin's importuning, the inactivity on the military front and Eden's personal sense that policy to the USSR was drifting aimlessly must be added a further factor in shaping the FO's attitude. Soviet demands that there should be an international reconstruction bureau were taken as a sign that this was an important issue for them, a view endorsed and expanded upon by Brigadier Skaife at the start of November. Although attached to PID, Skaife was regularly called upon to offer opinions on Soviet questions, and eventually this role was formalised by his being moved into FORD, alongside academics such as Humphrey Sumner from the RIIA. He was a Russian speaker, with experience of the country going back to before the First World War, and had been the first Military Attaché to the USSR in 1934. Skaife argued that Soviet reconstruction needs would be vast and would shape their postwar relationship with Britain. Their need for credits and imports, and for a peaceful international environment, were seen by Skaife to offer an opportunity for a successful collaboration.[121]

All these considerations were brought together in a series of meetings of senior FO officials between 14 and 19 November. The conclusions reached at these meetings demonstrate how perceptions of the USSR were developing and beginning to reshape Britain's policies. There was consensus that the Soviets were suspicious of British motives, and that they were, in Warner's words, 'very touchy' about being left out of any discussions on the postwar world.[122] The answer seemed to be a two-stranded military and political approach. There was regret that Ismay had not been able, as had been intended, to explain the military situation fully to Stalin. The Soviets felt their request for 25–30 Divisions to be sent to their fighting front had not been answered, and Sargent conceded there was something in this; though the suggestion was unrealistic, they deserved a clear explanation. Stalin was a realist who would face facts, it was claimed, and the reluctance of the COS to give such information had to be overcome.[123] An offer to relieve Soviet troops occupying northern Iran and to send a British corps to the Caucasus had in addition aroused deep suspicions that the British were aiming to subvert Soviet power in this region while they were distracted.[124] The COS were already beginning to feel they had given enough with no return, but the FO saw Soviet resistance as the main return. Moreover, fighting two separate wars did not seem strategically sound. Even Cadogan conceded, 'we shall have to have frank political and military discussions with the Soviet.'[125]

This preference for frankness was not matched for the political sphere, the second element of the problem. The trouble was that Britain's own views were still at an early stage, though already inhibited by commitments to the Americans. Little definite was known of Soviet thoughts about the postwar era, and this was a further problem.[126] The Soviets had publicly committed themselves to the Atlantic Charter, though stating that they would have stiffened the wording of some clauses and changed others, without specifying which. Stalin's statement of war aims on 6 November had been 'quite unexceptionable' denying as it did any territorial ambitions or intention of interfering in the affairs of other countries.[127] There was some discussion, however, of whether this was the limit of Soviet aims.

Warner felt Stalin was deeply suspicious of the British desire to cooperate; these suspicions were long-standing and not easy to allay. The problem with attempting to conciliate Stalin was that he would be likely to raise his demands; but if no response was made he would hoard up his complaints and use them as an excuse with his own people and the world (including impressionable British public opinion) in the event of defeat. Britain in any case needed Soviet cooperation in Iran, Afghanistan, possibly against Japan, and certainly if Germany turned its military forces westwards again. Britain must do what she could to reduce these suspicions. The problem was that Soviet peace aims might well run counter to Britain's. They might want restoration of their 1941 frontiers, control of the Dardanelles Straits, an opening onto the North Atlantic at the expense of Norway and large reparations from Germany. The Soviets had to be brought in to any discussions on North Atlantic security (which the Norwegians had proposed), but the problem was what they would then demand. Warner favoured frankness on the military question, and the offer of a meeting between Eden and Stalin. But since Stalin was heavily engaged in the defence of Moscow, this could not happen for some time, so they could have their suspicions allayed while avoiding embarrassing discussions.[128]

This pessimism was not reflected at the FO meetings that followed. There was a clear sense that reserve was now obsolete, and opinion was uncertain about the possibility of such wide-ranging Soviet demands. Senior officials concluded that Stalin could be satisfied with something indeterminate – some kind of 'Volga Charter'.[129] Cripps had asserted that it would be easier to get a satisfactory agreement now, while Stalin was weak, but the officials felt Stalin wanted an agreement because he feared he would be in a weaker position after the war and a wanted firm British commitment that would ensure he was not excluded from peace-making. It was believed the Soviets would want a warm water port, probably on the Persian Gulf, protection of their interests in the Baltic and Black Seas, and bases in Finland, Norway and the Baltic states. The principal Soviet aim, however, was described as security, and it was felt that if a workable international settlement was reached regarding protection against future aggression, they might not feel the need to resort to the absorption of the Baltic states, eastern Poland and Bessarabia.[130]

In contrast to 1940, the level of cooperation that could be gained with the USSR was beginning to seem a vital factor in the shaping of postwar arrangements. The ideal settlement, it was felt, would depend on Anglo-American-Soviet cooperation, but the extent to which the Soviets would be cooperative would be conditioned by Soviet exhaustion, and how far they felt dependent on American favours. Reconstruction needs might prevent the Soviets from Sovietising eastern Europe, though they might be in occupation of Europe as far west as Berlin at the end of the war. This made it even more important to treat the Soviets as equal partners now, and to try to get their agreement to the establishment of confederations in eastern Europe and the Balkans.[131]

Overall, the inclination of the FO was to avoid a specific and detailed treaty, while identifying a need to make a paper commitment beyond the mutual assistance agreement of 12 July. As Dew had noted on 3 November, this might help insure against Soviet isolationism after the war, but it might involve Britain committing herself to restoring a certain regime or frontiers. His inclination had been to go slow.[132] Stalin's 8 November message made this difficult, but all were agreed that a vague statement of principles was best; this 'Volga Charter' would, it was hoped, flatter the Soviets, convince them that they were to be treated as equals and that they would be one of the powers shaping the postwar settlement, while avoiding any prior commitment to the shape of that settlement such as might cause contention between Britain and the USSR or with other allies. Cooperation could then build gradually.[133] This was the policy recommended to the Cabinet, and approved after considerable discussion which reinforced the aim of avoiding an agreement on Soviet frontiers.[134] The difficulties if Stalin did raise this issue were not really confronted. Thus it came as a shock when Stalin did raise the issue as his main desideratum with Eden in Moscow. The inadequacy of what was offered to Stalin (he did accept the 'charter', but wanted something more concrete, albeit in a secret protocol) was only partly a consequence of the need to satisfy the Americans by avoiding commitments on frontiers. It was also a reflection of the vestigial unwillingness to consider seriously Soviet points of view which led the British to suppose that the Soviets would be satisfied with less territory at the end of the war with Germany than they started it with. Stalin was depicted repeatedly as a realist who appreciated hard facts, but the implications of this were not yet being thought through.

The position at the end of 1941 was that FO perceptions of the USSR, unlike those of the military, were in a state of flux, and indeed some confusion, as the old certainties were undermined. The alliance that few in the Government had wanted in June 1941 was now believed to be essential. There was lack of agreement on what exactly this should entail. This reflected a greatly broadened range of perceptions of the Soviet Union concerning key areas. The crucial question was whether the USSR was a potentially cooperative partner, and if so, whether the cost to be paid would in any way jeopardise British interests. The concepts which now began to appear as guiding principles were not entirely new, but for the first time they gained influence with the formulators of policy: with the Northern Department, Sargent, Eden and in the Moscow Embassy. The result in the medium and long term was that even the theories that pre-dated and helped form the 1940 view, which had been part of FO traditional thinking, were no longer unquestioned. The theories that security and sensitivity guided Soviet policy seemed more accurate. These two hypotheses formed a central part of the wartime assumption that the USSR was not only potentially cooperative, but was actively going to pursue a policy of collaboration with Britain.

3
'The New Russia'[1]

Views of Soviet foreign policy derived from images of the Soviet Union itself, far more than was the case for any other state. However, this aspect of the wartime image of the USSR has rarely been explored. Instead it is implied that the Churchill administration was naïve and ignorant about Soviet internal affairs; that its policy was based upon certain misinformed assumptions that bore no relation to reality, and were not based on solid analysis. Yet Churchill himself placed this aspect in the forefront when considering why good relations with the USSR now seemed possible:

> The tremendous victories of the Russian armies, the deep-seated changes which have taken place in the character of the Russian state and government, the new confidence which has grown in our hearts towards Stalin – these have all had their effect.[2]

The two major monographs on wartime Anglo-Soviet relations pass over views of internal developments lightly. Victor Rothwell asserts that the British suffered from 'an almost pitiful lack of knowledge' about the military and economic position in the Soviet Union. He contends that the Soviets released information on the German-occupied parts of the USSR only, and the British did not believe most of it, especially when it related to atrocities. Martin Kitchen gives little more space to British analysis of internal developments, apparently endorsing the customary approach, which is that comments about changes in the USSR were made in ignorance. Hence Churchill's remark is accounted for by his annoyance with the Poles, and there is no exploration of what he was actually referring to.[3]

The thesis of a cooperative USSR was explicitly based on a set of assumptions about domestic developments. Assumptions about Soviet reconstruction needs derived from a connected series of interpretations of what had happened in the USSR since the outbreak of war, which were taken to shed light on the nature of the Soviet regime and its fundamental motivations. There is, moreover, plenty of evidence that an effort was made to assess internal developments in the USSR, and to take advantage of the possibility of acquiring better information which was afforded by the increased number and intimacy of contacts. By examining British assessments of the Soviet military and of social and economic change, it can be seen how an overall impression developed of an undogmatic, flexible regime, with serious economic problems. These newly ascribed characteristics were at the heart of the thesis of a cooperative Soviet Union.

Sources of Information

An important factor in developing the wartime image of the USSR was the increased amount of information available. It was still limited, but was more extensive than before. The Embassy in Moscow (in 1941–42, most of the staff were evacuated, to Kuibyshev) was the primary source of information on Soviet internal developments. Embassy reporting was patchy in quality, and under Cripps relatively little background material was sent. The Embassy claimed in mitigation that Moscow was unlike any other diplomatic posting. There were few informal social contacts, and none of the political gossip that in other states provided so much in the way of insight into developments. The Embassy did its best to satisfy the demand for solid information. The quality of despatches on internal developments improved with the appointment of Cripps' successor, Sir Archibald Clark Kerr. If the selection of Cripps had been unfortunate, the choice of Clark Kerr was inspired. He had been a success at a number of difficult posts in non-democracies, culminating in his period in China from 1938 to 1942. He appears to have brought with him few if any of the anti-Soviet prejudices characteristic of many British diplomats at this time. For him the main drawback of life in Moscow was its drabness and lack of social life; but he seems to have come to Moscow with a fairly open mind. Clark Kerr's observations of the Soviet Union were to be perceptive, if couched often in colourful metaphors that may have lessened their impact.

Clark Kerr's deputy was initially Lacy Baggallay, formerly Head of the Eastern Department in the FO. Upon his death in 1943, he was succeeded by Jock Balfour, an equally astute reporter whose scepticism balanced Clark Kerr's optimism. Of the junior diplomats, John Russell and Jim Lambert, and later Thomas Brimelow and Frank Roberts, plus Charles Gifford and Thomas Barman, despatched by the MEW and the Political Warfare Executive (PWE) respectively, were contributors of perceptive observations. In 1944, Barman's work was supplemented by a press reading bureau, headed by George Bolsover of Manchester University (later Director of the School of Slavonic and East European Studies).[4]

The main sources for internal developments were newspapers, visual evidence such as dress, sudden appearance or disappearance of certain consumption goods and choice of theatrical themes. Much of it was therefore indirect, as Clark Kerr pointed out. The continual Embassy dilemma was to satisfy the Northern Department and other clients who were hungry for information and analysis, but who might easily place too much reliance on what was inference and informed guesswork. Lack of archives (burnt during the evacuation of Moscow in October 1941) and of trained staff to assess the press did not help. Both Ambassadors in their different ways chafed at the lack of social contacts in Moscow. Balfour and Clark Kerr noted later in the war that the contacts position occasionally appeared to be improving, but this never lasted, and Soviet citizens remained cautious of striking up acquaintances with foreigners, fearful of attracting the attention of the NKVD.[5]

The Soviet press, if read carefully and systematically, was actually a fairly good source. In its coverage it was more weighty than much of the British press, and there was plenty of statistical data and revealing articles to process, always bearing in mind their purpose and source. Churchill complained that Clark Kerr in despatching Soviet press material was sending 'froth and fluff'. The FO and MEW, however, found such material valuable.[6]

In Moscow, the main personal sources of information, in the absence of good contacts with Soviets, were other foreigners. Journalists found their task even more frustrating than the diplomats, as their reports were heavily censored by the Soviet Government. They tended either to develop a festering discontent, aggravated by personal clashes with the authorities, as did the *Daily Telegraph*'s Cholerton, or else went native, as did *The Times*' Parker.[7] The many British service personnel who were posted to the USSR as technical experts, on convoy support or other liaison duties, became equally frustrated. Such individuals, however, could provide plenty of information from contacts and experiences of a kind never available before to Britons in the USSR, in spite of the determined efforts of the Soviet bureaucracy to limit them. Their observations were all grist to the mill; and it can be seen from the above that much of this information was coming in to Whitehall from sources that were hardly pro-Soviet.

One source that does not qualify for this description was the SOE representative in Moscow from 1941 to 1945, Brigadier George 'Pop' Hill. Hill's eccentricities are well known; Clark Kerr nevertheless regarded Hill as the best informed of British personnel in the USSR about conditions and attitudes. He made plenty of contacts, including within the NKVD, while at the same time making no attempt to hide his interventionist past, indeed proudly displaying his Tsarist medals.[8]

The other major source for information in the USSR was the diplomatic community in Kuibyshev and Moscow. Views were exchanged regularly with the Czechs, whose Military Attaché, Colonel Pika, quickly gained a reputation for accuracy by predicting the outcome of the 1941 campaign. Bruce Lockhart regarded him as the best-informed of all foreigners in the USSR, describing him as objective and possessing extensive knowledge, while being under no delusions about the 'Soviet paradise' (unlike his colleague Fierlinger). The FO and MI3c came to attach some reliance to his reports. The Poles, who had tended to be pessimistic in 1941, thereafter lost credibility, being regarded as biased.[9] Contacts below the Ambassador level were close with the US Embassy. The Australian and Canadian Embassies (formerly High Commissions) passed on information and interpretations, and the Canadian Dana Wilgress was highly regarded.

In Whitehall, this material was supplemented by readings of the Soviet press and official pronouncements. Most of the information on the course of the actual fighting on the Eastern Front came from covert sources, principally signals intelligence about the German side; these sources also provided a certain amount of other information, particularly in the areas of interest to the MEW. The Soviets were inconsistent in the amount of information they were prepared to give on the fighting; occasionally full details of the German order of battle were given, but this was infrequent and depended on the political climate.[10] Information on the Soviet order of battle from the Soviets was even less regular. They would usually refer enquirers to the official communiqués. The JIC, however, were able to supplement the occasional information the Soviets supplied, and actually build up a fairly accurate picture of developments on the Eastern Front from about August 1941 from decrypts of German wireless traffic; and from late 1942, of decrypts of the German signals intelligence organisation, which was itself doing the same thing with regards to Soviet wireless traffic.[11] JIC reports and predictions regarding this front were usually prefaced with the statement that their contents were to be taken with reserve, in view of the lack of direct and reliable information from the Soviets.[12] Generally, their papers were remarkably accurate (not always true of those of MEW), and they need not have been so modest. Doing so, of course, helped to hide the ultra-secret source of most of this material. Actual visits to the front did happen more frequently than 30 Mission complaints would suggest, though often these were to quiet areas and were closely supervised. The major exceptions were Hill's trips in 1944 to Leningrad and to the front area in Byelorussia; he seems to have been free to see almost all he wanted and to talk to whomsoever he wished. In addition, some naval personnel went into combat on Red Navy warships.[13]

Whatever the limitations of these sources of information, and there were many, this still represented an unparalleled situation in comparison to that obtaining either before or after the war. With such new sources available, it is hardly surprising that images of the USSR should be modified, even without taking into account the actual changes that were taking place in the USSR itself.

A number of agencies and individuals in Whitehall were involved in processing information on Soviet internal developments. The main ones were the Northern Department, MEW Russian Section (later USSR section of German Europe and Russia Department, Enemy Branch), NID16 and MI3c. PWE and the Ministry of Information were interested too, from the point of view of propaganda and morale. The Northern Department received interpretations from all these agencies, and their extensive papers in the FO371 series in the Public Record Office are an invaluable source for their views as well as those of the FO itself, particularly in view of the patchy records of MEW and the limited amount of material released for the JIC and MI. Initial interpretation on this material was provided by Dew and Geoffrey Wilson, who joined the Northern Department in 1942. Wilson, a pacifist barrister of Quaker origins, was much closer than

Dew to the views of Cripps, whom he had accompanied to the USSR. He was one of the few diplomats not to be jaundiced towards the USSR by his stay in the country. Skaife was asked frequently to comment on internal developments, and emerges as far less critical even than Wilson. FRPS and its successor organisation FORD were intended to supply only historical and factual background, though often this spilled over into political analysis. This was fed into Northern Department discussions, but with the exception of contributions by Skaife on reconstruction, was not particularly influential. Material on internal developments mainly went only as far as Sargent, except that pertaining to morale, the military situation and the food crisis, which went right up to Eden. However, Clark Kerr's despatches were circulated within the FO and to the War Cabinet, so Churchill was familiar with the basic material, if not with the FO's commentary.

Stereotypes of Russians

British attitudes to the USSR were imbued with and to an extent even shaped by a set of racial assumptions. The key racial issue concerning the Soviets was whether they could be considered European at all. There were frequent references to 'Oriental' traits, which conjured up an apparently clear set of characteristics; though on closer analysis these traits were many and various, and at times contradictory. The most common use of the term 'Oriental' was to denote deviousness and cunning. Orientals were supposed to favour complex and convoluted plans, never quite mean what they said, expected to haggle and bargain, and distrusted apparent straightforwardness; they seemed to enjoy protracted and tortuous negotiations. To an extent, they were even 'inscrutable'. It was often remarked of Soviet officials how they adopted a stony-faced expression and were devoid of all apparent emotion when dealing with official business or negotiations, and this was explained as a consequence of their ethnicity. Anthony Haigh of the Northern Department summed up the prevailing view when he wrote: 'Russia has never had more than a veneer of Western civilisation and in the Soviet Union that veneer has been scratched off and Asia predominates.' Other Asiatic characteristics included a tendency to exaggerate and an obsession with prestige. But 'Oriental' could also mean an almost vulgar directness, crudity and lack of refinement. The ethnic theme was pushed furthest by Owen O'Malley, Ambassador to the Polish

Government, who wrote of the 'cruel and heathenish tyranny' of Russia compared to the Roman and Byzantine civilisations of eastern and south-eastern Europe. Churchill was to make similar comments. Lieutenant-General Martel, Head of 30 Mission in 1943, found the Asiatic idea to be the key to understanding the USSR; others too found aspects of it useful. Bruce Lockhart believed Russia to move between extremes of humaneness and cruelty, energy and laziness – Europe versus Asia.[14]

The ethnic Russians themselves were identified as possessing to the full the attributes of the Slav. This meant that they were taken to have a 'peasant mentality': slow-thinking and dull. It was a supposed Slav characteristic to have brief fits of frenetic activity, followed by a reversion to inactivity. 'The Russian temperament still finds sustained exertion distasteful,' wrote Clark Kerr, though they were capable of useful work in spurts of action. Skaife, certainly no anti-Soviet figure, found the Russian by nature to have a poor sense of discipline, a fact he thought well recognised by the Soviet authorities. They were presented as a stark ethnic contrast to the equally stereotyped Germans with their Teutonic thoroughness and machine-like efficiency. Baggallay commented in February 1942 that it was a good thing that they did not have the Teutonic characteristics as well as their own. He added that despite the success of factory relocation, 'the idea that they can really be efficient is ... difficult of acceptance. The imagination boggles at the idea, as at the idea of a land where two and two make five.'[15] Russians, it was commonly observed, were unmethodical. This was confirmed in a number of areas; by their unpunctuality, their lack of routine, the way their mechanics flitted from one unfinished job to another, the way their destroyers avoided the boring monotony of escort duty. Stalin himself encouraged the idea, saying to Cripps that Russians lacked order and method.[16] As Slavs, they were also blessed with a deeply romantic temperament and a simple love of country. Their tendency to denigrate foreign achievements led Dew to comment: 'as always, the Russian considers himself superior to anyone else.' According to Lockhart, Russians were traditionally xenophobic, partly a racial characteristic, partly a consequence of centuries of despotism; a sense of inferiority to the culture of the West competed with the Slav sense of messianic vocation. They had the Slav sensitivity to criticism and the Slav capacity for suspicion of the motives of others.[17] They were technologically maladroit, incapable of sophistication, but resourceful in improvisation. Their inefficiency and romanticism made them difficult to organise, and it was felt that the problems encountered by the Soviet Government in trying to industrialise and modernise the country before the war derived greatly from these racial characteristics.

The tyranny was therefore in a sense necessary; softer methods would not have succeeded. The Russians were anyway used to such methods throughout their history; such achievements as they had were due to an efficient autocracy able to harness their qualities while diminishing the effects of their defects. Russians, an SOE paper declared, 'want a bit of leading'.[18] Baggallay commented that 'Russian patriotism and self-sacrifice have always shone brightest at the worst moments even under rulers whose hand lay heavy upon them', and added that they bore hardship because they were accustomed to it.[19] There was indeed some sense that these ethnic characteristics had been overlain by further ones that were a consequence of the autocracy, particularly secrecy and unfriendliness towards foreigners. Prior to BARBAROSSA, Thomas Preston, who had been Consul in Ekaterinberg in 1918 and in Kovno in 1940, had claimed that under Bolshevism the Russians had become aggressive, stubborn, distrustful and offensive to foreigners and even physically shrunk, now being slovenly in gait and puny, compared to the giants of Tsarist days, and Collier and others had been ready to believe it. Such views went out of fashion after June 1941, when it now appeared the regime had done wonders with this unpromising ethnic material; Lambert, for example, found the USSR an improvement in efficiency terms on old Russia, though still with much ground to make up, inefficiency being characteristic of Slav peoples.[20]

New characteristics were observed in the war; an ability in improvisation and quick organisation to cope with new problems were remarked upon, particularly in connection with the relocation of industry and the organisation of reconstruction in the liberated territories. Russian improvisation was sometimes seen as a failing, especially in technological matters, but there was some appreciation of their resourcefulness under severe conditions, and of their ability to move quickly and decisively.[21]

The Caucasian peoples of the USSR were clearly identified as 'Orientals'. Georgians and Azeris were characterised in terms that seemed to put them on a par with Afghan hill tribes. In 1940, Butler had been puzzled by FO references to 'typical Caucasian behaviour' by Mikoyan, and was told by Collier that Armenians were the product of a semi-Oriental, commercial environment, which created a racial inferiority complex, suspicion and an indirect approach to any question. He suggested Butler could find out more by reading Lermontov and the 1914 *Baedeker* guide, which says much about the kind of material these racial stereotypes were based upon. These Caucasian peoples were seen as the source of the 'Georgian-Armenian ruling clique'; to observers this accounted for the 'almost oriental suspicion' of Soviet officials, the hard bargaining attitude and the refusal to compromise. It was, noted Lambert, a tyranny '*à l'orientale*'.[22]

It is notable how frequently references to such traits were made. At first they tended to appear as supporting arguments for the idea that the Soviets were no match for the Germans. Surprise resulted when the Soviets apparently rose above their basic ethnic nature. They still operated to explain certain behaviour. They also, significantly, served as a strong mitigating factor for Soviet methods. If the Slavs were inherently lazy and inefficient, then such methods were the only way by which Stalin was going to bring them into a state of readiness to face the German onslaught; regrettable of course, but the outcome was the right one – and of course, 'the Russians are not like us.'[23] If for them the end justified the means, there was cause to be thankful for the miracle that Stalin was able to achieve in bringing his people to be able to stand up to the efficient German war machine that had overrun so many others.

Soviet Morale and Self-confidence

As we have seen, the general expectation throughout the British Government, with few exceptions, was that morale within the USSR would quickly crumble after the first German victories. The regime's hold on its people was supposedly only sustained by terror, and this was no basis for popular resistance in modern warfare, when the autocracy itself was so inefficient. Having seen morale collapse in the face of the German *Blitzkrieg* in more advanced European nations, such as France, how much more likely was this to happen in the USSR, particularly among the non-Russian peoples who would be the first to experience German invasion. A breakdown of the transportation and communications system was predicted and the consequent shortages of food would, it was felt, quickly spread the collapse of morale to the major cities, including Moscow. In the first two weeks, this seemed close to realisation. Few expected an upsurge of patriotism to be possible after 20 years of Communism, even Churchill, despite the phrasing of his 22 June broadcast. Probably the first major concern in the FO, MEW and the military was to find evidence of the state of Soviet morale.[24] Only slowly did pessimism disappear, with signs that the regime had regained its nerve and that it was planning for a long war. The acid tests in this area were the determination with which the scorched earth policy was being carried out and the readiness to move resources out of reach of the Germans.[25]

It was observed that the successful defence of Moscow and the Soviet counter-attacks of the winter of 1941–42 did wonders for Soviet self-confidence. That Moscow held out and morale did not crack were attributed to the harsh measures taken. This was seen as a revelation of the unsuspected efficiency of the regime. Even more surprising, Stalin was seen to have taken a statesmanlike, popular stance by remaining in Moscow, and his combination of coercion and patriotic exhortation was increasingly seen as skilful and well conceived.[26] The regime, which had commonly been depicted in Whitehall as unpopular, was seen to have strengthened its standing with public opinion. As the war progressed, it became axiomatic in Whitehall that the regime's position after the war would be secure and unchallengeable, provided that it achieved victory and maintained good relations with the armed forces.

Soviet military morale was observed to rise, fall and rise again dramatically through 1942. In February, Stalin rashly promised his people that the war would be won in 1942, carried away by the successes of his winter counter-offensive.[27] The British did not share this confidence and in the summer both Stalin's increasingly frenzied pleas for a second front and rumours of disastrous collapses of morale on the Southern Front confirmed this view. The British received only fragmentary information of the harsh measures taken to stiffen the resistance of Soviet forces – the infamous Order 227 ('Not A Step Back') – but concluded that Stalin had acted personally and decisively to avert catastrophe.[28] From the time when Soviet forces counter-attacked at Stalingrad, Red Army morale was consistently regarded as excellent.

Uncertainty continued, however, about morale on the home front, and about the whole issue of the influence of public opinion. Central control of the communications media by the state and Party meant there was no obvious means for its expression. However, many of the Soviet Government's actions appeared to indicate a concern about public opinion and morale. There was some discussion by the British about the extent to which the evident needs and concerns of the populace would put pressure on the regime, and as to how the regime would respond. It was possible to argue that the war had shown the regime the advantages of liberal methods over blatant coercion. It was also possible to argue that having stirred up public opinion for the purposes of total war, it would be impossible for the Government simply to ignore its public immediately after the war. Skaife, for one, suggested that the Soviet Government would not even wish to do so, assuming that their professed aim of raising the lot of the Soviet masses was in some part genuine.[29]

The sacrifice of 'useless mouths' in the rationing system served to increase the constant perplexity as to how the Soviet people's morale remained as high as reports suggested.[30] It was felt that subjugated peasants could not have endured this situation without breaking. The solution was found in attachment to *rodina* ('motherland'), part of the deep Slav romanticism identified as an ethnic characteristic.[31] It was clear right at the start that as the JIC reported, the 'nationalist drum was being beaten louder than the communist one'.[32] Eric Berthoud, an MEW oil expert who was an active observer while in the USSR in 1941–42, suggested that patriotic feeling must have been very strong to overcome the debilitating effects of forced industrialisation, purges and labour camps. Others, in asking why the Soviets were doing so well against the efficient, well-armed Germans, agreed; the main reason had to be attachment to the motherland, which brought into play the toughness and resilience of a somewhat backward people used to roughing it. They were believed to be accustomed to a 'heavy hand' and being essentially an indolent people, responded best to firm treatment.[33]

On the other hand, it was felt in the Embassy and in the Northern Department that public opinion could not entirely be ignored by the Soviet Government. The emphasis on patriotism demonstrated clearly that in a war situation the Government had to anticipate and shape public opinion even more than in peace time. Public opinion may not have directly made decisions, but it could offer constraints on the regime's policy, and even on occasions shape the particular course followed. The essentially pragmatic regime would be concerned to initiate policies that stood a chance of success; and in that sense public mood was of importance. This was a logical conclusion; but it gradually and almost imperceptibly developed into the more contentious idea that public mood could actually determine the policy itself. Thus in 1944, Skaife felt that the constitutional changes giving increased autonomy to the republics were a result of popular pressure.[34]

One consequence was that British policy-makers – and this included Churchill – became very concerned that the Soviet Government educate its public about the Allies. One of the acid tests of the attitudes of the Soviet regime to collaboration with the Allies was the extent to which they publicly recognised the Allied war effort, and in particular the contribution made by Britain and the USA in the form of supplies to the Red Army. The resentment caused when this contribution was downplayed, denigrated or ignored was quite remarkable. Equally, the satisfaction with recognition was great. The complaint that the Soviets showed no gratitude is repeated again and again in documents of the period and in memoirs written subsequently. Often these comments were simply made to make the point that the Soviets *should* be grateful. On occasion, deeper concerns were voiced; amongst them that the Soviets were leaving themselves scope for a separate peace, that they were urging the Allies on to greater efforts, or that they were concerned about interest being shown in the Allies by the Soviet people, which might lead to unhealthy demands for reform.[35] With all these considerations in mind, except the last, there was concern to generate a pro-Ally mood. This was a desire for an accolade that could be of propaganda use at home, but it also stemmed from a genuine feeling that the Soviet people needed to appreciate the aid their allies were giving. This would help them to get over their dislike of foreigners, and implied that the creation of such a mood, even though it would clearly in the first place have been inspired by the regime itself, would apply pressure on the regime to be cooperative with the Allies.[36]

Developing Assessments of the Capabilities and Equipment of Soviet Armed Forces

It was to an extent inevitable that the image of the Soviet military machine would undergo a change, given the way in which the war developed. British public admiration for the Red Army knew few bounds. In view of the importance of the Soviet victories to British operations, it might have been expected that there would have been a corresponding attitude in Whitehall in official and military circles. The image of the Soviet military certainly altered, but by no means as far in the same direction as it did for the general public. Admiration was limited by continuing scepticism about the level of sophistication of the Soviet forces. The old image of the Russian steamroller proved very enduring. Soviet staff methods and technological expertise were still criticised. British personnel found it hard to understand how the Soviets actually managed to beat the Germans, about whom to the end the British military had a very high opinion. Indeed, annoyance was expressed in response to suggestions in the British press and from the Soviets themselves that their efforts had won the war; suggestions which the FO by contrast felt were justified.[37]

There was a number of factors that shaped the way that attitudes developed. One was the ethnic stereotype. This had always been influential on British military assessments and continued to be so. Another factor was the treatment of British personnel in the USSR. The lack of respect towards them, or gratitude for British efforts to help, and the failure to provide facilities for them to do their duties or live in what the British regarded as conditions of basic comfort, influenced the underlying attitude towards the Soviets as a whole. This reinforced the view that they were 'savages', in the words the Soviets attributed to Major-General Burrows, the Head of 30 Mission in 1944.[38]

A further factor was the nature of the information available. Much of it came from sources that with the exception of the Czechs were not friendly to the Soviets. These sources did little to redress the balance against the preconceptions in the WO regarding Soviet staffwork and inter-service coordination. Failings in these areas continued to be remarked upon throughout the war in MI3c and JIC commentaries. MI, 30 Mission and the Embassy all reported separately the opinion that junior officers were good, and that staffwork at the highest level was competent, but that in between, at Division and Corps level, it was, in Baggallay's words, 'rotten'. Training was seen to be rudimentary, especially in the Air Force, where the JIC described the situation as the 'survival of the fittest'. In 1942 the JIC thus praised Soviet morale, which had 'confounded the prophets', but felt that it was too much to hope that their fundamental weaknesses in planning, organisation and administration had been entirely overcome. On receiving their report the COS felt they were even then being over-optimistic.[39] Those who were able to make first-hand observations tended to confirm these conclusions.

The renowned defensive capabilities of the Soviet soldier continued to be asserted; but it was not until 1943, and then grudgingly, that his (or her) ability to maintain an offensive were conceded. The JIC at the end of 1942 described the Soviet soldier as first class in defence. Given a rifle and some food and ammunition he would prepare his own position with skill and fight until either he or his opponent was dead. There was great admiration for this quality, though at the same time a sense that it was a result of his 'primitiveness'.[40] However, these qualities could only delay, not halt, the powerful *Wehrmacht*. Soviet equipment was not rated highly, except for some Soviet aircraft, notably the Il-2 *Stormovik*. Naval equipment was believed poor, except the submarines, many of which were built from German designs. The Soviets were credited with the same characteristic as the Japanese; of being good copiers of other people's designs, but of tending to lack a grasp of the technical complexities. The only area where Soviet superiority to the Germans was conceded was in the area of clothing; there was great admiration for Soviet winter equipment.[41] Soviet successes from 1943 were seen at least partly to be a result of the influx of Allied matériel and the design lessons the Soviets would have learnt from it.

From the Soviet counter-attacks in 1941–42 onward, the question was posed as to how the Soviets had managed to hold their own and then defeat the Germans. As well as high morale and a deep, if romantic, patriotism, the military ascribed this to overstretch by the Germans and traditional Russian abilities in winter warfare. They felt that the revival of the political commissars (*politruki*) enabled the regime to use coercion to keep their troops fighting. Salutary measures were believed to have been applied after the Rostov débâcle in July 1942, and rumours abounded that the *politruki* had orders to shoot officers who allowed retreats. This was seen, however, as in the long run a weakness, and the British military felt a major problem with the Red Army was political interference that magnified the deficiencies of the higher command structure.[42]

There was considerable satisfaction, therefore, when it was announced that the system was once more to be abolished. Clark Kerr felt that this move was the result of a struggle between the Army and the Communist Party, and that the Army had gained valuable ground. There was widespread interest in the relationship between the two, now that the Army was assuming such an important role. Party membership in the armed forces before the war had not been high, and it was assumed there was military resentment about the purges. The *ukase* of 17 July 1941 restoring the *politruki* had been seen as a sign of Party concern to maintain its control, even at the risk of efficiency (taken as the reason for abolition after the Finnish War). The Soviet High Command (*Stavka*) was not likely to be happy with this. The new abolition suggested that the Army had scored a notable victory in internal power politics, though Clark Kerr noted that the Party was also developing its influence in the Army by making enrolment in the Party by soldiers much easier. It was certainly reported as pleasing to units at the front, and in the Navy too, when abolition was extended there.[43]

However, on reflection, analysts in Whitehall disagreed with Clark Kerr. The Northern Department, MI3c and NID16 agreed that there were three main reasons for the reform. First, to increase efficiency by removing the impediment to commanders' actions. Second, to remedy the shortage of officer personnel caused by war losses and the expansion of the Army. The Soviets announced that many of the *politruki* would be retrained as line officers. Third, it was felt that there was an attempt to identify the Army and Party as partners in the same cause, without one needing to supervise the other. It was not, therefore, a victory of the Army over the Party.[44]

Service observers in the USSR were anxious to counter the impression given in the British press that the commissars had completely disappeared; all that had happened, they felt, was that an anomaly had been removed. The political officers who now served with units would do the same job their predecessors were doing in practice since BARBAROSSA – acting as morale officers, with their main task the prevention of cowardice and defeatism; still giving political instruction, but unable to interfere with command decisions. It was reported from North Russia that their naval counterparts continued to sport their special badges and to throw their weight around in the Red Navy Club at Polyarnoe. The difference was that the new 'deputy captain' no longer stood at his captain's shoulder and reviewed his decisions. Air Vice-Marshal Babington, head of the Air Mission in 1943, who had a low opinion of the intellectual capability of the Soviet soldier, felt the continued existence of the political officers, far from being a disadvantage, might have been crucial to Soviet successes that year. Clark Kerr agreed the high morale in the forces in 1943 was a result of the activities of the new political officers. Generally it was felt that a potentially damaging system had been modified, to give a simpler and more efficient line of command, which would remove the fatal tendency to indecisiveness on the part of commanders always conscious of the *politruk* examining their actions.[45] All agreed that it was an important development, indicating the regime's flexibility and willingness to make changes to increase efficiency, and demonstrating that the regime was prepared to trust the military to know its own business best. Since political interference had long been seen as a major weakness of the Soviet armed forces, the image of those forces' effectiveness increased with abolition.

Thus, in accounting for Soviet victories, increased efficiency was conceded, though there were distinct limitations to this. The emphasis was still on the virility of the individual Russian soldier. The military saw a major Soviet strength to be vast manpower reserves, though both the FO and MEW felt that this could be exaggerated, as the Soviet economy was fully mobilised and there was by 1944 no manpower surplus available.[46] It was still aspects of this kind that were stressed. The Germans continued to be seen to have the edge in terms of sophistication. Soviet tactics were observed to evolve beyond direct frontal assault, but they were not credited with much ingenuity in terms of attack, though their defensive techniques were much admired.[47] The abilities of the Air Force were seen to be limited to ground support, and the absence of a bombing force indicated their lack of capabilities or ambition. It was believed that the Allied strategic bombing of Germany and the invasion of Italy had played a crucial role in giving the Soviets air superiority in the east; little credit was given to Soviet air actions for this. Naval tactics were seen as limited and lacking in offensive spirit. Naval liaison officers in the Black Sea and North Russia saw a good deal of Soviet units, and were not impressed by their equipment or their methods.[48]

Thus, the main Soviet strengths were numbers, bravery, inspired improvisation, resilience in the face of huge losses on the part of front-line soldiers and some fine supreme commanders. These were, however, accompanied by deficiencies at the brigade and divisional level and by poor doctrine in coordination of different arms of service. The British military were reluctant to acknowledge that the Soviets had, or could have, defeated the Germans unaided, though when it suited them, they were prepared to assume a Soviet military machine of unlimited capabilities and resources.[49]

The Revival of Nationalism, Patriotism and Tsarist Practices

The suppleness of the regime evidenced by the reform of the *politruk* system was not an isolated instance. It was one of a number of developments that were carefully noted. Whitehall resisted the notion put forth in some areas of the press that the USSR had moved wholesale away from Communism, but such developments were seen to be more than just transitory. While to an extent expedient, they were not necessarily short-term. In addition, and probably most significantly, they were indications of the nature of the Soviet re-gime; under Stalin it appeared to be undogmatic, pragmatic and responsive to changing circumstances, free from any ideological straitjacket. This was nowhere more noticeable than in the revival of nationalism and particularly the conscious reference to the pre-Revolutionary past in an uncritical, indeed laudatory, way.

Long-term observers of the Soviet scene, such as Skaife and Dew, were aware that the regime had for some time been using patriotic themes to bolster its public support. They saw this as a consequence in the first instance of the victory of Stalin over Trotsky, supple-mented by the perception of the growing threat from Nazi Germany.[50] They were not therefore surprised at the use of such themes by Stalin at the start of the German–Soviet conflict. By 1943, how-ever, they found the extent and direction of this phenomenon had gone far beyond what had previously been observed. Moreover, to those focusing on the USSR afresh and with an image formed in the earlier days of revolutionary internationalism, including Churchill, these developments seemed all the more noteworthy and pointed to the possibility of wholesale reform within the USSR.

The Soviet Government began by reminding its citizens of the past feats of the Russian people in defending their homeland, par-ticularly in the Napoleonic period. References to fighting for Socialism, or for the 'workers' paradise' were notable by their absence. In-stead, the achievements of the builders of the Russian Empire were recalled as an inspiration, with due regard to the deeds of ordinary Russians. Aleksander Nevski, victor over invading Teutons, was naturally given special prominence. The new bravery awards to go alongside the Order of Lenin and the Order of the Red Banner were named after Suvorov, Kutusov and Nevski. When he visited Leningrad in 1944, Hill observed that Suvorov's tomb had been transformed into a shrine.[51]

All this was remarkable enough, though explicable in terms of wartime propaganda. However, it seemed that the regime felt it had hit upon a rich vein of supportive material, for it did not stop at words and images, but began to revive old practices of the pre-Revolutionary era that had been swept away after 1917. Significantly, this was done with overt reference to the Tsarist past.

This began first with the Army. At the start of 1943, soon after the abolition of the *politruki*, the wearing of epaulettes (*pogoni*) was revived. These had been hated symbols of the old regime, emblems of rank and privilege torn from the shoulders of officers during the Revolution and discarded as having no place in the army of the proletariat. Now they were reinstated, following closely the pre-Revolutionary pattern, so that anyone over 40 might recognise them, with a clear reference in the *ukase* to restoration of the traditions of the glorious Russian Army of the past. No mention now of that army's role as defender of the *ancien régime* and enemy of revolution. Again, it was noted that steps towards this change had been made before the war, for instance, with the revival of Cossack units and distinctive regimental uniforms. This however was clearly a reform of much broader scope. The open reference to tradition struck many observers as highly significant and symbolic of the categorical movement of the Soviet regime away from its revolutionary status to the government of a traditional nation-state.[52]

That this meant more than simply decoration was soon apparent. Further *ukases* made clear that deferential behaviour was expected from junior officers and other ranks towards their superiors; a strict code of behaviour was laid down on saluting and the proper deportment expected of a Red Army officer, which would not have been out of place in any monarchist army. Tsarist rank nomenclature was reinstated, and use of the word *offitsier* was revived, instead of *tovarisch komandir*. Observers noted that use of the term *offitsierski sostav* in the press clearly implied the existence of an officer corps along the old lines. The establishment of officers' clubs and the reinstatement of batmen (officers' orderlies), were additional signs of this return to tradition.[53]

This was interpreted as a further attempt at improving efficiency, by improving discipline and building an *esprit de corps*. It was also seen as another attempt by the Party to win favour with the military, while at the same time, political figures were given uniforms and rank, associating the Party with the Army's glory.[54] Such developments clearly, however, had broader social significance, in the positive references to the pre-Revolutionary past and the introduction of the trappings of privilege.

Traditionalist, nationalist reforms were observed to continue apace through 1943 and 1944. A noteworthy example was the national anthem. The revolutionary *Internationale* was replaced by a patriotic song. In announcing the change, *Pravda* declared that the old anthem was no longer relevant in view of the 'radical changes' that had taken place in the USSR; as clear a statement as one could wish for that the revolutionary days were over. There was not a single reference to revolution or Socialism in the anthem; instead it was a call to national pride.[55] Thus the war was observed to be spawning many wholesale changes in the USSR, changes that were openly in contradiction to the declared aims of the Bolshevik state in the years immediately following the Revolution. The big question in Whitehall was what significance to attach to these changes.

'The Elimination of the Classless Society'?

The FO, MEW, Ministry of Information and MI watched carefully for signs that the war was bringing changes in Soviet social organisation, particularly in the direction of liberalisation, or a movement towards a more 'normal' organisation of society; specifically involving private property and the development of a class system. Any such changes would be important indicators of the nature of the regime and the ideological motivations of its leaders.

Baggallay introduced this topic in a despatch of 25 February 1942. He commented that the Soviet system was open to those with talent, regardless of birth; there was privilege, but it had to be earned. Thus the 'classless society' that the Soviet Union claimed to be was not devoid of differences in status, but membership of groups was fluid.[56] However, this proviso tended to be ignored subsequently, and any sign of groups acquiring privileged status was regarded as a new development and one of deep significance.

By the end of 1942, Clark Kerr and Skaife were both drawing attention to social changes that seemed to be part and parcel of the revival of various traditional practices and the whole issue of the appeal to the Russian (Tsarist) past in Soviet internal propaganda. The introduction of the new military orders was 'another link in the chain which is being slowly reforged with Russian traditions of the past'. Clark Kerr noted the changes were publicly justified in terms of continuity with tradition, now seen as an adequate reason on its own, quite apart from the increased efficiency that was also supposed to result.[57] Dew commented:

It is certainly significant that in the interests of efficiency the Soviet Govt feel able to dispense with outworn ideological ideas and to re-shape and re-cast so radically. The officers will form

another 'class' and we have gone a step further towards the creation
of a bourgeoisie.

Dew noted that such trends dated back to 1935; the process was
merely accelerated by the war. Such a perception lent strength to
the idea that these were more than wartime expedients and would
be permanent; even more so if they proved successful in the war
in firmly establishing the regime, as they seemed to do.[58]
The tendency to eliminate the more obvious revolutionary crudi-
ties, as the Kuibyshev Chancery put it, certainly did seem striking.[59]
A wholesale system of deference and rank was being introduced, it
seemed. This was only natural for the Army, particularly in view of
its earlier problems with morale, but the significant thing was that
this was spread much wider through Soviet society. If this was a
militarisation of Soviet society, then it was also clearly a stratifi-
cation according to distinct gradations of rank. According to Balfour,
writing in 1944, the blending of the Leninist doctrine of a classless
society with ingredients from pre-Revolutionary times had reached
a stage approaching the old Russian notion of *chiny*, or categories
of rank, to produce a highly stratified form of society based on
service to the state with rewards and privileges which corresponded
to the value of each category to the community as a whole.[60]
Developments in the education system reinforced this impression
most strongly. Reform of education had been one of the fundamental changes wrought by the Bolsheviks. They saw it as the
foundation for future social progress, and had as a central principle
the idea of free education for all, with equal opportunities for males
and females in a co-educational system which aimed to produce
skilled industrial workers, professionals and intellectuals. Any
alteration to this system was regarded as highly suggestive of the
regime's broader views of future social development in the USSR.
The wartime period saw many such changes, seen again by some
as continuations of a shift under Stalin away from the ideology of
the early Revolution. Dew commented on the fact that the regime
felt able to refer to the continuity of the new Suvorov schools in
the liberated territories with Tsarist Cadet Schools with no explanatory
propaganda; 'The regime has travelled a long way in recent years.'[61]
Other reforms seemed to underline this fact. The old stress on
equality had all but disappeared, to be replaced by differentiations
of privilege in every walk of life. Dew compared these developments to what Bonaparte had done in France in replacing the old

class system with a new one.[62] Skaife wrote of the 'steady progress of the Soviet Union towards the elimination of the classless society'. He added that 'the emphasising of sharp distinctions between those in authority and those under authority is noticeable in all walks of life'.[63] By the start of 1944, it had become a commonplace in Embassy reports and Northern Department commentaries to refer to this development; it had become an accepted fact that the new grades of *chiny* meant that the USSR was becoming a highly stratified society. Furthermore, it was observed to be an increasingly conservative society in terms of the values extolled by the Government regarding discipline, deference and family values.[64]

The central question to be answered was whether any of these changes would be in any way permanent. The view that these reforms had begun around 1935 implied that they would, as they could not be seen as a wartime expedient. Some of the reforms in education, such as the increase in discipline and the rejection of revolutionary theories of education, were believed to have long been desired by Stalin; the war simply provided him with the opportunity. Other reforms were designed to rectify deficiencies the war had thrown into greater relief. The establishment of a Faculty of International Relations at Moscow University was taken as evidence that there was concern about training the next generation of Soviet diplomats. It was seen as part of a broader anxiety about the consequences of the narrow education formerly purveyed; Clark Kerr believed that Stalin was taking energetic and decisive measures, unbound by revolutionary dogma, to rectify the situation.[65]

The general feeling by the middle of 1944 was that the basic pattern of Soviet society had been permanently reformed and now conformed to Stalin's own vision. If the reforms brought increased efficiency then it was clearly in Stalin's interest to retain them. The regime was believed to be more firmly established than ever before, so there was no pressing reason to revert to old ways. By appealing to the strong Russian sense of patriotism and tradition, by reviving the system of reward and the possibility of passing on social position to children, Stalin, it seemed, had found a better basis for his regime and established his power on a more solid foundation than ever before; he had at the same time moved Soviet society wholesale in the direction of the kind of social organisation the British political elite felt comfortable with. If these changes were not new, what was new was that the attention of a wider range of British policy-makers had been drawn to them.

There was curiosity as to how much further these reforms would go. Skaife drew highly optimistic conclusions from the departure from revolutionary values in a long memorandum in December 1942. He concluded that the developments, though socially conservative, meant an increase in individual liberty, and he detected a 'humanising' of the regime. He felt there was a chance at least that the reforms would continue, until Soviet social organisation approximated to that of the western democracies. It was to be expected that there would be a concurrent move towards political liberalisation.[66]

This was further than his colleagues in the FO were willing to go, in December 1942 or later. While accepting and endorsing many of the conclusions Skaife drew about the elimination of the classless society, the Northern Department were more cautious in predicting future change. Even Wilson, often held up as the arch-optimist in the FO, did not base his arguments on the idea that the Soviet regime would become capitalist, if this meant private ownership and control of land and industry. On the contrary he asserted that the present system was so taken for granted and had so proved itself in the war that change was inconceivable. Trimmings might change, but they were only trimmings.[67] As Dew commented, there was a distinct limit as to how much reform the regime could instigate or permit and retain its control. Thus, while a cash economy had been allowed to develop, and most forms of private property were allowed, there would continue to be restrictions on private commercial enterprise, and the regime would not relinquish the right to control the economy from the centre, nor to dispose of resources and deploy labour as it saw fit. This implied an element of coercion, and the basic apparatus of the secret police-informer system was not expected to disappear.[68]

In the Embassy there was also caution about the theory that the reforms went so far as a movement towards liberal democracy. Balfour agreed that the war had accelerated new domestic trends in political and ideological spheres. Since it had been decided to build 'Socialism in one country', the state had used the principle of 'from each according to his ability, to each according to his work'; this had been found to work best with an inequality of wages. Consequently the Communist ideal appeared to have been lost, but it had not.[69] Clark Kerr felt reforms of a traditional or military sort might be preparations for mobilisation of the population for reconstruction, but was reluctant to speculate too far on where they might eventually lead. He would report changes, but hesitated to draw long-term conclusions.[70] Bruce Lockhart at the end of the war was to warn of the dangers of believing the USSR had departed from Communism.[71] The analysts in the Embassy and Northern Department had not succumbed to this temptation, though they did correctly point out that there were different forms of Communism. They *did* feel that greater freedom for the populace would have an impact on Anglo-Soviet relations. Patriotism, or as Hill put it, 'realism', had replaced revolutionary ideas. John Wheeler-Bennett aptly described the USSR as now a 'military-socialist state'.[72] A Soviet Naval officer explained how they were restoring the best of their traditions, while not going back on their principles, as some foreign newspapers were suggesting.[73] This became the view of the more perceptive observers in Moscow and the FO; it was a sign of the maturity of the regime.

The changes were, however, seen to be significant, if not in the way newspapers were suggesting, and no longer believed to be irrelevant as Dew had thought at the start of 1942.[74] Others in the FO, and elsewhere in Whitehall, including to a degree Warner, tended to be even more impressed by the changes, which seemed to them to depart from the ideology of the Bolshevik Revolution, failing to understand the dynamic nature of Soviet ideology, shaped by the inclinations of its leaders. Having a static model of 'Bolshevism', they thus attached great importance to the changes they could see taking place, particularly the encouragement of intense nationalism, the revival of traditions and the emphasis on discipline in the militarisation of many aspects of Soviet life. Particularly striking were changes taking place in the regime's attitude to religion.

Religion

It was clear right from the start of the Anglo-Soviet co-belligerency that the treatment of religion in the USSR was going to be an acid test for many in Britain (and the United States). When Maisky made a statement in September 1941 to the effect that there was freedom of religion in the USSR, the furore in the press demonstrated the particular significance attached to this issue. Within the Government, Maisky's statement was criticised as tactless as much as for being inaccurate. However, there was also a sense that the treatment of religion was as strong an indication as anything of the nature of the regime in the USSR.[75] Soviet policies towards the Russian Orthodox Church were to prove something of a yard-stick, becoming a welcome sign that the regime was flexible and tolerant. Changes in Soviet religious policy, viewed with caution, came to occupy an important place in assessments of the 'liberalisation' of the regime.

Initially, the Northern Department had no time for disingenuous Soviet claims about religious tolerance. They were quite firm in the opinion that the Stalin Constitution was a dead letter in religion as in so many other of its civil rights provisions. The churches were open, to be sure, but their activities were strictly circumscribed by the state. The active persecution that had followed the Revolution had ceased by 1936; priests were granted the vote, for instance. Dew pointed out that the fact that churches were open was not a sign of any change, as some misinformed members of the public felt: they had always been open, and since there were few of them, they were usually well attended. However, church-goers were penalised in a number of ways. There were strict financial constraints applied, and most important, the Church was not allowed to proselytise, run schools or engage in any activities that were not strictly liturgical. State-sponsored organisations, such as the Anti-God Society, maintained anti-religious propaganda in newspapers such as *Bezbozhnik* ('Atheist'), and priests were openly mocked.[76]

The Russian Orthodox Church adopted a patriotic stance after the German invasion, and offered its full support to the Red Army and the Soviet Government. It exhorted its followers to resist the Germans and supported the call for partisan activity. The contrast with the attitude of the churches in the Baltic states, which initially regarded the Germans as liberators, was not lost on the Kremlin. The decline in active persecution, which, as Dew noted, pre-dated BARBAROSSA, was speeded up. The FO, aware that the momentum of the anti-God movement had been fading, did not regard this development as particularly significant at first.[77]

This scepticism was strongly in evidence up to the end of 1942. Small changes were observed – the extension of the curfew at Easter 1942 to allow the faithful to attend midnight services was noted as unprecedented.[78] Clark Kerr demonstrated the continuing reserve about such developments in a despatch in September 1942. He depicted the change in attitude to religion as pragmatic, with both a domestic and an international dimension, and felt it was too early to conclude from these signs that a fundamental change in the attitudes of Soviet leaders to religion had taken place.[79] Dew was of similar mind, and not at all convinced that religious tolerance was in any way permanent. A request from the Metropolitan of Kiev for an exchange visit with the Church of England was treated cautiously. It was seen as another attempt to influence opinion in Britain and the US on this sensitive issue. Even Wilson, who usually rejected such methods, advocated a hard bargain in this instance. Dew and Warner thought this a transparent propaganda stunt, though Sargent saw it a sign of grace that the Soviet authorities would wish to propitiate the Church leaders. Cadogan was very sceptical, writing that 'deathbed repentances are not very convincing', and stating that he had little faith in a real change of heart by the Soviets towards persecution of the Church. Eden was equally clear that this was a political not a religious gesture. It is noticeable, however, and characteristic, that once another department, the Treasury, questioned the wisdom of an exchange of visits, the FO strongly defended the view that there were advantages.[80] The Soviet acceptance that an Anglican delegation could go first was one of the factors that by the start of 1943 was beginning to dispel the prevailing scepticism.

Through 1943, the feeling grew stronger in the FO that these religious changes were of some lasting significance. For one thing, the Soviet Government was believed to understand the utility of the Russian Orthodox Church as an instrument of its foreign policy; not only in the effect on attitudes in the US and Britain, though that was clearly important, but also in the countries of eastern Europe, as a major means of promoting pan-Slavism.[81] Domestically, the more tolerance was allowed, and the more church attendances increased, the harder it would be to revert to persecution afterwards. In view of the Church's open support for the regime, this hardly seemed necessary anyway. With the regime's advocacy of traditional values in many areas of social life, there seemed to be much less at issue between Church and State than in the post-Revolutionary period. Signs were searched for that the new attitude would be permanent. Major test issues were the establishment of a regular Church organisation and sanction for the education of a new generation of priests. Developments took place during 1943 in both these areas.

It became evident that the old attitude of aggressive anti-religious propaganda was dead. President Kalinin demonstrated this in May 1943 when he exhorted Red Army soldiers to desist from mocking the religious. The regime, he said, did not endorse religion, but such beliefs were solemnly held and should be respected. Such a remarkable public statement could not but have an effect; Warner regarded it as very suggestive.[82] It was followed later in the year by weightier evidence that a new, long-term position for religion in the Soviet state was being established. At the time of the Archbishop of York's visit in September 1943, it was announced that the Patriarchate, vacant since 1925, was to be revived, and the Holy Synod (*Sobor'*) was to be re-established.

Overall, this change gave rise to great optimism. Clark Kerr was much more hopeful in reporting the Archbishop's visit and in his despatch on religion of October 1943, than he had been in September 1942. Freedom of worship, he felt, was increasing, it was no threat to the regime and he could see no likelihood that the authorities would want to arrest this development. As in other areas, the rulers of the USSR, 'nothing if not opportunist in their approach to problems affecting the welfare of the Communist State', had proved flexible, adaptable and undogmatic; certainly not losing control, but recognising the needs of their public and being big enough to allow them. They were reacting to a genuine religious revival and to the support for the war effort offered by the Church; 'the process of promoting untrammelled facilities for religious worship – in itself an integral part of the trend towards a revival of Russia's historic traditions – has already gone too far to be easily arrested when the immediate occasion for it has passed.' This was without the regime relinquishing its commitment to scientific materialism.[83] Skaife saw a further reform, the re-establishment of training institutions, to be of importance; the Soviet Government had accepted publicly that the Church could be a binding force in the state and had a permanent place in Soviet society.[84]

Thus by the end of 1943, British scepticism regarding the Soviet regime's attitude to religion had been greatly reduced. The increased tolerance towards the Russian Orthodox Church and the explicit acceptance of its place in Soviet life by granting it educational facilities clearly were of a piece with the other changes involving the return to pre-Revolutionary practices and the elimination of the classless society. It could now be believed that the acid test had been passed, because such reform was consistent with these other phenomena. Conversely, the regime's attitude to religion was taken as a firm indication of the deep-seated nature of the changes and the earnestness of the Soviet Government in making them. The significance of the public sanction of an ideologically heterogeneous body by the Soviet regime appeared great. Thus in making the statement cited at the start of this chapter, Churchill was expressing an increasingly firm perception within the FO and Moscow Embassy, and a broad sense within his Government that the changes in the Soviet Union presaged well for the future. Since Churchill read Clark Kerr's despatches, such a statement was based on observation and interpretation, not just wishful thinking. Optimists like Skaife apart, the FO itself had been reluctant to believe in a change of attitude, most clearly in the case of religion, even when in 1942 they would have liked it to have been true. Permanent officials were not prone to optimism about the USSR, and their acceptance that changes were taking place reflected their belief that the evidence was good and the analysis plausible.

The Dissolution of the Comintern

For many individuals within the policy-making elite, the Comintern more than any other aspect of the Soviet regime represented the revolutionary aims of the founders of the Soviet state. It was the instrument of interference in other countries' affairs, in Europe, in India and most importantly in Britain itself. It was through the Comintern that British Communists were believed to receive their orders from Moscow, which made them in effect tools of Soviet foreign policy. While close observers of the Soviet scene identified the Comintern with the Trotskyite wing of the Bolsheviks, to most, Stalin was seen to be as culpable as the others for its activities. When the wartime collaboration began, the existence of the Comintern and its deeds became a matter of some interest. Treatment of this issue would reveal much about Stalin's intentions and motivations. It cannot, however, be said to amount to an acid test, for the abolition of the Comintern in May 1943 did not alter many individuals' views, with the exception of the uninformed general public, which relied on the excitable reaction of much of the press.[85] The most that can be said is that for those who were already so inclined, it reinforced the impact of other evidence that Stalin's motivations did not encompass a quest for world revolution, that he was a realist prepared to be flexible and that the reforms taking place within the USSR were genuine.

There was general agreement that the organisation was practically defunct. The most satisfactory foreign policy dimension seemed to be that Stalin was anxious to please his allies and to make an impression on them by removing such a long-term bogey. The symbolic importance of the Comintern meant that, in publicly abolishing it, Stalin was admitting that its mission was outdated and the concepts it was based upon were no longer applicable, or indeed were erroneous. The sense that the Comintern had been for some time of peripheral importance to Soviet foreign policy meant that there was little inclination to see this as heralding any change in Stalin's diplomacy. MI3c, Clark Kerr and the Northern Department agreed it was mainly part of the 'nationalistic' policy Stalin was now pursuing, fitting in with Stalin's policy of 'Socialism in one country'. The Comintern's activities had become obstructed by the war, but it had really become obsolete once official Soviet relations with other countries had improved. Cadogan, rather surprisingly, saw this as a really positive move: while obviously the Comintern could be revived at will, he thought it must be seen as a sign of a real desire by the Soviets to cooperate with friendly countries in the reconstruction of Europe. It was a genuine symbol of a Soviet desire to renounce any subversive aims in the postwar era. It was also a sign they recognised that 'Russian patriotism and a new won self confidence is to mean frank cooperation on the basis of equality with other nations and not a resort to backstairs endeavours to attain Russian aims by international sabotage and revolution.'[86]

Labour and TUC leaders were much more cautious, suspecting that this was a subtle attempt to aid infiltration by British Communists into the labour movement by enabling them to claim they no longer had any ties to a foreign power. Warner found Labour's attitude to be ridiculous; they could see nothing in the abolition except an awkward problem regarding the Communist Party and believed that this was the motive.[87]

There was interest as to how this move would be taken within the USSR. It would be more popular with the Army and the general populace than with the Party and particularly elements of the NKVD. A certain amount of shock and resentment was reported. Old Communists were seen as bitter about the sacrifice of a cherished principle, coming as it did at a time when many revolutionary practices were being swept away. This supposition added to the strength of the developing thesis of two or more schools of thought within the Soviet machine, divided on issues of reform, cooperation with the Western capitalist powers and the future mission of the USSR. Dew felt quite positive; significant effects might flow from events such as this within the USSR. Old dogmas about the behaviour of capitalist governments (now allies) and workers (German workers were not opposing their Nazi leadership or class enemies) were being exploded. There would be a great deal of discussion about the dissolution among the Soviet intelligentsia, and Party propagandists and agitators, as publicity had been widespread; 'official interment of the Comintern will help to dissipate some more doctrinaire cobwebs and to induce a more practical outlook towards the outside world.' It did not, however, mean that Stalin would not support leftist regimes in Europe, nor that Communist Parties would not continue to follow Soviet directions slavishly.[88]

Soviet Postwar Reconstruction Needs

One of the central perceptions in the composite image of the USSR formed within the British Government in this period concerned postwar reconstruction needs. Its roots lay in the pre-war assumption of Soviet economic weakness, and in the 1940–41 tenet that the regime was desperate to avoid war because the economy would not be able to withstand the pressure. Thus, from the moment of the German invasion, attention was focused on the economic condition of the USSR, which might be the key to continued Soviet resistance.

The destructive nature of the campaign was soon obvious. The scorched earth policy attracted interest, initially as an indication of whether the Soviets were serious in their resistance. Reports on its effectiveness varied. Poles from the Ukraine claimed that the destruction had been slight. Others were more impressed. Generally, the FO and MEW accepted that more had been destroyed in the towns than in the countryside. Skaife pointed out that destruction was much more noticeable in towns; one could not expect the wholesale destruction of crops to be very widespread, as this was extremely difficult to achieve. The point that was missed was that livestock was being slaughtered on a large scale. To him, scorched earth was effective, and in autumn 1941 he was among the first to draw attention to the probable consequences. He was already assuming a large postwar reconstruction problem for the USSR and exploring the implications of this for Anglo-Soviet relations. He was to keep this theme alive throughout the war.[89]

Skaife was not alone in making assumptions about the level of destruction. Others referred to Soviet reconstruction needs as vast, and saw no need to elaborate on the point, so obvious did it seem. The food shortages reported in 1942 bore this out. However, the theory was not just based on assumption and supposition. The Russian section of MEW Enemy Branch produced a number of assessments on this issue. There was a large amount of statistical data available, and the Russian section felt it had enough from which to form reasonable working hypotheses.[90] Most of it came from Soviet published sources. The Soviet bureaucracy was addicted to statistics, and published a great deal of detail about crop yields, industrial output and so on. This had to be treated with care, though it is not true to suggest that the statistics always gave an exaggeratedly rosy picture. The figures were often published as an indictment of underproduction or inefficiency. A huge amount of criticism of those in authority was published: local officials, factory managers, *kolkhoz* bosses and the like. This was possible despite the state control of the press, because the Kremlin itself was exempt from the criticism, indeed its decisions were universally depicted as correct; any shortfalls were thus easily blamed by this method on inefficient or wrong-headed subordinates. This characteristic of the Soviet system meant that a careful reading of the press could reveal much about the internal workings of a state renowned for its secrecy.[91] It was awareness of this situation that prompted Warner in 1942 to suggest a press reading bureau in Moscow and a central clearing committee in Whitehall to deal in a coordinated way with the information processed by different departments; in fact the latter reform was only instigated in 1946 with the formation of the inter-departmental Russia Committee.[92]

Another source for the MEW assessments was secret information. Most of this came from decrypts of German signals, though this was not openly acknowledged on these papers, which had wide circulation. Reports from travellers in the USSR and MEW agents supplemented this material, though in an impressionistic rather than a quantifiable way.[93] Until late 1943, the MEW's clients were primarily the military. Most of their queries were concerned with the Soviet capacity to wage war against the Germans, rather than speculation on postwar needs. None the less, the economic material they assembled in these estimates served to underpin and confirm the assumption that individuals had begun to make when the Germans invaded; that the destruction of the Soviet economy was vast and fundamental.

From the outbreak of war, anxious attention in Whitehall was focused on the food situation. With the related issue of transport, this was seen to be the Soviet Achilles' heel and the crucial factor in the Soviet–German conflict. The MEW regularly reported to the

COS and Cabinet on the situation. Unawareness that most workers were fed in works canteens, thus receiving one square meal a day, meant that the situation, which was anyway very bad, looked even worse because levels of rationing were used as a guide to the availability of food.[94] Throughout 1942 the food situation appeared desperate, especially to FO analysts.[95] The MEW were a little more optimistic, though they probably underestimated the burdens caused by refugees having to be catered for in deficiency areas.[96] While there was disagreement between the FO, Embassy and MEW as to how much Soviet productive land had been lost, all agreed that there was hardship and famine, especially for dependants and agricultural workers, and that Soviet advances in 1943 actually made the situation worse. Food for devastated, doubly scorched areas would have to be supplied from existing resources.[97] This situation was aggravated by the transportation situation and the inevitable priorities given to the needs of the Red Army out of limited railway capacity – needs that multiplied as that army advanced westwards.[98]

In a number of areas, however, the Soviet economic infrastructure was found to be working much better than expected. The evacuation of factories was characterised as a feat of foresight, planning and efficient execution. Scattered hints that dismantled factories were rotting in railway sidings were ignored. The fact that the railways continued operations at all occasioned surprise.[99] It was acknowledged that this was only done by a strict set of priorities which sacrificed supply of the cities to the needs of the Red Army. That this did not bring the expected collapse was put down to the endurance of the Russian people as much as the power of the regime to suppress discontent.[100]

All this, however, did not outweigh the awareness of the destructiveness of the war in the east. For two years the USSR was without both its main food-producing area and its main modern industrial districts in the Donetz and Donbas. The MEW believed that the loss of population to evacuation or to German atrocities in these areas was great. In May 1943 it was estimated that 1.5 million out of 46.3 million had been lost due to 'abnormal mortality' (German measures) and 7 million transported to Axis Europe. Balfour believed mortality in the Ukraine to be even higher, and that Nazi atrocities had reduced the population there by 12 million.[101] The real scope of Soviet problems only became apparent as they pushed back into the German-occupied territories. Up to that point, the loss of people balanced the loss of food production; but now there were many more mouths to feed and immense destruction to make good.[102]

Once again, MEW and the Northern Department were impressed by the evidence of careful planning as reconstruction was seen to begin immediately the Red Army advanced into the Ukraine. Plans for the revival of agriculture were swiftly announced.[103] However, against this, it was clear that the damage could not be repaired quickly, whatever Soviet skills in improvisation. In October 1943, after nine months back in Soviet hands, industrial plant at Rostov was reported to be operating at 5 per cent of pre-war output. Apart from the rehabilitation of industry, the two other major problems were seen to be housing and livestock. In the Smolensk *oblast'* it was reported that 70 per cent of the surviving population were living in trenches or caves. What housing stock there was, even in areas that had not been occupied, was woefully inadequate. It was believed that crop production could be revived fairly easily. Livestock was another matter. Scorched earth and the needs of war had scoured the countryside of pigs, cattle, sheep and especially horses. The shortage of horses was particularly serious as they were needed for ploughing in the absence of tractors. These deficiencies could not be made up quickly.[104]

The basic idea that the Soviets would have vast postwar reconstruction needs rapidly became an unquestioned assumption. It was predicted to be the main preoccupation for postwar Soviet policymaking. Thus, Baggallay suggested the Soviets would devote their main energies to reconstruction of their own devastated areas. Whole towns would have to be rebuilt, whole areas refertilised, whole populations resettled. They might require German labour and assistance from the Allies, though they would prefer to put their house in order themselves. The pace would be slower than before, because the population would desire a greater measure of comfort and happiness. Churchill wrote in his 'Morning Thoughts' in early 1943 that the USSR had suffered 'horrible devastation' and reconstruction would occupy them for many years.[105] The MEW felt that production in the heaviest industrial areas had been virtually eliminated, and 'the crippled industrial economy . . . can be totally restored only after years of unremitting effort.'[106] By 1944 it had become a commonplace that the task of economic reconstruction was enormous. Experts and inexperts treated this idea as axiomatic, and domestic preoccupation was regarded as a fairly certain limitation on Soviet enthusiasm for interference elsewhere.

Three important issues raised by this situation occupied the attention of British analysts; how long the reconstruction would take, what its main focus would be and what effect it would have on Anglo-Soviet relations. Estimates of the duration of reconstruction greatly varied, which was hardly surprising, given the number of unknown and unpredictable variables, such as the degree to which Soviet consumer demand would be met, the amount and type of reparation exacted from Germany, and the regime's sense of security (affecting level of conversion from armaments production). Some estimate was needed, given the potential influence of the reconstruction issue on Soviet foreign policy. The MEW took ten years as a reasonable hypothesis, in advance of information on Soviet priorities or participation in world trade. In ten years, it was felt, the Soviet economy could be back to pre-war levels of production, provided sufficient resources could be diverted to peacetime activities from arms manufacturing.[107]

The Soviet Government, however, was expected to aim for better than this; it would not to be content until the standard of living of the average Soviet citizen was on a par with his western European counterpart, and Soviet products had reached the same standards. The size of this task was taken to be colossal. The Post Hostilities Planning Staff (PHPS), in collusion with the FO, put it thus:

> The full exploitation of her vast untapped resources of natural wealth will be a long process, perhaps extending to twenty years. If it is safe to prophesy in any way as to the probable policy of the USSR, it may be said that she is more likely to expend her energy and resources upon achieving these aims towards a higher standard of comfort, liberty, culture and contentment of her people than to follow a policy of external aggrandisement.[108]

The JIC shared the view that the Soviets would desire to raise standards of living as well as rebuild and develop industry and agriculture, though feeling that the start already made would enable good progress to be made in less than five years.[109]

Public opinion was seen as particularly significant in this area. For years, the regime had justified austerity and sacrifice, forced collectivisation of agriculture and industrialisation, in terms of better living conditions in the future. Now there were war sacrifices as well. The question was, to what extent would the postwar actions of the regime be conditioned by the aspirations of a war-weary people for some of the material rewards they had been promised? This would be a more potent desire even than political freedoms. Would the regime be able to continue with a policy of guns not butter? To an extent, it recognised such aspirations by allowing free sale of merchandise which was outside the quotas. This was not a black market; it was officially sanctioned, and allowed peasants to sell any surpluses they produced on the plots they farmed themselves in addition to their work on the collective farms.[110] Townsfolk with money could supplement their meagre rations and the peasants earned cash, some of which the state took in forced loans, the rest of which was saved. The accumulation of wealth in this way meant pent-up demand for consumer goods from the pre-war period was aggravated still more.[111]

Assessment of the level of pressure this put on the Government depended on an individual's idea of how much the ordinary Soviet person was aware of standards of living outside the USSR. Skaife pointed out that many remembered the pre-Revolutionary era. Those who read the Embassy's propaganda sheet, *Britanski Soyuznik*, could observe British standards from the illustrations.[112] On the other hand, there was the innate Russian pride in Soviet achievements. Skaife felt that the regime would have to put much effort into the improvement of standards of living. The Soviet people, he argued, had been promised 'better things tomorrow' since the Revolution, and the demand would become impossible to ignore after the war was over. He suggested that the Soviet Government actually shared this aspiration. Stalin in particular, with maybe ten years of power left, would want to be remembered as the man who had made the Soviet state secure and the man who had redeemed the promise of a better life made in 1917.[113] Since the Soviet economy had always been geared towards preparation for war, they would need help in switching to consumer production.[114]

This theory was the basis of Skaife's belief that the USSR would follow a policy of cooperation with the West after the war. In the debate on this issue, not everyone accepted his full thesis. Colonel Geoffrey Vickers, Deputy Director-General of the MEW responsible for economic intelligence, accepted the importance of rehabilitation needs as an influence on Soviet postwar policy, but disagreed that consumer demand would be met. The concentration, he argued, would be on heavy industry. In any case, instead of buying goods from the West, which Skaife saw as the basis of a 'positive policy' of postwar cooperation, the Soviets would prefer the estab-

lished route of self-sufficiency, if necessary requiring continued sacrifices from their population. This would be supplemented by whatever
they could get from Germany in terms of reparations, transfer of
plant and forced labour.[115] Wilson agreed that the Soviets would
seek to avoid trade except on the most advantageous terms, and
pointed out that the centralised nature of the Soviet economy was
such that they could move to consumer or peacetime production
at least as quickly as the West. Gladwyn Jebb, Head of the Economic and Reconstruction Department from 1942, agreed with him
that though the Soviet Union would not be self-sufficient, its
degree of dependence on outside trade would not be so large as
the havoc in the USSR might cause one to suppose. They would
certainly want to keep their indebtedness to a minimum.[116]

Overall, Wilson shared Skaife's optimism and hopes about postwar economic collaboration, writing that regardless of whether
consumer demands would be met or not, if the Soviets were happy
with Britain's wartime aid, it should be possible for Britain to help.[117]
Warner was more cautious, but it was generally felt in 1943 that
the Soviet hope for British help would encourage them to be cooperative. An inter-departmental committee on postwar trade with
the USSR was set up, and concluded that while self-sufficiency was
the preferred Soviet policy, it involved high economic cost, and
they would not follow this policy if the international position was
satisfactory. The Soviets might need to compensate consumers for
pre-war and wartime sacrifices, and furthermore a class had grown
up with purchasing power (richer peasants and higher state employees)
which would have an inflationary effect if not checked by imports.
The Soviets would prefer not to do this, but might have to.[118]

There was general agreement that after the war the energies of
the Soviet Government would be directed towards rehabilitation –
including reconstruction of houses, factories, power plant, bridges,
railways and port facilities. This would need a durable peace. Warner
was almost alone in suggesting that the Soviets could limit the
amount of resources devoted to this task, as they could control
public opinion. All the same, he accepted that all other things being equal, the Soviet Government would not be able to drive their
population so hard and would want to raise the standard of living.[119] Despite Warner's caveat, by 1944 an important shift of
emphasis had taken place. The idea that the Soviets would welcome British help, if convinced the British were cooperative, became
transformed into the notion that the Soviets would themselves be

cooperative in the postwar era because of their need to concentrate resources on internal development. They would need a peaceful environment for this, and cooperation offered the best way to solve the problem of security against Germany. Less was said of their cooperating because they wanted help in that development.[120] Partly, this may have been because, by 1944, it was clear that Britain would not be able to supply much of that help. Thus, despite Wilson's personal hopes, this aspect was played down. The fundamental thesis of the importance of reconstruction needs was, however, taken as certain in the FO's arguments in favour of the thesis of postwar Soviet cooperativeness in 1944.

The reconstruction thesis was the product of the various inter-pretations of Soviet internal developments made by different agencies of the Government. There continued to be discussions of certain aspects of it, such as the role of consumer pressures. However, there was a degree of consensus on fundamentals, shared by many, includ-ing the military. In looking at internal developments, there was no inclination to ignore the totalitarian aspects of Soviet society. There was certainly an element of grudging admiration for the capacity for war mobilisation such a system offered. Skaife's hopes that the war and cooperation might lead to a humanisation of the terror were shared, but it cannot be said with any great degree of expec-tation. No one echoed George Hill's optimistic suggestion that the liberties in the Stalin Constitution would be real in ten years. Hill also depicted the labour camps as an exigency of war. Balfour was more typical: when noting all the changes and the restoration of traditional values, he reiterated that the traditional form of Russian government was autocracy, and this was not about to disappear. The USSR would continue to be a 'jealously watchful police state'.[121]

The widespread dissemination of the important reconstruction thesis reflected the fact that in 1942, and increasingly in 1943, there had been dramatic developments in the USSR, which had come as a surprise in the light of the prevailing assumptions of those who had not closely observed the Soviet scene. Whatever continuing scepticism about individual aspects of this remained in different agencies, this added up to a genuine feeling that the USSR had become a nationalist, traditionalist state, with an increasingly con-servative attitude towards social organisation, individual behaviour and personal morality. Since these had been areas where the Bolshevik state had been found especially wanting, undoubtedly perceptions of these changes fuelled a general transformation of image. The

stereotype of the Russians as inefficient and slothful had been undermined as they rolled back the highly respected *Wehrmacht*, though
it had not disappeared entirely. Losses and shortages were known
to be vast, and it was reasonable to assume that the making good of
these would be a first priority. A mobilised, proud, but war-weary
people would be a new factor. In the acid test area of religion, the
Soviet regime had, it seemed, committed itself beyond what was
necessary purely for the conduct of the war.

Perception of these developments directly influenced individuals'
views of the attitudes and role of Stalin, and of the aims and
motivations of Soviet external policy (shaped and driven by internal needs such as morale and reconstruction), and helped create
an assumption that the USSR could be expected to try a policy of
postwar cooperation. Furthermore, these internal changes, representing clear evidence of the move away from the revolutionary
ethos, made such cooperation far more likely actually to work. The
USSR did not need to have gone so far as to become a liberal democracy for this to be credible. The jury was still very much out at
the end of 1944 on the issue of 'liberalisation'. There had nevertheless been a genuine shift in image, based on real observed changes,
not wishful thinking, or even, for the key actors like Sargent, Warner,
Eden and Churchill, a desire to look on the bright side. This change
in image crucially shaped responses to the question of whether the
USSR could or should be a partner in wartime or postwar cooperation.

4
Wolf, Bear or Retriever Puppy?

This chapter outlines the development of perceptions of Soviet external policy from the end of 1941 to 1944, examining the broad conclusions built on the security axiom established in 1940–41. Three alternative Soviet foreign policies were identified. These can be summed up as first, the 'bear' – hostile and aggressively expansive, either from revolutionary or imperialist motivations. The second alternative was the 'lone wolf' – isolationist and uncooperative in the organisation of European security, intent on gaining security by the Soviet Union's own actions and resources, creating a defensive *glacis* in eastern Europe and leaving Britain to deal with the German problem. The third was what Clark Kerr described as 'a wet retriever puppy in someone else's drawing room, shaking herself and swishing her tail in adolescent disregard for all except herself' – cooperative though likely in the initial stages to be uncouth in its methods and behaviour, through both ignorance and the self-confidence generated by victory.[1]

The core assumptions that will be discussed here have all been acknowledged by historians before, but there has not been much analysis of how they developed. In particular, the underlying image of the USSR has not been explored. Nor has it been seen that the third option implied that cooperation would not always be smooth, and that it would not be of the same intimacy as that with the US, without making collaboration unattractive to British policy-makers. Such optimism that existed was by 1944 definitely a qualified optimism. The sensitivity thesis is usually brought up only to be dismissed as evidence of the delusion of British policy-makers. Yet the thesis was the product of much discussion and observation and deserves more understanding. The issue of how responsive Soviet policy-makers were to external matters, such as the tone and content of British policy, was particularly important, and played a significant part in the debate on how to handle the Soviets. A major area of uncertainty was whether Soviet behaviour, if it was uncooperative in its daily manifestations (as it often was), was any indication of the possibilities of long-term cooperation. Looked at superficially, evidence of displeasure at specific Soviet acts can mistakenly be taken to indicate nascent Cold War attitudes. Fuller examination of underlying perceptions reveals that this was not the case.

These points have tended to be obscured by either a predominantly narrative approach, by the focus on Cold War origins, or by concentration on specifics (countries such as Poland or issues such as aid). As an alternative approach, this chapter eschews narrative and makes no attempt to get involved in the intricacies of British dealings with the USSR over specific countries, except where general principles can be inferred. Instead, focus is on the development of interpretations regarding the overall shape of Soviet foreign policy in the context of the alliance.

Uncle Joe

The key issues of British wartime and postwar collaboration with the USSR all centred on the enigmatic figure of Stalin. The prospects for the cooperation that all regarded as important, no matter how distasteful, depended to a great deal on how Stalin was viewed. The image of Stalin established in the policy-making elite in the pre-war years and strengthened in 1939–41 offered little prospect for any sort of cooperation. From the autumn of 1941, however, Stalin began to be seen in a different light. A new side of Stalin was revealed by wartime contacts. The continuing perception of him as a 'realist' was the foundation for an increasingly firm and uncontested view of him as rational and sagacious. Historians have tended to pour scorn on what they see as a travesty of the real Stalin – the 'man-monster' of the purges; to see it as either delusion or over-optimism. Negative characteristics were not, however, lost sight of, though many of them could be seen as qualities in a war leader. For British policy-makers the central question was whether Stalin could be cooperated with. The answer to that question had to be sought in Stalin's personality, his motivations and the nature and scope of his power in the USSR. It was focus on these areas, informed by greatly increased personal contacts, which drew attention away from the acts of terror and established an image that did not exclude character defects, but tended to accentuate the positive.

Stalin's realism increasingly came to be fused with an admiration for his intelligence, which became almost a mystique; some policy-makers, including Cadogan, seem to have developed by Yalta an inferiority complex towards Stalin, in terms of their belief that he was far-sighted, extremely well-briefed and knew exactly what he wanted.[2] There continued to be references to Marxist aims, but this was a minor theme, and the emphasis in discussing Stalin's motivations was his oft-quoted realism.[3] Stalin's intelligence and grasp of both broad essentials and arcane detail impressed in direct proportion to the degree to which he was seen previously as a simple-minded peasant or a Georgian brigand. He could quote to Beaverbrook the exact horsepower of a Spitfire and demonstrate a grasp of the com-plexities of the Indian political and social situation that put Roosevelt's ill-informed generalisations to shame.[4] Nearly all the British who met him in this period formed the impression of what Churchill described as his 'cool, deep wisdom'. Stalin also came to be seen, despite the early disasters of the Red Army, as a military genius.[5]

However, while Stalin's realism was universally assumed, other traits were identified, which looked at logically appear to operate in contradiction to that theory. In two ways in particular Stalin was assigned sensitivities which were far from 'hard-headed'. He was assumed to be sensitive of his status as a world leader and to be highly suspicious. Stalin was characterised as a man eager to be accepted on the world stage with other world leaders. Observers commented on his egotism, though it was not manifested in so extravagant a manner as Hitler's or Mussolini's. Baggallay, for example, believed Stalin wished to go down in history as one of the great Russian figures.[6] He was frequently seen as 'the suspicious Bruin', though it is worth noting that the attribution of rationality meant that the depth of these suspicions was underestimated. A suspicion about Allied postwar intentions was not irrational, in British eyes, in the way that suspicions about British dealings with Rudolf Hess were, and the latter were discounted.[7]

Stalin's basic aim continued to be seen to be personal survival. Beyond that, Bruce Lockhart's formulation, that his motivation was to make the Soviet Union the greatest country in the world by a process of internal development – the continuation of 'Socialism in one country' – accurately summed up the feelings of most in the British Government, particularly as it did not preclude external interventions to safeguard and further that development. Stalin was believed not to subscribe to theories of world revolution, though as Cripps put it, he was 'like all of us, not averse to being a missionary of his own form of government, which he thinks to be the best'. Eden now found Stalin to be the political descendant of Peter the Great, rather than Lenin (or Genghiz Khan, as he had thought earlier).[8] The Stalin cult was now based on his identification with Kutusov and Suvorov, whose pictures replaced those of Marx and Engels in his Kremlin office. When Churchill wrote of 'the deep-seated changes' in the character of the Soviet state, he emphasised 'the new confidence which has grown in our hearts towards Stalin'. The observed transformations in Soviet society were believed to be directed from the centre, and the conservative thrust of them to correspond to Stalin's own preferences.[9]

By 1944, the idea was firmly entrenched that these concerns of Stalin had led him to decide on a policy of cooperation with the West. Any suggestion of Anglophobia in Stalin's motivations had long since disappeared. He might seek reinsurance in eastern Europe, with limited objectives, but collaboration was his first choice. This conclusion was based not on an idealistic vision of Stalin, but on an assessment of how he would view his interests, and took as evidence Stalin's public speeches and his cooperative behaviour at the conferences at the end of 1943.[10] The supposition that BARBAROSSA established a fundamental enmity towards and fear of Germany as Stalin's central motivation was a significant ingredient of this latter assumption.[11]

It was not forgotten what kind of regime Stalin presided over, but on making his acquaintance, he did not appear as a monster. Eden told Dalton that he tried hard to think of him as dripping with the blood of his opponents, but somehow the picture would not fit.[12] Many testified to Stalin's approachability and charm. Stalin had, as Churchill noted, 'that saving sense of humour, which is of high importance', a redeeming trait the more impressive for being unexpected. Going on appearance and demeanour, the general impression, according to Eden, was 'quite a nice and gentlemanly fellow!'[13] He seems to have enjoyed these meetings with foreigners, especially Churchill, since, as Clark Kerr pointed out, there was no one in the USSR with whom he could converse as an equal. By contrast, as Eden observed, 'the strange animal ... seems to lack humour on paper'.[14]

Stalin was often found amenable to clearing up small problems when no change whatsoever had been got out of his subordinates. His public pronouncements, while it was seen they could easily be reversed since he was not directly accountable to public opinion, were believed significant, and to be a brake on his future freedom of action. This is not to say that there was no awareness of his darker side and of the uncooperativeness of which he was capable. However, the personal image, particularly his sagacity and realism, inevitably influenced views of his policy, and deficiencies in manners could be ascribed to his peasant upbringing and inexperience of diplomatic niceties – an explanation Stalin himself thoughtfully provided to Clark Kerr on their first meeting. It appealed to both Churchill and to the FO, reinforcing as it did their own tendency to condescension towards the 'civilization' of the Soviets.[15]

Thus, while not suggesting the British Government was converted to a roseate view of Stalin and his USSR similar to that of the fellow-travellers of the 1930s, it is clear that new images of Stalin, based partly on new perceptions and partly on new twists being given to old ones, permeated the assumptions on which much of British wartime policy and postwar planning was made. Stalin had moved from being a murderous despot to a sagacious and fairly benevolent patriarch. This image of Stalin was at the very heart of the thesis of the cooperative Soviet Union. It became accepted wisdom in the FO, and also a constant ingredient of Churchill's attitude. Interestingly, the Americans came independently to very similar conclusions, and on both sides of the Atlantic elements of the Stalin image were strong enough to persist even into the Cold War era.[16]

In a sense, the new Stalin image was also produced by comparisons. It was when measured against the other dictators that Stalin appeared humorous, charming and lacking in affectation. It was when compared to the other Soviet leaders or those like the NKVD who had not modified their behaviour towards foreigners that he was the soul of cooperativeness and openness. The perception that the Soviet autocracy allowed for the existence of different power-centres – Army, Party, Government – was an important factor underlying this.

'Behind the Horseman Sits Dull Care'

Information on Stalin's associates was never plentiful. Exact functions, status in the pecking order, political leanings and personal character were all unclear. These individuals remained shadowy while the character of Stalin, and the subordinates with whom British personnel had direct contact, became better known. Prior to BARBAROSSA, they were seen as Stalin's cronies – mostly from the Caucasus and invested with the ethnic characteristics of that region.[17] Lack of contacts with important figures meant that these images tended to persist, except that they became distanced somewhat in people's minds from Stalin himself as national war leader. The imputation of genius given to Stalin certainly did not spill over to the other leaders.

The one with whom there was most contact was Molotov. He became the antithesis of Stalin. He was viewed as a cold, emotionless figure. He had been seen as part of the pro-German faction, and never quite lost the image of being anti-British. Partly this was personal: Cadogan found him to have the 'grace and conciliation of a totem pole', and Macfarlane wrote, 'the more I see of him, the more I distrust him. I try not to be biased by the fact he is one of the most unpleasant creatures I have ever met.' It was unclear what his personal standing was, but most felt, as Churchill put it, 'he counts for a lot'.[18]

Unlike Molotov, Vyshinsky's reputation improved. Harold Macmillan, who worked closely with him for a time, found him good company and a competent, able and not unfriendly colleague.[19] He was, however, clearly of the second rank, and the more powerful Kremlin figures remained little known. There was little social interaction with the other members of the State Defence Council (GKO) or the Politburo, such as Zhdanov, Beria, Malenkov, Kaganovich or Shcherbakov. Some of them obviously had power-bases.[20] It was assumed that Malenkov represented Party interests on the GKO, and was an *eminence grise*. Shcherbakov was clearly a rising star, amassing eight posts by 1944.[21] Beria and Zhdanov were seen as powerful behind-the-scenes actors, with power-bases in the NKVD and Leningrad Communist Party respectively.[22] The existence and obvious power of individuals such as Beria or institutions such as the Red Army led to the conclusion that they had some influence.[23] From this assumption derived an important element in British perceptions of the USSR during the war, the 'two schools' theory.

While Stalin's victory over Trotsky was seen to have signalled the end of one important debate on foreign policy within the Soviet regime, outside observers had perceived continuing signs of debate during the 1930s. The issue was, basically, cooperation with Germany, as a continuation of the Rapallo policy of the late 1920s, or realignment with Britain and France in collective security measures against Germany. Maxim Litvinov was identified as the leader of the group favouring the latter. Eden had perceived two schools in the Kremlin when he visited in 1935, a fact to which Litvinov himself drew his attention. Litvinov's replacement by Molotov in May 1939 was commonly taken as a sign that Stalin had finally decided to go for the German option.

Thus, it was an accepted principle that there could be warring factions, each seeking to influence Stalin's policy, within the basic framework of the autocracy. During the Nazi–Soviet Pact period, this potential opposition was believed to have been eradicated at the centre, and now included only fringe figures like Alexandra Kollontai and possibly Maisky. BARBAROSSA threw this situation into flux again. The Army was now important, as were national as opposed to Party institutions. Stalin's status appeared to separate him from purely Party leaders. The key question of how much to cooperate with the western powers was back on the agenda.[24]

It was therefore natural when Soviet policy exhibited inconsistencies that the idea should be revived that there were two groups (or more) influencing policy. The general conclusion from Churchill down was that Stalin was in the 'cooperative' school. Thus evidence that an uncooperative attitude was still present at the top seemed to demonstrate that members of the formerly pro-German school had not lost their power, and that an isolationist or non-cooperative group had now formed, with sufficient political standing to influence Stalin's actions.

This idea thus had a respectable pedigree, and was not simply a product of frustration at Stalin's soft/hard tactics at summit meetings. Stalin himself had hinted to Cripps that a pro-German school existed in July 1941.[25] Cripps and Macfarlane raised the idea of a 'Kremlin gang', implying that there were two schools of thought on cooperation. Macfarlane suggested that Stalin was being given biased advice on the quality of British intelligence material, and that Stalin had not approved the obstructionism that 30 Mission was experiencing: 'I am not at all convinced that Stalin either realises or approves the existing situation.'[26] Cripps placed the blame on Molotov: 'I have a feeling it may be that Molotov is acting as the main channel through which all political information reaches Stalin both as regards internal and external affairs and that he is still adopting the anti-British attitude which I commented on in the past.'[27] At the Moscow Supply Conference, Beaverbrook had responded to such theories by deciding to concentrate on Stalin, believing that his subordinates had either kept him in ignorance or themselves were not aware of Allied efforts. Eden's experiences in Moscow in December seemed to confirm this judgement; he found Molotov 'particularly unhelpful'.[28]

Churchill concluded in Moscow in August 1942 that there were indeed two schools of thought in the Kremlin. When he encountered problems with Stalin during the conference and became temporarily disenchanted, Churchill depicted Stalin himself as the problem in conversations with Colonel Jacob, Clark Kerr and his doctor, Sir Charles Wilson (later Lord Moran).[29] However, he also raised the possibility that Stalin at the second meeting might have been placing views on record about the second front for the benefit of the Commissars:

> We asked ourselves what was the explanation of this performance and transformation from the good ground we had reached the night before. I think the most probable is that his Council of Commissars did not take the news I brought as well as he did. They perhaps have more power than we suppose, and that he was putting himself on the record for future purposes and for their benefit, and also letting off steam for his own.

Churchill was convinced, as were many others, that Stalin's 'surefooted and quick military judgement' meant he himself knew that the British case was sound. But he did not want to be seen by his colleagues to acquiesce in this too easily. Churchill's aide, Desmond Morton, though no expert on the USSR, had already put forward the idea that there was internal policy debate, and Churchill was aware of Cripps and Macfarlane's comments on the subject. US envoy Averell Harriman supported the idea in August 1942.[30] It was clearly an idea that Churchill found appealing, for he was to revert to it on a number of occasions. Churchill's final dinner with Stalin may well have convinced him of Stalin's interest in cooperation; if this was so, then when relations soured, it was concluded that powerful individuals were exercising an influence behind the scenes. The fact that these individuals were shadowy but undoubtedly grim – people like Beria and Malenkov – made this the more credible.[31]

The FO were considering similar ideas in the last months of 1942. It was entirely reasonable to make the assumption that this was an important time for future Soviet policy. Since it had become an accepted idea that the autocracy still allowed scope for debate at the top level then it was possible that individuals in the GKO and Politburo would feel free to express divergent views in policy discussions. Inconsistencies in Soviet policy, which had always had the image of decisiveness and single-mindedness, suggested this was so. The image of Stalin meant that the alternative – that Stalin himself was indecisive – was not considered.[32] Official endorsement of these ideas was given in a circular memorandum prepared in the Northern Department at the end of 1942 and signed by Cadogan. The Soviets were to be informed on all major matters of foreign policy to avoid bad blood in view of their decision to cooperate:

> Stalin's speech of November 6th last may safely be taken as announcing to the Soviet Union the decision of the Soviet Government to give the policy of collaboration with this country and the United States of America a trial. This pronouncement, following on a period of somewhat strained relations over the 'second front' issue, probably represents a major decision of Soviet policy, taken after a period of much doubt and indecision and possibly of some internal controversy.[33]

In February 1943, Maisky revived interest in the theory by telling Wilson directly that there were a number of 'highly-placed people, though not perhaps the highest placed' who suspected that Britain was deliberately holding back against the Germans, and that they were able to prevent cooperation taking place. He said this feeling was especially strong in the Army. Dew thought the Soviet Government probably saw this to be not undesirable, and after 25 years of propaganda there were unlikely to be many pro-British elements. Wilson thought Maisky was trying to show there were two schools in the USSR and that Stalin was having an uphill fight to convince those who were against cooperation. Warner instructed Clark Kerr to take this up, by assuring Stalin no one soft on Germany had any influence in Britain. This might throw light on the reports that there was an influential party opposed to 'Stalin's policy of cooperation with the democracies in general and this country in particular'. Stalin's response caused some interest; he said there were indeed such elements – he described them as enemies alike of the USSR and Britain – but most of them had been dealt with. This caused a flurry of telegrams, the upshot of which was the conclusion that Stalin had been referring to the 1937–38 show trials, though the connection to cooperation with Britain was unclear.[34]

Opinion in the Embassy on the two schools theory was to be cautious after Cripps had left. Thus, Clark Kerr reported to the JIC in December 1942 that a 'certain section' in the Soviet Union feared the possibility of British cooperation with Germany after the war. On the other hand, he told the COS at the same time that Stalin had freedom of action in the USSR; there was some sort of council behind him', but what he said usually carried the day.[35]

Continuing inconsistencies in Soviet policy during 1943 kept the two schools theory very much alive. Stalin may have taken the decision to opt for cooperation as his prime policy, while maintaining a freedom to reinsure, but it was felt that dissatisfaction about this was still alive in influential areas of the Soviet hierarchy, especially in the Politburo. These elements at the very least were believed to wish for a heavier emphasis on reinsurance. More extreme elements were seen as out-and-out isolationists, representing a long-standing trend in Russian foreign policy and reflecting the continuing deep distrust of foreigners. Churchill wrote of 'two forces in Russia; a) Stalin himself, personally cordial to me, b) Stalin in Council, a grim thing behind him, which we and he have to reckon with.'[36]

The Northern Department and Naval Intelligence Division (NID) found that the 'old mentality' regarding cooperation seemed very much to be persisting amongst lesser officials. The Embassy believed that the fundamental attitude of those who were the real authorities in the country – the NKVD – had not changed since the war began.[37] NID were firmly of the opinion that what they persisted in calling the GPU was hostile and powerful. While Stalin might well desire good relations, subordinates were purposefully not carrying out his orders: 'Stalin is not himself a completely free agent.' Rushbrooke, the Director of Naval Intelligence (DNI), noted in September 1943 that 'as long as the GPU functions it will be difficult to obtain confidence – for their own selfish ends they do not want it and unfortunately Mr Stalin is not so all-powerful as to be able to stand up to this evil body as he might like to.'[38] The way that Stalin excused and distanced himself from such behaviour when it was brought to his attention reinforced the idea that he had his hands full in leading the Soviet regime in this unaccustomed direction.

The theory was thus useful to account for the obstructiveness of the Soviet bureaucracy, which was often cleared up after direct appeal to Stalin.[39] Certainly Stalin's subordinates seemed much less willing to get involved in cooperation than he did (probably for good reason, as the Embassy pointed out; they were less likely to be punished for stalling than for giving something away without specific instructions). The theory meant that Stalin could be absolved of guilt for unpleasant telegrams and for bad turns in policy. It was actively encouraged by the irrepressible Maisky, who himself was placed in the cooperative school. This idea rested on two perceptions; that the sagacious and realistic Stalin had firmly decided by the start of 1943 that his best interests lay in trying cooperation with the West, so long as certain security desiderata were met, and that the Soviet system, excessively centralised as it was, still allowed scope for differences of opinion and encompassed a certain time-lag in passing on the attitudes of the highest one to subordinates. The FO and Intelligence departments found it a useful explanation for apparent inconsistencies in Soviet policy, particularly for anti-western articles in the Soviet press.

Churchill, bewildered at the inconsistency of his personal relationship with Stalin, on which he based much of his Anglo-Soviet policy, continued to find the interpretation persuasive. At the 'Tolstoy' meeting in Moscow in October 1944, he again saw evidence that there was behind-the-scenes debate:

> I am sure there are strong pressures in the background, both party and military... we have talked with an ease, freedom and intimacy never before attained between our two countries. Stalin has made several expressions of personal regard which I feel sure were sincere. But I repeat my conviction that he is by no means alone. 'Behind the horseman sits dull care.'[40]

Cold War images of Stalin led to this interpretation being derided as naïve (and its significance ignored), but it is now apparent that the idea was not entirely baseless. There was in fact some room for debate in the Soviet political machine. What was further from the mark was the image of Stalin's own consistency, vision and decisiveness.[41]

The Security Motive

The strongest element of consensus within the Government on Soviet policy was the belief that its prime aim was security. Security had developed from being seen as a minor theme in Soviet policy motivations to a major one during 1940–41. This assessment became firmly established from thence until beyond the end of the war, with few significant dissenters. Stalin's main aim was characterised time after time as securing the survival of his own power, of his regime and of the Soviet Union.[42] Most Soviet external policy actions were fitted into this interpretation, which was highly flexible and could accommodate a wide range of Soviet behaviour without being discredited. Skaife, Wilson, Lockhart and others asserted that Stalin wanted if possible to divert Soviet productive capacity away from armaments and manpower away from the armed forces in order to continue the internal development of the USSR. Thus, his preference would be for a security policy which removed the need for the USSR to maintain itself as a beleaguered fortress. If there was a reasonable prospect that security could be achieved by means other than a high level of armaments, then he would try it.[43]

Predominance of security did not mean that the USSR had ceased to be seen as an expansive power. The expansive urge was, however, interpreted to be defensive, the main aim being protection of the integrity of the Soviet homeland and ultimately the provision of sufficient security for internal development. The policy options for the Soviets ranged from halting their advance on their 1941 frontiers and building up their internal strength while their allies were engaged with defeating Germany, through the exercise of some form of control through mutual assistance pacts, bases arrangements and the sponsorship of friendly governments, to prolonged military occupation with or without communisation, to provide a defensive *glacis*.

While there was uncertainty within the British Government regarding these options, there was basic agreement in 1941–42 that Soviet policy was directed primarily at gaining security against Germany – by defeating her and ensuring she would not pose a threat in the future. This was formalised in the Treaty and represented what seemed to be a strong bond of common interest which would make wartime and postwar collaboration possible. In 1942 there was hope that the whole issue of eastern Europe could be left to the peace conference.[44] By the end of the year it did not appear

that this was going to be possible. Consciousness of Soviet freedom of action increased with the victory at Stalingrad. This produced
a concern in the FO to discover what Soviet war aims were. Doing
this would hopefully also serve to allay Stalin's suspicions that the
British wished to leave everything for the peace conference in the
hope that the USSR would then be weak and exhausted. Churchill
preferred that these matters should be left alone, for they could
easily become divisive while the issue of the war was in doubt.
Clark Kerr opened discussions in February, but they were then
stopped.[45] The consequence was that uncertainty persisted throughout
1943. It seemed obvious that the Soviets would want friendly governments on their borders. Their neighbours must on no account fall
under German influence. What friendly governments would mean
in practice was not, however, certain, and little concrete evidence
of Soviet plans could be gleaned; though it was assumed that Stalin
had plans of some kind (most thought two, one of them a
reinsurance). It did seem unlikely that, as Jebb put it, Stalin would
be able or want to 'absorb 110 million tempestuous Balkanics'.[46]

The Soviet freedom of action in this region caused concern; temptation would be great. The Southern and Central Departments frequently
referred in a vague way to Soviet 'designs', in areas such as the
Adriatic and the Dardanelles, in addition to the clearly stated ones
in Eastern Poland and Romania.[47] Eden and Cadogan in particular
could not rid themselves of the thought that it would be open to
the Soviets to 'bolshevize' a great deal of eastern and south-eastern
Europe.[48] They were answered by Northern and the Moscow Embassy
that the Soviets were too 'realistic' to try to impose Communism
in areas where it had no natural roots. They would prefer to erect
'popular front' governments which could draw on popular support,
but which, as left-leaning governments, would not be anti-Soviet.[49]

The primacy of the security motive that the British assumed in
Soviet policy calculations meant, however, that the central issue
for the Soviets was seen to be Germany. Past Soviet policy was
interpreted as a series of varied efforts to deal with this overriding
problem.[50] The key assumption, with which most agreed, was that
the Soviets were rid for good of any inclination to follow an
entente policy with Germany. There was, of course, one scenario
in which such a policy could feature, and that was the establishment
of a Communist Germany. By 1944 it had come to be concluded,
however, that Stalin would not want this – here the Central
Department agreed with Northern – for such a state, with its industrial

potential and organised manpower, might easily prove uncontrollable. It would soon become a threat to Stalin's ability to use international Communism as an instrument of Soviet policy, as well as endanger Soviet security. Sargent was sure that Stalin 'was aware that the eternal German was waiting to bite the hand that fed him'. A subservient German state was far preferable. The difficulties of controlling such a large country as Germany by force were obvious, especially if the Soviets would prefer not to keep a large proportion of their manpower under arms. The Soviets seemed faced with a dilemma, which gave a strong incentive to prefer a third option; cooperation with their Western allies to keep Germany restrained.[51]

The general inclination was to accept the idea that the Soviets, while preoccupied with their security, were realistic about the measures necessary, which would therefore be limited. They might still be very large, however, and this is where their sensitivities towards their allies were seen to be crucial. To limit themselves, particularly when expansionist options opened up to them, would depend on their confidence in their allies. Thus, considerations of Soviet sensitivity and suspicion became central to analysis of Soviet policy.

Soviet Sensitivities

While assumptions about Soviet security motivations had grown in strength during 1940–41, there had been little sense in the policy-making elite that there was any need to take into account any Soviet sensitivities. As 'grim realists', the Soviets were not influenced by such factors: balance of forces was what counted. All this underwent a marked change in the alliance period and belief in Soviet susceptibilities was to be a vital element in shaping Britain's perceptions of Soviet policy. The range of Soviet susceptibilities that was considered expanded beyond specific suspicions about Allied aims to a sense of psychological, even pathological sensitivities. By 1944 these had become bound up in the debate on the key issue of the Soviet response to external stimuli.

Few would disagree that there were mutual Anglo-Russian suspicions dating back at least 125 years, nor that there was an intense suspicion of all foreigners. Suspiciousness was commonly taken to be a characteristic inherent in the ethnic make-up of the Soviet leaders, and historically of the Russian political systems. In the Soviet period it had been reinforced by Leninist doctrine and by the attempts of the British to destroy the Bolshevik state at birth. To Cripps and others who were critical of inter-war British policy, the situation had been made worse by appeasement, which appeared to them to give Germany a free hand in the east and thus secure peace in the west at Soviet expense.[52] Alongside this, there were seen to be suspicions that derived from specific foreign policy issues – these were easier to understand and hopefully easier to deal with, and if they were assuaged then in time the habitual suspicions would be reduced. The principal suspicion that caused concern was that the British and Americans intended to play the same 'mutual exhaustion' game that had been attributed to Stalin earlier. Expressions of friendliness and admiration were viewed as mere camouflage for determination if not to destroy the USSR, then once more to keep it in isolation behind a *cordon sanitaire*. British perception of this suspicion was in evidence soon after BARBAROSSA. In so far as the suspicion derived from the British inability to supply relief in the form of military operations, it was understandable, and officials in the FO saw that the failure to supply information and discuss plans fed these suspicions and that close Anglo-American cooperation fuelled them further.[53]

These suspicions were seen to have an impact at every level of policy-making. It appeared, for instance, from comments in the Soviet press and from Maisky that the Soviets held their own version of the 'two schools' theory: that elements in Britain – usually cited as the 'Cliveden set' – were still inimical to the USSR. In SOE it was felt there was a vicious circle: Soviet perception of British suspicion produced Soviet suspicion.[54] This acute sensitivity about British policy was a nuisance, particularly as importance was being attached to peripheral figures or newspapers over which the Government had no control. It was a perverse sign, though, that the Soviets were serious about cooperation; why else would there be such concern about the British commitment to it?

The discussion of how to respond to the demands Stalin made to Eden in December 1941 shows Soviet sensitivities to be at the centre of the debate on Soviet policy, where they were to remain for the duration of the war. When he returned from Moscow, Eden firmly believed that Stalin's frontier request should be granted. He had given no prior hint that he looked favourably on such a demand, and he knew the Cabinet wished to avoid discussion of the topic. The sensitivities he had come to perceive led him now, however, to claim that it would be impossible to get any kind of collaboration if Stalin was not satisfied on this. Moreover, here was the chance to assuage Stalin's long-standing suspicions. Eden told the War Cabinet:

> It must be remembered that, if we won the war, Russian forces would probably penetrate into Germany and that at a later date she might well want more than her 1941 frontiers. It would seem that Stalin's keenness on our recognition of the Soviet 1941 frontier was partly due to Russian suspicion of our country and partly because he wished to be sure that we were prepared to treat with Russia on equal terms.[55]

Churchill disagreed with the point about Soviet sensitivities. He asserted that concessions never had any effect on realists like the Soviets and this especially applied to political measures in a relationship that he conceived, and believed the Soviets also conceived, to be based on military interests. These interests were strong and separate from political matters. It was part of Soviet character to try to gain political advantage from the situation, but if it was not forthcoming this would make no difference to their military policy. They would accept that their bluff had been called and far from being detrimental it would increase respect for the British as defenders of their own interests.[56]

Beaverbrook shared Eden's view of the importance of Soviet suspicions. He particularly wished to make sure that nothing prevented the Soviets from whole-heartedly continuing the struggle and believed that Britain should make large concessions to achieve this. His reading of the Soviets during his Moscow mission was that they were extremely sensitive to outside stimuli: British actions could crucially affect their continued will to fight and their readiness to take the war to the enemy.[57]

Attlee's refusal to accept the point about Soviet sensitivities brought him into open opposition to Eden and Beaverbrook, and provoked one of the few instances when the War Cabinet was openly divided over a Soviet issue (resulting in Beaverbrook's resignation). Until the end of 1941 the Labour leaders, with the exception of Dalton at the MEW, had played little part in the formulation of policy towards the USSR. The frontiers issue was the first to draw a strong response from them. They had concurred in Churchill's policy thus far and Attlee had supported Soviet supply requests in the Defence Committee.[58] However, their perception of the USSR had been solidly established by the events of autumn 1939 and they were unconvinced that a policy of political concessions could build goodwill. The Labour leaders did not press their opposition once Churchill changed his mind, accepting his view of the pressing reasons for doing so.[59]

Some officials, such as Cadogan and Cavendish-Bentinck, were doubtful at this point about the chances of Soviet survival and of the cooperative intentions of Stalin, and felt that a concession on the frontiers was not necessary, once the 1942 German offensive began.[60] The Northern Department, however, thought the issue was Stalin's acid test of British sincerity. Eden agreed, and one of the fundamental divisions within those parts of the Government which shared the cooperative assumption began to be in evidence at this time.[61] There were those who, though they came to it from a variety of perspectives, agreed that the main problem with Anglo-Soviet relations in the past had been British policy. Thus many of the difficulties now were of Britain's making. This view was marked in individuals on the Left, but was also held by others who followed Cripps interpretation such as Wilson and Jack Ward of the Economic and Reconstruction Department, and some distinctly non-Left figures, notably Beaverbrook. Their policy contributions were to be imbued with the belief that what was necessary to bring lasting Anglo-Soviet cooperation was a carefully formulated British policy, because the sensitive Soviets were deeply affected by outside factors. This hypersensitivity led the Soviets to certain uncooperative behaviour, but did not mean that they were inherently uncooperative. What was important was that Britain should pass the tests they were setting to discover whether British cooperation was a realistic possibility.[62]

The majority of the professional policy-makers did not accept that past policy had been wrong, nor that all the faults in the present were on the British side. But significantly many of them, including Nigel Ronald (Superintending Under-Secretary for the Economic and Reconstruction Department), Jebb, Sargent and Warner, together with non-professional diplomatists like Lockhart and Eden, accepted some of the interpretations offered by the Crippsians, as a result of their own belief in the security and realism axioms, and in particular accepted the hypersensitivity theory – argued persuasively by Lockhart, the bridge between followers of Cripps or Beaverbrook on the one hand, and the establishment on the other. In particular, Soviet suspicions were of central concern. Eden later in the year spoke for most of the FO when he wrote:

If we can contrive on all possible occasions to *treat* the Russians as partners & do so as a matter of course we stand the best chance of breaking thro' this crust of suspicion. We can never wholly succeed; but we *must* succeed far enough to make cooperation possible, or this war may have been fought in vain.[63]

However, it was also felt that the Soviets often manufactured such grievances in an attempt to win concessions.[64] The problem was determining which concerns were genuine and which were simply try-ons. This had to be done without aggravating genuine suspicions, or poisoning the atmosphere. The effect of this perception, because of the way such suspicions were now seen, was to diminish considerably the negative effect of Soviet behaviour, for the operation of suspicion meant that even ostensibly uncooperative actions fitted into the overall interpretation of Soviet cooperativeness; the way to avert such actions was to reduce suspicion.

Developments in the Perception of Soviet Sensitivity

Stalin explained manifestations of a less than cooperative spirit by Soviet officials in terms of their inexperience and the lack of adequately trained personnel. While this was seen by the British to be somewhat disingenuous, it was not dismissed out of hand for it corresponded to their own assessments of Soviet personnel, and it sounded like a cry from the heart by Stalin, striking because it was not usual for the Soviets to highlight their own inadequacies. Those who took Stalin's (and Maisky's) apologies for Soviet behaviour at near to face value concluded that the Soviets now wanted to break out of isolation. Wilson and Clark Kerr likened the Soviet desire for inclusion in Allied decision-making to the desire of 'country cousins' to join a London club.[65] In putting the issue in this way, Clark Kerr was expressing the common view that the Soviets felt excluded from decisions that materially affected them. The FO felt that this was a rational attitude from the Soviet point of view.[66] The metaphor also, however, had a further dimension, in that it encapsulated a sense of a more pathological, psychological attitude: a Soviet desire for the respectability that membership of the international community brought. They resented their pariah status, not only because it was a material danger, but because of a desire for their power and legitimacy to be acknowledged.

This thesis of a psychological dimension to Soviet sensitivities, which coexisted strangely with assertions of hard-headed Soviet realism, developed gradually. In April 1941 when Cripps had stated that the Soviets would let affronts to their *amour propre* shape their policy, it had received short shrift from Collier and his colleagues, and from Churchill, who all held that the Soviets judged matters purely from the standpoint of their practical interests.[67] This position was not maintained after June 1941, even though realism was still emphasised. By the time of the February 1942 discussions of the frontier issue, *amour propre* was now acknowledged as playing a role. That the Soviets desired the USSR to be treated as an equal for its own sake was implied in the FO's Cabinet paper on the frontiers, WP(42)48, and in Warner's remarks that the Soviets resented being singled out for special treatment, even though they were in fact peculiar.[68] Bruce Lockhart linked such attitudes to traditional Russian xenophobia, strengthened by the humiliations of the previous 24 years. Lockhart's views are notable for their exclusion at this time of any influence of ideology, for their ethnic assumptions about 'Russian' character and the patronising tone, however much he wished to avoid it. He was also, however, arguing that past relations need not be a guide to the future and was trying to find a policy that would get the best out of the Soviets.[69]

The psychological point was explicitly recognised in a War Cabinet telegram to Halifax on 26 March 1942, though only as an element, at this point, of the sensitivity about damage to practical interests. The telegram stated that the issue of the recognition of the 1941 frontiers

> has a psychological character which derives from the fact that for 20 years the Soviet Government has not been in relations of equality or confidence with any of the great Western Powers.[70]

The perception of this sensitivity about the Baltic states issue was subsequently to be broadened into a general theory concerning the overall conduct of the Soviets in the alliance, but here, already, was an idea of sensitivity to exclusion and a Soviet search for signs of acceptance – not just for the practical gains but as evidence of status.

Further development of the psychological point did not take place until 1943, with the introduction of the notion that the Soviets

had an inferiority complex. This had been an expression used occasionally before to explain Soviet clumsiness in international affairs,
with the implication that the cause of this was at least partly the
treatment of the Soviet Union as an international outcast. Since it
was not entirely complimentary it had rarely been used by Soviet
sympathisers, but it was to be advanced by Maisky in August 1943,
and at this stage it fitted in sufficiently with perceptions of Soviet
sensitivities, and also the reality of their continuing exclusion, to
generate some discussion, though still little sympathy. It was indeed too close to a long-standing theme of Maisky's – that Soviet
uncooperativeness was due to past mishandling and hostility by
the British – to gain much acceptance at this point. Maisky complained that a British superiority complex caused them to tread on
Soviet toes and made the Soviets, with their inferiority complex,
feel they were being treated as uncouth country cousins. Clark Kerr
refuted this argument in discussion with Maisky, though he did
write to the FO that Britain was holding the Soviets at arm's length;
they were indeed treated as country cousins, though they had earned
their place on the club committee. Maisky had appealed to Clark
Kerr that the British should bear Soviet psychology in mind. He
cited the peculiarities of the Soviet system and the immaturity of
the regime to explain the restriction of personal contacts.[71] He complained to Eden on 31 August that the British were not trying their
hardest to win the war and that some people in the USSR were
apprehensive, though at present these people were unimportant.
He added that suspicion was easily aroused in Moscow, though often
not justified, as he knew with his greater knowledge. He was thus
pleading for patience and sensitive handling. This was the legacy,
he claimed, of an unhappy past which had the effect of making
his countrymen scrutinise any British or American action to see
whether any slight was intended. The Soviets wished to be treated
as absolute equals. Maisky ominously linked the matter to the issue
of two spheres of interest in Europe or one. The Soviets would
prefer treating Europe as one, but this meant that the right of each
of the powers must be admitted to take an interest in all parts of
Europe. It was clearly the developing Italian situation which he
had in mind.[72]

Dew remarked that it was an admirable alibi to be so sensitive
and have an inferiority complex as a justification for a permanent
grouse. Warner agreed, commenting that whatever the excuse in
each case, the British were always asked to show understanding of

the Soviet determination to have their own way.[73] Maisky's attempt to put across a sense of general sensitivity of a psychological rather than material nature thus met at this time little response in Whitehall, though the established idea of resentment about exclusion from decision-making remained. Despite the answers he made to Maisky, Clark Kerr had, however, become convinced that there was something in this idea and feared it might affect overall policy, much of which was a matter of building or sustaining mutual confidence for which there was no historical foundation.[74]

Signs of a shift in the FO attitude began to become more evident later in the year. While still seeing the Kremlin mind as working in a cynical, opportunist way, Dew on 15 October postulated a quest for respectability as an important factor in Soviet policy-making. He believed Soviet suspicions to be genuine, even though misguided. He felt as did many in the FO before the Moscow Conference, that the Soviets had not yet fixed their policy; they had been moving towards collaboration, but their actions could still bear two interpretations, cooperation or unilateralism. However, a factor in shaping a movement to cooperation was the desire for respectability; the Soviets would prefer approval of their territorial gains (the 1941 frontiers) to be gained from the Allies rather than from the Germans for this reason.[75]

The Soviet demeanour at the Moscow Foreign Ministers Conference in October 1943 (especially the cordiality of Molotov) and the enthusiasm about its results in the Soviet press gave a great boost to such theorisations. Clark Kerr ascribed Soviet behaviour to the fact that they felt they were admitted for the first time and on terms of complete equality to the most intimate counsels of Britain and the United States. The fact that Secretary of State Hull and Eden went all the way to Moscow stirred their vanity. They were surprised by their allies' candour. Satisfaction of their *amour propre* was demonstrated in the rise in confidence and the quality of cooperation, and this served to confirm that such things were influential. Clark Kerr warned that the situation was still delicately poised, and the British should be careful to take no liberties, even at the cost of some forbearance. Eden similarly remarked that he had not before the Conference fully grasped the extent to which the Soviets had genuinely felt excluded: it was important now to bring them to feel equals.[76]

It was in 1944 that this notion received fullest consideration as a factor in shaping Soviet foreign policy actions and responses. Interest in the idea needs to be seen in the context of the sense of Soviet freedom of manoeuvre and the tendency to try to seek clues to Soviet policy objectives in Soviet day-to-day behaviour, in the absence of other sources. Interestingly, it was Wilson who sounded a note of caution about this. He warned against getting too excited about the post-Teheran Conference mood in Moscow, or too depressed by Soviet obstructiveness and discourtesy. He developed the theme of Soviet inexperience in international affairs. One should not, Wilson warned, take Soviet professions of cooperation at face value. By this he meant that one should not assume that because they were committed to cooperation, they would immediately start behaving in every respect like a civilised Western nation versed in all the diplomatic niceties. The Soviets, he wrote, were only now emerging as a Great Power; Britain could not reasonably expect them to exercise that power with a moderation which the British learned after two or three hundred years and according to rules drawn up by themselves. By habit, Soviet methods were more robust and brutal than those of their allies. Mixing pragmatism with the condescension that usually accompanied British discussions of the inferiority complex theme, he saw the nature of possible cooperation in a 'realistic' light – it was not necessary to think and act the same, to hug one another as friends, to have a meaningful alliance. Attempts to get on such terms with the Soviets, for instance by Churchill's telegrams to Stalin, had failed, because the Soviets had not responded in kind (and Wilson implied were culturally incapable of doing so at this stage). To Wilson, backgrounds and methods were irrelevant, it was interests and intentions that mattered, hence his postscript, 'too bad Molotov and Stalin were not at Eton and Harrow. What can we do about it?'[77] He was convinced the Soviets wanted to be reasonable but influential members of the 'club',

> even though they think that some of the rules are damn silly and want to change them. They are members now, but are not allowed into some of the rooms and I'm worried that they may get fed up with waiting and being mucked about and may go off and start another club of their own. The fault seems to me to be about equal on both sides but I think you've got to go on going out of your way to make the new member feel at home if you want to keep him inside.[78]

With the Americans becoming concerned at signs of unilateral action by the Soviets, Sargent demonstrated that he shared much of Wilson's viewpoint. Bad incidents, he wrote, arose out of ignorance and clumsiness, not ill-will. Cooperation between any two governments was difficult and the Commissars and other Soviet officials had been taught for 20 years their duty was not to cooperate with foreigners. First efforts to unlearn this were very clumsy, for their ignorance was profound and qualified personnel were lacking: 'there is no evidence to show that the incidents from which we have been suffering are due to the fact that the Soviet Government do not wish to co-operate'. Eden noted that he hoped that this was the real explanation – he at this time was in a state of some uncertainty, interpreting Soviet unilateral actions in their dealings with the Badoglio Government in Italy to indicate dangerous ambitions, but arguing to Churchill (who himself in the Italian case drew different conclusions) that there were few instances in which the Soviets were actually not cooperating after their own fashion.[79]

The theory, however, was not incorporated in the FO policy papers of summer 1944, in which references to sensitivities were limited to specific Soviet suspicions of Allied treatment of Germany. Clark Kerr, though, was developing the theory and voiced it in a colourful fashion in his despatch of 31 August. Looking at Soviet foreign policy as a whole, Clark Kerr wrote that the available evidence pointed strongly to the conclusion that 'the whole approach of the Soviet Government is strongly influenced by a morbidly developed sense of inferiority'. The Soviets were prompt to take offence at criticism and were imbued with an 'almost desperate' determination that the USSR should be thought no less respectable, cultured or efficient than the countries of the West. They limited visits to factories and the front to avoid unfavourable comparisons. As was commonplace, Clark Kerr found this feeling of inferiority, often accompanied by sullen mistrust and an abnormally sensitive pride, to owe much to inbred ethnic Russian characteristics. This had been given a nearly pathological bias after 1917 by acute resentment at the attitude of the rest of the world.

Clark Kerr added that whereas before the war the Soviets had been regarded by western opinion as well-nigh bandits, they were now treated as honourable equals by the governments of their great allies. Stalin and his associates accepted their new status 'with becoming pride'. Internal reforms showed a desire to strengthen this respectability. They were, however, 'as sensitive of their reputation as is a prostitute who has married into the peerage':

it seems safe to infer that the tactics and perhaps strategy of Soviet foreign policy will depend in no small measure upon whether the Soviet Government are satisfied that the Western democracies are treating their country with all the deference to which they now consider her entitled by virtue of her military victories and newly found prestige and respectability. It is no exaggeration to say the most important thing about the Moscow Conference was that it was held in Moscow.[80]

Clark Kerr felt that the Soviets believed there were influential circles who still looked upon the USSR as an international outlaw, which explained the Soviet demand for unanimity in the UN Security Council. They were resolved not to be thought less worthy of confidence than the other Great Powers:

> Having until very recently been judged unfit for the structure of an international order, they aim today at seeing themselves as 'the stone which the builder rejected, the same has become the head of the corner'.[81]

Similarly, he remarked regarding the Soviet reaction to Burrows' alleged 'savages' remark, that 'these people have memories as long as the elephant's vindictiveness when their sense of inferiority has been pricked.'[82]

Overall, no one in Whitehall took the inferiority complex idea as far as this, though elements of it were certainly endorsed; the desire for respectability, sensitivity to real or imagined slights, ignorance of proper forms of behaviour, arrogant assertion of their own achievements. Sargent was among those who felt the 'savages' point was germane and it was widely accepted that there was some such psychological dimension to the Soviet suspiciousness. The basic idea of extreme Soviet sensitivity to external attitudes was firmly established in the FO and in the Embassy.[83]

The most important aspect of these new considerations of Soviet hypersensitivity was the link to security concerns in sensitivity about British policy towards Germany. A central precept of the 1940–41 view was that Soviet policy was outside British influence, driven by an internal dynamic. Strong internal forces remained in the 1941–44 interpretation, but now the Soviets were seen to be extremely sensitive and likely to shift their whole policy in reaction to British actions and attitudes on certain key issues. The Soviets were perceived to be deeply suspicious about the Anglo-American desire to cooperate and therefore sensitive to any signs to the contrary. If they felt that the British and Americans were attempting to 'gang up' on them, dictate the policy of the Grand Alliance and impose their own post war settlement, then they would be tempted at the least to attempt a 'reinsurance policy' as a concurrent alternative, or else to turn their backs entirely and retreat into isolation. Their commitment to cooperation, despite its foundation in self-interest, was not therefore irreversible and could be shaped by their sensitivity about others' motives and commitment. The theory of sensitivity and its linkage to the security motivation is critical to understanding the nature of the British image of the USSR in the alliance period, and of the policy that flowed from it.

Lone Wolf

The Soviet alternative to cooperation given most attention by British policy-makers in 1941–43 was isolationism. It was a distinct possibility that Soviet leaders would be satisfied with their minimum war aim: the recovery of Soviet territory. Whether they made this choice depended on a number of variables, the major ones being their attitudes towards Germany and towards their allies, and the strength and outlook of the Red Army. Uncertainty about these factors meant that a separate peace between Germany and the Soviet Union was something that could not be discounted, though concern ranged more broadly than that, for such limited aims carried serious implications for Britain.

An isolationist tendency was identified as a long-standing element in Soviet policy. Partly, it had been forced on them by the interwar *cordon sanitaire*. It had been enhanced by the policy of 'Socialism in one country', which was believed to have focused Soviet attention internally. The only foreign policy requirement for this was security from outside interference. In the context of the war, Dew dubbed this tendency the 'lone wolf policy'.[84] That the Soviets would go their own way in response to the Allies' apparent unwillingness to treat them as equal partners in the war, or a refusal to accept their basic war aims, was seen as a highly possible outcome at times.

Bruce Lockhart, in his memorandum on Stalin's 1942 Red Army Day Order, saw Stalin to have the lone wolf policy as an option, feeling that at a pinch he could do without Britain, and that he was considering it because they had rejected his modest political demands and did not seem to accept the concept of equal sacrifice in the war.[85] Baggallay saw it as axiomatic that the Soviets would not make a separate peace unless Germany was unable to renew its attack in the foreseeable future, but did see in Stalin's Order hints of an isolationist policy: the threat that the Soviets would only fight to free themselves.[86] This possibility seemed more dangerous, because it was more likely than that Stalin and Hitler could agree terms. Sargent agreed that Stalin was not hinting at a separate peace, but the possibility had always existed that he would stop on his frontiers; indeed, he might have difficulty urging the Red Army to go further.[87] The theme was central to the discussions of frontier recognition in early 1942. Halifax was told that a separate peace was a possibility, but was not expected. The proposed concession was not designed to stop such a development, for it could not do so: the object of discussions would be to find out whether the Soviets aimed to defeat Germany or merely recover their lost territory.[88] The Anglo-Soviet Treaty was not designed to prevent a separate peace, but to bring the USSR out of isolation in the interest of postwar Europe. Frank Roberts of the Central Department noted the main aim was to ensure the Soviets did not repeat their Rapallo policy.[89]

It was certainly believed possible that Stalin was capable of concluding a separate peace, should Hitler offer acceptable terms, though as he came to be viewed as more trustworthy this belief faded (the increased anti-German, as opposed to anti-Nazi tone of Soviet propaganda supporting this change). The corollary of this was, however, much more worrying and came to appear relevant whenever the Red Army scored some victories; the Soviets would either cease fighting once the Germans had been expelled from the USSR, or make their own settlements of eastern European questions and not take any interest in collaboration with the western Powers. The Allies would be faced in the first instance with a Germany still intact and with armies in the field, and in the second with the destruction of hopes of building up strong independent units in the east with the German problem still unsolved. Should the US also withdraw into her own region, then Britain would face the problems of European reconstruction and German resurgence with no powerful ally.[90]

These were regarded as real possibilities because of Soviet suspicions and their overriding concern to achieve security against

Germany, which would lead them to take whatever course seemed most likely to achieve it. Soviet policy-makers appeared to have a definite choice of policies involving a greater or lesser degree of collaboration with the Allies, and a choice of exactly what their war aim was to be: expulsion of the Germans (by force or negotiation), the removal of the 'Hitlerite' regime, or occupation and destruction of Germany itself. Linked with the question of whether they would continue the war with Germany beyond their frontiers was whether they would prefer to rely on their own resources to ensure their security, and take unilateral actions in the limitrophe states. The victories of the summer of 1943 and the advances that followed opened up their options. There was a rough-and-ready consensus that actual Soviet objectives were limited and rooted in the quest for security. Jebb was of the opinion that while the US was ripe for expansionist activity, 'Russia will, I feel pretty certain, retain her state socialistic machine, and I very much doubt whether this is really suited to any form of "imperialistic" expansion, even if this was going to be the instinctive Russian urge after the war – and I personally do not believe it is.'[91] The signs were anxiously read to discover what the Soviets had decided. The evidence was not definite, but the broad conclusion the FO reached by the start of 1944 was that Stalin had decided to relegate independent action to the status of a reinsurance policy.[92] By contrast, the US State Department suspected the Soviets favoured unilateralism.[93] Theories of sensitivity meant that uncooperative actions were not necessarily viewed as clear evidence of such a policy – and the idea of the reinsurance policy implied that some measures would be taken to have it ready and that there were certain fundamental actions that would be taken whether a lone wolf or a cooperative policy was to be followed. In addition, it was thought that the Soviets had probably only made provisional decisions about post-war policy; as pragmatists they would wait to see how things shaped for a year or so after the end of the war before finally committing themselves.[94]

The USSR as a Potential Enemy

The prospect of Soviet isolationism carried within it the possibility that Soviet policy would move a stage further, to hostility towards Britain. Stalin's Anglophobia had been a central part of Maclean's thesis in 1940, and the mutual exhaustion theory was founded on the idea that Stalin saw that his best interests lay in the reduction of British (as well as German) power. After BARBAROSSA, Stalin's need for allies against the overwhelming German threat meant that this option of Soviet policy was no longer considered an active one. Stalin was seen as driven by security motives, and ideological factors no longer appeared in British analyses. Through to the end of the Churchill Coalition, there was to be no serious advocacy of the idea that Stalin saw that his interests at present lay in hostility towards Britain, beyond the possible coolness in relations that might follow from the lone wolf policy. However, this did not mean that this was entirely discounted as a possible scenario for some point in the future.

Given the strategic position of the USSR, particularly if a German defeat was postulated – and this was the only reasonable basis for planning – the issue of possible Soviet enmity arose as soon as postwar defence issues began to be discussed. Defence planning had to consider possible enemies and if the destruction of the war-making potential of Germany and Japan was assumed there were few choices left at the level of major powers. In early 1942, before the Anglo-Soviet Treaty strengthened belief in Soviet commitment to cooperation, the FO desired that the implications of future Soviet enmity be considered. The military at this point were reluctant to do this, having no inclination to speculate about a postwar world that was a long way off.[95] A consequence of this mood was that the Military Sub-Committee (MSC) that was set up to discuss military aspects of postwar problems was isolated from the established services planning organisation.[96]

Later, the military were more ready to consider this Soviet option as a possibility; concurrently the FO were coming to believe Soviet sensitivities were such that if they sensed the British were planning on this basis they would opt for unilateralism. The COS and their planners accepted the need for cooperation with the Soviets as much as the FO, but their experience of wartime liaison was not salutary. This led them at the best of times to be less than optimistic. It is clear that by mid-1943 they were approaching the Soviet question differently from the diplomatists. In August they began to consider the problems of postwar strategy, and in order to do so, enlarged and upgraded the MSC into the Post Hostilities Planning Sub-Committee (PHPS/c).[97] From the first PHPS/c papers it is obvious that the military had become concerned with how Soviet and British interests might clash in a postwar world in which they would face each other as victors in many areas. Any consideration of strategic interests has to consider potential enemies, but the particular channels their investigation followed owed much to their view that the USSR not only possessed the means, but also that there was sufficient uncertainty about its intentions that it had to be considered as a potential enemy. The non-inclusion of the USA in such studies indicates that assumptions about intentions were as important as means in this selection. Furthermore, they felt that the options available to the Soviets, their past record and their present equivocal attitude to the actual conduct of cooperation made this a reasonable assumption.[98] The first PHPS/c papers dealt with specific subjects rather than broad strategy. They made no global assumption about a Soviet threat; the USSR was simply dealt with as the power against which a defence had to be maintained in a certain area and in a certain scenario.[99]

At this time the COS were sensitive to the 'awkward repercussions' if it became known outside official circles that they were engaged on such studies, and for their part the FO accepted the need for contingency plans. Jebb noted that the Soviet attitude was a basic factor in any postwar plans. If a friendly USSR was assumed, then some involvement by it in Middle Eastern security would have to be contemplated, for example. If there was any possibility of the USSR being unfriendly, plans needed to be ready. Warner thought the present omens were favourable; but that cooperation would continue to the end of the war was 'on test'. British policy was certainly to go all out for Soviet cooperation, and the response was encouraging; a friendly and cooperative USSR should be the working hypothesis. Britain, however, needed alternative plans to meet the possibility of an uncooperative USSR. The FO assumed this would be kept secret.[100] The important point for the FO was that they should guide this process, for postwar strategy was on an awkward bureaucratic interface between diplomatic and military planning. The FO were thus involved in the production of the PHPS/c's major Soviet appreciation, 'The Probable Long-term Impact of Russian Strategic Policy on British Interests'. In its predictions of Soviet policy the paper reflected the feeling that the Soviets had made a definite step towards the adoption of the third policy option, cooperation, at the Moscow and Teheran Conferences. The military were not immune to such feelings, and apart from some comments by the JIC on matters of detail, the COS expressed no major objections to the paper.[101] They did, however, feel uncomfortable with policy predictions as well as delays caused by FO involvement in drafting. Future papers were to avoid estimates of Soviet policy and focused on what the Soviets *could* do if hostile.[102] Even this was to cause disputes with the FO, such was the strength of the conviction that had developed there regarding the cooperation option.

The Third Option: Cooperation – and How to Achieve it

The FO had come to the conclusion that Stalin was interested in cooperation in November 1941. From thence, the principal British concern was whether he was changing his mind, and how to dissuade him from doing so. The option of collaboration with Britain over the long term was viewed as an attractive but also a risky one from Stalin's point of view. After Eden's experience in Moscow, it was concluded that Stalin was testing British attitudes with his frontier demands. Stalin was assumed to be realistic enough to see that in the event of victory, the Allies could not prevent him taking what he wanted in the east. His demands must therefore have some other motive: a test of sincerity, with future collaboration in mind. This in itself indicated to some what his present inclinations were – to experiment with cooperation and see how far his allies would meet his basic security requirements. The acid test idea was agreed within the Northern Department, and appealed to Sargent and Eden. Cadogan was more sceptical, but this was the viewpoint argued in Cabinet by Eden, where it proved eventually to be persuasive.

In this forum, Eden argued for a particular way of handling the Soviets, drawn from his long-standing inclinations, reinforced by his experiences in Moscow, and showing signs of influence from Cripps and Beaverbrook. Interestingly, Eden put forward his arguments for concessions to secure long-term political cooperation before there was much debate in the FO on what method was best to secure cooperation under the circumstances then prevailing. He and Sargent developed their ideas quickly from the formulations of November 1941 into the arguments put to the War Cabinet in January 1942, leaving the rest of the FO to catch up. Thus, FO discussion of the meaning of 'cooperation with the Soviets' – of what the British wanted from it and how to achieve it – came after Eden had already made the case for concessions to the Cabinet.[103]

Having come to the conclusion that Stalin was considering war and postwar cooperation with Britain, the problem the FO officials saw was how to bring about working cooperation with such a difficult and sensitive ally in a form that met British needs. In this debate, assumptions about the USSR played a central role. British policy was shaped by views of how the Soviets would respond to certain types of action or treatment, and by views of what kind of cooperation Britain needed, in terms of duration and degree of intimacy. Cripps and Beaverbrook both argued that the way to secure the right kind of cooperation was by convincing the Soviets of British sincerity by granting concessions and treating them as equals. Beaverbrook was principally concerned with making wartime cooperation work: Cripps had always looked to the long term, and Eden returned from Moscow both convinced of Soviet suspicions and of the need to take positive measures to ensure cooperation would last into the postwar era.

After Cripps left the Embassy in January 1942, the Chargé d'Affaires, Baggallay, sent a number of telegrams which questioned the effectiveness of such an approach. Writing at a time when Soviet confidence was sky-high as a consequence of their winter offensive, he believed that Soviet self-centredness and contempt for weakness would mean that this approach could not be the foundation of a workable cooperative relationship. He argued on the basis of the old concept of the Soviet respect for strength: this meant that public adulation of them needed to be reduced, and concessions should be linked to performance of cooperative acts, not made in advance of them.[104]

Warner picked this up and saw the need for a careful policy, not only to bring out Soviet cooperativeness, but also to institute actual collaboration: as a practical matter, not an abstract concept. To Warner, this meant being both firm, as Baggallay suggested, but also frank. He believed the essentially *ad hoc* policy pursued thus far had been simultaneously too concessionary and too uncooperative. He felt the British should not seek to buy cooperation, for he assumed the Soviets were drawn to it in their own interest, but on the other hand, the British should be cooperative themselves. Soviet needs had not been considered and they had not been brought into any real consultation. Policy should combine 'frankness' and 'firmness': this meant drawing them into discussions and planning, while not shrinking from speaking to them as one would to friends, stating frankly British views and interests. This derived from the key perceptions of the Soviets – that they distrusted gestures of goodwill, respected strength, but were also highly sensitive about being excluded from Allied decision-making.[105]

Bruce Lockhart used the same terms – 'firmness' and 'frankness' – but placed more emphasis on the need to satisfy Soviet needs and desires. His emphasis on Soviet sensitivity chimed in with Beaverbrook and Eden's views, and his extensive and apparently authoritative formulations supplied the latter with a theoretical foundation to what were effectively gut feelings. Lockhart persuasively argued that the only way to treat the Soviets was as the government of a Great Power like the USA. He was the first person of any real influence in Whitehall to put forward a 'therapeutic trust' argument; the Soviets if treated thus would then try to behave appropriately. If patronised, however, they would only behave badly. He endorsed Harriman's view that

> the only way is to purify our own hearts. If we suspect them, ergo they will suspect us. This is not far from my old formula of 1918: treat them like civilised beings and decent people, and they will try to behave like civilised beings. Treat them like gangsters and they will out-gangster gangsterdom.[106]

As Sargent put it, this did not mean Britain should 'try to propitiate Stalin by one-sided sacrifices and surrenders'. It did mean creating a sound basis for future relations by an alliance to cover the war and postwar reconstruction of Europe, which meant making some concessions to achieve it, 'but if we want to prepare our relations with the Soviet Govt. against the more difficult period ahead of us, such concessions will be well worth while', so long as Stalin made some too. This would form a foundation of confidence and goodwill on which to build Anglo-Soviet cooperation, and which would help when difficult issues arose.[107]

To deal with Soviet suspiciousness and xenophobia Lockhart recommended 'polite but firm directness'. At present, he thought, Britain had no policy to the USSR, nor to Europe as a whole. Soviet suspicions were if anything increasing. They felt they were fighting in isolation and that they had no share in the inner counsels of the Anglo-American alliance. 'They are treating me', Stalin would think, 'as they treat their natives and negroes.' The variety of approaches covered by the term 'firmness' is indicated by Lockhart's recommendations. To him, 'firm directness' did not involve the rejection of Soviet demands nor tough bargaining. The Soviets, he argued, should not be treated as inferiors. Britain appeased the Americans, but did not appease the Soviets. It was necessary to understand

Soviet psychology and examine the conditions on which the partnership that Britain needed with the USSR had to be based. His
suggestions therefore involved going further than Warner: giving
the Soviets their security demands, an equal say in the conduct of
the war, the pooling of resources and a role in the European peace
settlement. It was unpleasant having the Soviets at strategic talks,
but it would be even more unpleasant having them walk out
of the partnership. Lockhart's doctrine was to 'give concessions
graciously now, and not have them dragged out of us later'. The
perception of Soviet sensitivity on which Lockhart built this rec-
ommendation was to be a strong factor in promoting this particular
approach over the other 'straight talking' aspects of the frankness
method.[108]

Warner had wished to forward a paper containing his and
Baggallay's ideas to be agreed upon as policy. He was overtaken by
the Cabinet's decision after further reflection to accept Soviet frontier demands, in order to start building Soviet confidence in
cooperation.[109] To Churchill, the halting of the Soviet offensive and
the prospect of further German advances in the summer made this
seem necessary, though he was not enthusiastic, and Attlee raised
no objection. Warner noted that it was decided not to proceed with
any directive on doctrine.[110] No reason was given, but this was
clearly inopportune, as a change in attitude to one that would appear
less forthcoming would dispel all the potential advantage of the
concession. The perception of Soviet sensitivity caused the problem.
The concession was to be made to gain confidence – an essential
prerequisite if a frankness policy was not to appear retaliatory or
confrontational. But this then meant that until confidence could
clearly be seen to be established, a less accommodating line was
difficult to initiate without raising the suspicions again. The dilemma was to appear repeatedly: erstwhile builders of a sound, frank
relationship along the Baggallay–Warner lines, including most FO
professionals, were continually having to deal with the initial bad
impression created in the first months after BARBAROSSA, when
British policy was imbued with the belief that unpleasant decisions
(for example, on declaration of war on Finland) could be avoided
because the USSR would be quickly defeated and the Soviet regime
disappear; subsequently the primary task always appeared to be to
expunge Soviet suspicions. Without this, neither 'firmness' nor 'frankness' could be initiated. Consequently, the Government now
proceeded to enter negotiations for a Treaty without an agreed

doctrine on how to handle the Soviets; policy in this area continued to be improvised and nothing was done to dampen down public adulation (which was driven by domestic factors) nor to build a more 'regular' relationship such as would permit of frankness and the occasional argument, without this being interpreted as having fundamental effects on the issue of cooperation.

Given the perceived importance to Stalin of his frontier demand as a test of British attitudes, it was considered a major triumph to achieve the Anglo-Soviet Treaty in its final form with no mention of frontiers in it. This soon had an effect on attitudes without reference to the special circumstances that brought the Treaty about; the American attitude and the Soviet preoccupation with assurances of a second front in 1942 after the shock of defeat in the second battle of Khar'kov. The Soviets seemed to have moved to a more accommodating position by affirming their commitment to postwar cooperation without a *quid pro quo*.[111] This increased the hopes and dampened the fears evident earlier. The positive feeling was increased by relief that a domestic political crisis had been avoided.

By the autumn of 1942, the British had finally begun seriously to consider postwar plans. The issue of whether the USSR could be assumed to be a cooperative power was central. Anglo-Soviet relations soured in September and October 1942. Even though this could be attributed to Soviet anger about the suspension of Arctic convoys after convoy PQ17 suffered disastrous losses, and their anxiety about the outcome of the battles at Stalingrad and in the foothills of the Caucasus, there was concern within the FO that the Soviets might be reconsidering the commitment and that they were examining the lone wolf option.[112] There was therefore great satisfaction when Stalin appeared to come out in favour of the cooperation policy in his speeches in November.[113] It was concluded, from these public statements and some satisfactory telegrams to the Prime Minister, that after some debate within Soviet ruling circles, Stalin's preference for cooperation had prevailed.[114]

The outcome of the first FO considerations of postwar planning, under the auspices of the new Economic and Reconstruction Department, was the Four-Power Plan. This assumed the best way to avoid a repetition of the failures of the post-First World War settlement was to base any international organisation squarely on the realities of power. Central to the plan was the assumption that the Soviet Union would be one of the leading powers in the postwar world and would cooperate with Britain and the United States in

preserving the peace. This was based principally on two foundations: Stalin's speeches, and the conclusion that the lone wolf option
would be the more costly policy to the Soviets and would not offer
a comprehensive solution to the overriding problem of the containment of Germany. Soviet desires were described as two-fold:
to seek to erect some barrier against 'Europe' so as to be able to
restore the Soviet 'paradise' in peace, and to make every effort to
ensure that Europe was not united against them again. This meant
'making quite certain that the power of Germany is effectively smashed
for as long a period as possible'. The confidence of the statement
in the Four Power Plan paper was a reflection of the strength of
the assumption about the way Stalin's security and reconstruction
needs would make the possibility of cooperation with Britain
attractive.[115]

The strength of the security perception did not mean that there
were not many questions that remained unanswered for the FO
professionals and for Eden. The Northern Department were concerned with the practice of cooperation; Warner and Dew were
sceptical about how this would work.[116] Warner warned that while
the Soviets might be cooperative, they were still capable of a lot of
what would seem from Whitehall 'mischief making', though they
should still be involved as much as possible. Warner's attitude, like
those of most his colleagues, was never free from hints of ambiguity
and conflicting emotional and intellectual inclinations, for he was
also concerned to avoid the impression of 'ganging up' with the
Americans to the exclusion of the Soviets, and asserted that it was
important to have the Soviets involved in practical collaboration
from the outset.[117]

Although maintaining his tone of scepticism, Warner continued
to assert through 1943 that the Soviets wanted cooperation. More
fundamental doubts were expressed by Cavendish-Bentinck and
Cadogan, who wondered whether the Kremlin would consider a
collaboration policy more profitable than a *volte face* (that is, a
peace with Germany and possibly even a return to a Rapallo policy).
However, Sargent and Eden endorsed the Northern Department view
that the Soviets were extremely unlikely to return to the German
option: this left a choice between isolation behind a *glacis* or cooperation (both directed against an inimical Germany), and the Soviets
seemed to be inclining towards the cooperation option.[118]

Generally, therefore, FO discussion of the third Soviet option
through 1943 focused not so much on the basic desire of Stalin for

good relations with the British, as on what this meant – what kind of cooperation would he want, could the British accept, or indeed themselves want, and how could Soviet policy be tested as to its cooperativeness. The limitations of personal contacts made this difficult to do, especially since ideology was not regarded as a helpful guide to Stalin's actions.

The diplomatists found the interest in agreements on war aims that Stalin expressed to Clark Kerr in February 1943, and his discontent at not being consulted about Allied decisions, to be evidence both that he wished for cooperation and that his sensitivities meant that the sooner some structure of cooperation was created, the better.[119] The ultimate result was the European Advisory Commission (EAC), which Eden succeeded in getting established at the Moscow Conference in 1943; though in practice a forum for frustration rather than cooperation, its establishment was seen as a step forward in the long process of accustoming the Soviets to 'normal' diplomatic cooperation.[120]

The thrust of perceived Soviet views of their interests was seen to point to cooperation, but there was less clarity about what was meant by 'cooperation' and what it would involve. Churchill saw it as a wartime comradeship, though a more distant one than that with the USA. He was not interested in involving them in structured three-power cooperation, for their obsession with the second front would damage Anglo-American intimacy as well as produce strategic decisions he wished to avoid.[121] The FO generally seem to have envisaged some kind of consultative arrangement that would produce a joint benign oversight of, but without close intervention into, the states east and west of Germany – hence their enthusiasm for a 'self-denying ordinance' on involvement in eastern Europe, which was supposed to mean neither Power would reach unilateral agreements with states in the region.[122] Some, such as Wilson and Ronald, thought this was not enough, and were examining the possibilities of trade and cultural links.[123] The aim of this was much the same as the consultation idea – to get the Soviets used to normal intercourse between states, in the hopes that this would prevent such differences as were bound to emerge from ruining overall relations. Cooperation would have sufficiently strong foundations to withstand occasional disagreements, as seen in relations with the USA.

It was not clear, however, what was the best way actually to bring working cooperation into being. Dissatisfied with Churchill's *ad hoc* policy, which combined concessions and adulation with a refusal to discuss issues like the second front frankly with the Soviets, Warner and others pressed for a firm but fair policy that was rational and reciprocal on the individually mundane but cumulatively important matters that tended to arise, especially military ones; not to close cooperation down, but to make it more productive and sound.[124] The key words were still 'firmness' and 'frankness'. They derived from an essential belief in the possibilities of cooperation (what Warner called the 'broad strategy'), but a belief that methods until then had been counter-productive: they might keep contention at a minimum, but they could not lay the foundations for the give-and-take of real cooperation.[125] When they advocated 'firmness', FO officials did not mean hard bargaining. Warner feared that Churchill and Eden tended to see this in the crude terms of the old controversy dating back to the Beaverbrook mission about bargaining or not bargaining.[126] There were subtle differences, resulting from the admixture of the old view of Soviet policy as self-interested and realist with the new perception of their desire for cooperation, with also a concern to mitigate the effect of their sensitivity and suspicion. The differentiation from bargaining, which derived from the same doctrine of self-interestedness, was too subtle for some; notably Martel, appointed head of 30 Mission at the start of 1943 as part of the COS's attempt to get better liaison.[127]

The military certainly thought cooperation could be improved, though they believed it would always be limited. To them it mainly meant the Soviets providing more intelligence and better cooperation over issues connected with running the convoys. They were not inclined to give credence to the idea of Soviet hypersensitivity. They accepted the stereotype that the Soviets, as Asiatics and realists, respected a firm interest-based approach and like anyone with a propensity to bully responded best to strength. Any sensitivity they possessed would be manifested in suspicion at gratuitous acts and declarations of goodwill. Brooke and his colleagues wanted relations on a fairer basis in which Britain did not do all the giving. The military therefore emphasised 'reciprocity' as the correct method for handling the Soviets. They rejected the Soviet point of view, for which there was some sympathy in the FO and in SOE, that the relationship was asymmetrical, in that the Soviets were already doing far more than the British in the war effort, and that therefore if the British could not get involved in large-scale ground combat, they should give what they could in other ways.[128]

As a concomitant to 'firmness', the Embassy and Northern Department pressed that it was important to discuss all matters frankly with the Soviets, including unpleasant ones; the problem with the concessionary policy was that the avoidance of contentious issues had meant that virtually nothing was discussed with the Soviets. Now, Clark Kerr, Wilson, Warner and Lockhart felt that more openness in confronting and thrashing out issues would improve cooperation, which implied disagreements would not be serious, at least not so far as to imperil cooperation.[129] Eden liked such an approach to cooperation, built around plans and agreements, and called it 'belling the cat'.[130]

The most prominent new factor was the belief that a regular rather than an *ad hoc* relationship was possible with the Soviets. In a sense this paralleled Churchill's belief that he could establish a useful working relationship with Stalin – though in 1943 he still eschewed paper commitments for the postwar era and sought to build the relationship purely on a fighting partnership against Hitler.[131] The FO officials for their part wanted to clear up their uncertainties of Soviet postwar intentions: doing so had the two-fold function of putting cooperation into practice and clearing potential areas of future dispute. They came up against Churchill's reluctance to discuss such contentious issues, and the fact that the British had vague ideas themselves about postwar political aims. The Atlantic Charter and the agreement with the Americans not to agree any territorial changes until after the war implied a preference for the *status quo ante bellum*. There was reluctance to develop British attitudes any further. This left the British to react to events and to appear to be standing in the way of change.[132] Without British decisions on what their own views were, there was simply no scope for a 'frank exchange'; instead, policy continued to be based on avoiding issues and responding to problems as they arose in ways that would not rock the cooperative boat in the short term. There was therefore no follow-up to the February 1943 Clark Kerr–Stalin talks.

'Frankness' implied treating the Soviets as equal and trusted allies: indeed making a special point of it in view of their suspicions. But as Lockhart had found earlier, the thesis of sensitivity worked both ways: they wanted to be treated fairly, with nothing kept from them, but they were also very suspicious and easily offended by unpleasant things which in the normal course of cooperation would occasionally have to be said to them. The idea of Soviet hypersensitivity regarding British policy and their own prestige implied certain possible effects that were too dangerous to ignore. As issues arose it seemed sensible to soft-pedal on 'frankness' for the sake of not upsetting existing cooperation, even on such a major matter as the Katyn massacre.[133] The Soviets, it was still felt, would be highly sensitive about a change of direction in British policy. They would not understand the subtleties of the change of approach and would think that British policy was hardening in preparation for the postwar world, and would shape their policy accordingly. While the Soviet decision for cooperation was seen as still a provisional one, it seemed prudent to be careful – and later in 1943, after the Moscow and Teheran conferences when Soviet policy seemed more firmly set, it did not seem wise to provoke contention when cooperation was proceeding better.

In the absence of information regarding long-term Soviet policy, actual Soviet behaviour was still taken by Churchill and Eden and the military as a guide. Many in the FO did so too, though there were also warnings against drawing too large conclusions from this. Equally, the assumed Soviet fear of 'ganging up' and their desire to be involved remained part of the everyday currency of debate. These facts explain why the course, character and outcome of the Moscow and Teheran Conferences were construed to indicate the result of the internal Soviet policy debate and a new stage in the Soviet commitment to cooperation, and why at the start of 1944 the prospects seemed bright.[134] It was not so much that categorical evidence was provided at these conferences of the direction of Soviet policy in important acid test areas, for it was not and much remained unclear. What was influential was their general demeanour of co-operativeness.[135] A War Cabinet discussion on 25 January indicated the strength the cooperative assumption had gained, particularly since the context was a pessimistic discussion about Poland. Moreover, a story in *Pravda* repeating separate peace rumours had raised British hackles. Despite this the Cabinet agreed that there was no ground for thinking the Soviets would not stick to any agreements reached, nor that they took Treaty obligations lightly: they 'had much to gain by maintaining the good relations established at the Moscow and Teheran Conferences', and generally there was every reason to believe that the USSR wanted to cooperate with the US and Britain.[136]

There was thus at the start of 1944 a complex of assumptions about the USSR producing a rough agreement across the War Cabinet and the FO that the Soviets could be involved in postwar cooperation; cooperation in terms of a political alliance. The actual process of this cooperation had not really been discussed, nor its limitations. It was not clear to what extent the British and Soviets were expected to get politically mixed up, or their spheres to be separated, though there was lip-service to the idea that 'Europe is one'. The shape and purpose of future military cooperation was even less clear (though it was clear one of the limitations was military secrets, including atomic research). These issues all needed to be worked through, and much of the debate in 1944 was concerned with them, building on the basic assumption that Stalin was cooperative. This left plenty of uncertainty as to the kind of cooperation he or the British wanted. It is clear, however, that the cooperative option, whatever that amounted to, was believed to have become the favoured one for Stalin. While alternative policies were open to him, and he had continuing tests of Allied sincerity on which cooperation was contingent, it met his security needs, his internal requirements, and not least, satisfied his vanity by placing him at the centre of direction of world affairs. Stalin was seen to favour cooperation as his best option, but not because he loved his allies. Relations could at times be difficult, and there would not always be a meeting of minds, but as Churchill particularly felt, this was a relationship based on a strong common interest, not sentiment or culture.

While it was clearly in British interest that the Soviets engage in cooperation, the belief that the FO and Cabinet had come to accept by the start of 1944 that the USSR would give cooperation a try was based upon a range of perceptions of the USSR that logically supported such a conclusion, not just wishful thinking. Recent research in Soviet archives suggests that this conclusion was a reasonable one to make. The Soviet Government had indeed made a decision to make cooperation with the Allies its prime policy, though this was, as Warner perceived, 'on test'.[137] The conclusion was not accepted without doubts or careful examination of the various Soviet policy options, and few of the professionals or politicians had put aside all their reservations. However, by the end of 1943, the basic point was established for the FO, Eden and Churchill, and the alternative Soviet policies for the time being at least appeared unlikely to be followed.

5
'Probable Tendencies of Soviet Foreign Policy'

During 1944 the thesis of Soviet cooperation was developed to its fullest extent. A range of papers was produced in the course of an extensive, if unstructured, debate on the assumptions that might safely be made about future Soviet policy. Within the FO there was plenty of caution, though in communications to representatives abroad and to other parts of the Government, points were stated more firmly. The crucial core perceptions were well established, however, not only in the FO, but wider in the Government; particularly the security motivation and Soviet concern about reconstruction and internal development. What were less certain, and about which individuals were uncomfortably aware that they still had only imperfect evidence supplemented by deduction, were the details of specific Soviet policies and the course of the assumed policy debate in the USSR.

Further Analysis of the Cooperation Option

Between October 1943 and April 1944 the FO Departments worked on a paper to provide the PHPS/c with guidance regarding Soviet policy. This required the FO to formulate conclusions on issues about which there had been some uncertainty. The final paper explored the extent of knowledge about Soviet external policy and its motivations, and identified 'probable tendencies'. Eden found it 'remarkable'. The central tenets were the product of the debate and analysis that had been proceeding since November 1941, and drew on key assumptions that had been established earlier, in the 1940–41 period. The Soviet Union was now characterised, in contrast to the early 1940 view, as immensely strong and well organised, provided that satisfactory reconstruction took place. It was stated that though it was difficult to predict Soviet policy, there were certain fixed points. Internally, the USSR would remain highly centralised, with public ownership and planning of the means of production. Its major interest would be reconstruction and further development. Externally, the primary Soviet policy would be the search for security against the Power or Powers that might threaten these internal developments, and the especial fear would be of a German recovery. Since it was further assumed that Soviet leaders were realists, not ideologues, this produced the assertion that security would be attempted through cooperation with Britain and the United States. In the pre-war period foreign affairs had been subordinated to internal needs. With their domestic preoccupations aggravated by the war, the Soviets were unlikely to follow a purely expansionist policy. Their overall aims were nationalistic, not those of world revolution, though they would not become capitalist. The Soviets could be expected to want their 1941 frontiers, friendly governments in eastern Europe and effective measures to restrain Germany. They would be suspicious if right-wing governments were set up elsewhere in Europe. The war was seen to have consolidated the hold of the regime, while at the same time strengthening the movement away from revolutionary dogma back to the traditional organisation of society. It had provided the chance to remove for good the threat from Germany and Japan, and had given the USSR the chance to get on terms of equality and cooperation with the remaining world powers, thus providing the opportunity to concentrate on internal problems without fear of external aggression or counter-revolution. While tending to apply simple but drastic tests of the real intentions of foreign countries, including allies, the Soviets were depicted as satisfied that cooperation was the best assurance of security, so long as the British and Americans did not threaten their internal development nor fuel their suspicions about a *cordon sanitaire* in eastern Europe such as would prevent them from dealing with any German problem. The theses of Soviet sensitivity, sense of inferiority and suspiciousness were also woven into the analysis, with some acknowledgement that methods should not be seen as a guide to aims. Even if the Soviets decided on a lone wolf policy, they were unlikely to take actions that would risk involving them in a major war for at least five years. Sargent added that any friction with the British would not be ideological but over the treatment of Germany.[1]

There was a note of caution in the statement that long-standing suspicions made it necessary to begin building confidence during the war to prevent deterioration thereafter. The reasons why it might become difficult were the ethnic Russian capacity for suspicion and the legacy of at least 125 years of Anglo-Russian hostility, the progress of the USSR to self-sufficiency and impregnability, and the difference of outlook between a 'war-weary, liberal and kindly Britain' and 'a vigorous, intensely nationalistic Soviet Union'. The present wartime situation of mutual need therefore offered a chance that must not be missed. The FO were clear that though Soviets were realists, their estimate of their interests depended upon their assessment of the threats from and attitudes of others. This shaped FO recommendations on how to handle the Soviets and was the source of much of the acrimony in the subsequent dispute with the COS.[2]

In a further paper, the possibility of differences of opinion in the Soviet decision-making elite and the need to encourage the cooperative elements was stressed.[3] The overall sense in the FO was that Soviet policies were developing along favourable lines, but were not firmly fixed. Unwelcome aspects could still appear, without necessarily being signs that cooperation had been rejected, though clearly requiring careful British responses.[4] There was a sense that these were still best guesses, as Warner pointed out in a minute on a dissenting paper from O'Malley, but the weight of opinion after Teheran was that cooperation was the preferred Soviet option, conditional on their perceptions of British policies.[5]

These points were developed further in response to views outside the FO, notably those of the military and of Duff Cooper, now the British representative with the French National Committee, and a strong advocate of the formation of a western European group led by Britain. One of his central justifications for such a policy was the potential of the USSR to dominate Europe. He wrote that the 'Bolshevik bogey' was a bogey, but had been succeeded by a real Soviet danger. The Soviets had it within their means, he thought, to subjugate the whole of Europe. Duff Cooper claimed the alliance with the USSR would be a case of the wolf lying down with the lamb, and drew comparisons with Hitler, Kaiser Wilhelm II and Napoleon, to which Eden countered, 'but what do the Soviets want?' and rejected the analogy. The FO generally accepted the need to develop a Western grouping, but rejected the idea of building it as a defensive measure against a Soviet threat, though they did wish

to limit Soviet influence, and saw that the group would inciden-
tally offer a useful defence against the USSR as well as Germany.[6]

Jebb found Duff Cooper's despatch 'masterly', reflecting as it did
his own views on western Europe, but added: 'we think it extremely
unlikely Russia will attempt the domination of Europe.' Harvey's
response was to agree that the principal uncertainty was the Soviet
Union. The test of the alliance would be treatment of Germany.
There was risk of estrangement, since Soviet policy would be tougher
than British public opinion would endorse. The Soviets might then
fall back on the alternative of a Communist Germany, but more
likely was that they would simply entrench themselves in eastern
Europe, stubbornly and uncooperatively. He believed Duff Cooper
was right to advocate a western bloc, but that he did so for the
wrong reasons. The USSR and France were natural allies against
Germany for geographical reasons, and France, the Low Countries
and Norway could share in the task of controlling Germany. This
need not make Stalin suspicious, for he had suggested such an
approach to Eden in December 1941. Without the Anglo-Soviet alliance there was the risk of the division of Europe with Germany
playing one half off against the other. With it, the more effectively
west and east Europe were 'articulated for cooperation' the better.
Britain should keep western Europe from Germany as the USSR would
keep Poland and Czechoslovakia, both systems bound by the Anglo-
Soviet alliance. Thus, to Harvey, the bloc scheme, which the FO
favoured, could only work to Britain's interest if over-arched by an
Anglo-Soviet collaboration, not as an alternative or reinsurance against
its failure.[7]

Sargent agreed with Harvey that the western bloc would be welcome as part of an Anglo-Soviet system against Germany but as a
defensive system against possible future Soviet aggression would be
a dangerous experiment that might precipitate the very evils it was
intended to guard against. Eden summed up the centrality at this
point of the relationship with the USSR in FO thought, writing
that the Anglo-Soviet alliance was 'the arch of our policy with close
association with Western Europe the Western buttress'.[8] A western
group was seen as a good way to avoid a power vacuum in Europe
which the Soviets would feel they would have to fill in their own
security interest; the perception that the Soviets feared disorder was
at this time a stronger influence than fear of Soviet expansion for
ideological reasons. Plans should be based on including both Britain and the USSR in European cooperation.[9] The Anglo-Soviet Treaty

was to be the basis of Britain's European policy, providing the link that would assuage Soviet suspicions of an exclusive bloc and assure them that the bloc was directed against Germany, even though it was considered that if the World Organisation failed and the Soviets stopped cooperating, a western bloc would then (but only then) be some defence against the USSR as well as Germany.[10]

The FO was to state the same view in response to the PHPS; their policy was to make the Anglo-Soviet Treaty a reality, draw the Soviet Union into closer collaboration in world affairs whenever possible and desirable, and oppose any renewed tendency on its part to withdraw into isolation. It was founded on the concept that after the war the Soviets would be primarily interested in peaceful conditions on their borders (for internal development), and coloured by fears of the lone wolf policy and an ongoing internal Soviet policy debate. British consciousness of their own weakness, fears about containing Germany and uncertainty about American post-war policies strengthened the resolve to fix upon this policy and increased the importance of ensuring in every way possible that British actions did not jeopardise the possibilities of its achievement. The genuine perceptions of Soviet sensitivities and suspicions then came into play to shape FO reactions to others' recommendations.[11]

The Cooperative USSR Thesis is Put to the War Cabinet

The definitive FO view on Soviet policy was put to the War Cabinet in two major papers, WP(44)304 'Soviet Policy in the Balkans' and WP(44)436, 'Soviet Policy in Europe'. The Balkans paper was compiled by the Southern Department, which now included Dew. The original impetuses for this were Eden's worries about Soviet policy in Italy and the broader expression of concern coming from Churchill. When Churchill expressed such views however, implying a large Soviet aim in the Balkans and beyond, Eden had attempted to moderate such views, and conversely, on the Italian issue, Churchill had been much less concerned at possible Soviet incursions.[12] The FO characteristically sought to lay out authoritatively what was known and what could be guessed about Soviet aims in this area, which would provide guidelines to lessen extravagant swings of opinion between optimism and pessimism.

The analysis of the Balkans issue was founded on the assumption that Soviet policy was based upon realism and directed towards achieving security for the Soviet state and regime. It was considered that the Soviets were certainly seeking to acquire a dominant influence in the Balkans, though Eden warned that there must be care to guard against the supposition that a clash of interests was inevitable. Britain should build up her influence but avoid a direct challenge or a suggestion that this was a direct counter to Soviet influence. This was in line with the image of the USSR outlined in the Probable Tendencies paper. WP(44)304 distinguished between the spread of Communism and of Soviet influence:

> The Russians are, generally speaking, out for a predominant position in South-East Europe, and are using the Communist-led movements in Yugoslavia, Albania and Greece as a means to an end, but not necessarily as an end in itself.

As far as Greece was concerned, the Soviets had agreed to let the British take the lead, though if things did not work out well there they might yet fish in troubled waters. While voicing concern and discussing policies to counter excessive Soviet influence, the FO were trying to place Soviet actions in perspective; in terms of historical Russian security aims, and in terms of a Soviet Union not seeking to propagate world revolution nor confront British interests.[13]

This intention was not always picked up. Cranborne, the Colonial Secretary, commented that Soviet policy was a danger everywhere, and that the principles in the Balkans paper needed to be applied in Europe as a whole. Cadogan and Eden agreed on the need for a paper defining British policy to Europe as a whole.[14] The task fell to Warner, and the result was a paper on Soviet influence in Europe and the extent to which purely British influence could be maintained against it. So WP(44)436 arose out of the concern being voiced by many outside the FO, such as Duff Cooper and Cranborne, about the likely expansion of Soviet influence in Europe after the war. The FO shared that concern, but on the basis of the core assumptions they had formed about Soviet policy they did not share the pessimism of these individuals. The paper served the dual purpose of laying out a very broad strategy for the maintenance of British influence and also of assuring those who were apprehensive that there were good reasons for not taking a pessimistic view of the situation. Thus the paper did not arise out of a mood of wild optimism; there was sober caution, as Warner had pointed out to O'Malley, and awareness of the speculative base of the analysis. Only certain points seemed definite, but they added together to suggest a strong possibility that the Soviets would try cooperation, at least for five years.

The argument was based on the reconstruction and security theses. The main Soviet aims were described as rehabilitation and internal development. The search for security was shaped by the threat of a revived Germany: 'both the Soviet Government and the Soviet people must dread the possibility of German recovery.' There might be friction over Soviet behaviour – 'they deal in drastic methods' – and they would be affected by their perceptions of British and US attitudes towards Germany and the countries between Soviet Union and Germany:

> their aim of working with us to keep Germany down and their desire not to combine Europe with Germany against Russia would almost certainly suffice to restrain them both from using the methods of undisguised power politics in their dealings with other countries and from trying to exercise an undue influence in their internal affairs.

Emphasis was placed on the idea that there were two schools of thought in the Soviet policy-making machine; the cooperative school led by Stalin was seen to be in the ascendant, but all depended on the Allies giving satisfaction in the treatment of Germany. The hand of the collaborationists should be strengthened by paying regard to reasonable Soviet demands and consulting them freely and frankly. It was open to Britain to reduce any danger by dextrous diplomacy as well as taking preventative measures.

The FO did not depict Soviet policy in over-idealistic terms, though there was surprising optimism over the prospects for Poland. The Soviets could be expected to seek to extend their influence, though they would not Sovietise territories beyond their 1941 frontiers. An important attitude ascribed to the Soviets was that they would see it was only Germany – and Japan – that could be a direct menace, whereas the other Powers neither could nor would wish to do so. Stalin was a realist not an ideologist: 'before and during the war the emphasis in Russia has entirely and necessarily been on efficiency, discipline and achievement, not on political theories.' Thus, in the case of Italy,

> if the Soviet Government are interested in post-war Italy and are resolved to exercise influence there, this is not merely or

even at all because they wish to impose a Communist regime on Italy, but because they will see in a strong Communist party the best guarantee against the danger of Italy being drawn back into the German orbit.

Cooperation was their prime policy and other policies would be tailored so as not to harm it. There would still be rivalry with Moscow, and the attractions of the Soviet line to Europeans would have to be counteracted; the problem was to do this without jeopardising cooperation and the FO were concerned to keep control of this process, especially when the idea of a western bloc was being raised in different quarters. If this was achieved, the forecasts based on these assumptions about Stalin and his policy were 'on the whole favourable', for the Soviets would 'wish to avoid directly indisposing the Anglo-Saxon democracies by undue interference in European countries'.[15]

The Debate between the FO and the Military

While the FO were developing and refining this interpretation, they were involved in exchanges with the COS/PHPS/c, ostensibly over the issue of the potential enmity of the USSR. The debate, however, did not really hinge on this issue, for the FO agreed the USSR might be an enemy at some point. It was the perception of Soviet sensitivities that created the gulf between the FO and the COS. The FO believed the Soviet attitude towards cooperation would be crucially affected by their perception of the attitudes and intentions of their allies. The COS disagreed with this basic assumption. Furthermore, FO officials and Eden were annoyed that the military should plan on the basis that most likely scenario was that a FO-directed, Cabinet-approved policy would fail.

The PHPS/c's first paper on Soviet policy, PHP(44)13(O), had reflected the Northern Department's positive feelings about Soviet cooperativeness and the limited, realistic nature of their policies. The JIC concurred, though they voiced some doubt about the assumption that the Soviets would not under any circumstances countenance a revival of German power, even if under their control. The PHPS/c fully accepted the reconstruction thesis; the JIC view was that while rehabilitation of Soviet liberated areas would take at least five years, development elsewhere in the USSR had been going on all the time. To overestimate the need for rehabilitation, they warned, might lead to an underestimate of Soviet defensive potential. The PHPS/c concluded that the Soviets would give cooperation a try.[16] However, they went on in subsequent papers to look at worst cases. They made a political assumption to discount the chances of US enmity and a further one to assume Germany and Japan would have been rendered powerless.[17] They saw the USSR as the only power with the capacity to be an enemy, though the PHPS/c and PHPS papers never made much attempt to assess that capacity, making instead sweeping assertions about Soviet capabilities quite at variance with the thesis of Soviet devastation. Soviet aims were assumed to be security and internal development, but there was no certainty that the Soviets would not be a threat in less than ten years, nor that a world organisation would successfully guarantee Britain's defence.[18]

After May 1944, the Committee became a Staff of the COS, the PHPS, with the intention of bringing it closer into the machinery in an analogous role to the JPS. It was restaffed with younger officers. Jebb was retained as Chairman until he was withdrawn by the FO in August in disagreement over the presentation of the USSR in PHPS papers. Even before that his position had become somewhat anomalous. Despite the changes the PHPS did not really become integrated with existing machinery. It was somewhat out on a limb through its involvement only in future strategic matters rather than operational issues and it had no link to the Intelligence departments either.[19]

The PHPS continued to accept the assumption that the Soviets would need at least ten years to reconstruct. Basing themselves on PHP(44)13(O), they also assumed the Soviet Union would at least try cooperation. This did not prevent them considering the possibility of Soviet expansionism, nor of the Soviets continuing their traditional policy of causing trouble in places vital to the British Empire. They clearly saw the USSR as at best a difficult partner, and in any event as a potentially disruptive force in the postwar world. One of the PHPS's inherent assumptions was that despite its domestic needs, of which the Northern Department made such a point, the USSR would concentrate much of its effort in the reconstruction period on building up those areas of its armed forces in which it was deficient – a strategic bomber force and an ocean-going navy. Thus while agreeing that there would be a reconstruction period, they had a different conception of what the order of priorities would be.[20]

It was on the basis of these assumptions that Britain's defences appeared so vulnerable. There was no technical appreciation in the PHPS papers of the actual Soviet capability to achieve such rearmament after the devastation of war, either in terms of industrial capacity or technological knowledge. The implication was that it would be given a high priority, as a natural course of action for the Soviet regime. There was no qualitative assessment of Soviet arms or the likely deployment of Soviet forces – they were credited with unlimited resources and the ability to develop them all simultaneously. It is no wonder that the USSR appeared such a dangerous foe. Each regional survey assumed unlimited Soviet forces would be available and deployable in that sector, without regard to needs elsewhere. None of this bore any relation to what had been learned about the Soviet forces or internal economy during the war. There was no indication of how the USSR was going to build such huge forces and simultaneously improve the road and rail infrastructure of the country to the level necessary within ten years. These broad assumptions were perhaps the natural result of poor information (though it was not non-existent and there is little reference in the papers to factual evidence or cross-referencing to the many relevant MEW or JIC papers) and of the worst-case scenario which encouraged consideration of the worst imaginable situation. They were, however, a serious weakness of the papers which brought the more tendentious political assumptions into greater prominence and prompted FO reactions that these papers were 'childish' and 'preparatory school stuff'.[21]

The military staffs as a whole had developed a grudging admiration for Soviet military achievements. At the same time a patronising attitude was evident towards the Soviets personally and on matters of technology. The strength of the Red Army was its numbers and the ruthless way it was handled which made up for lack of sophistication in other fields. The PHPS papers implied that this situation would not last and Soviet manpower resources and morale would be backed by increasing technical progress. This sat uncomfortably with the continued tendency to regard Soviet technology as low-grade and to see the educational and intellectual deficiencies of the Soviet soldier to be a real impediment to such progress. The JIC set out to provide the PHPS with some guidance on this issue. Their paper, JIC(44)366(O), was described by Sloan in the FO Services Liaison Department as 'explosive' and it was given very restricted circulation. Ward (Jebb's deputy on the PHPS), however, found it 'most interesting and valuable' and, since paragraph 2 endorsed the FO view, thought it ought to cool the heads of the PHPS, though he doubted it would.[22]

The JIC's paper was such as to satisfy both sides of the argument; indeed, it illustrates the different approaches that kept the servicemen and diplomatists at loggerheads. In commenting on probable Soviet intentions, the JIC strongly reiterated their previous approval of the FO's views, to the extent of directly quoting three paragraphs of the 'Probable Tendencies' paper. However, they then went on to discuss capabilities. There was a serious need for a well-informed discussion of what the Soviets were capable of achieving, based on predictions of reconstruction needs, industrial output, physical resources and transportation infrastructure. The JIC paper, despite the fact that there was a certain amount of information available on these issues, fell some way short of this, though it did set out some general comments that were at least better based on factual assessment than those of the PHPS. The paper assumed that conscription would provide the USSR with massive manpower for land and air forces, and claimed there was evidence, not cited, that the Red Navy would be expanded into a formidable force. On the basis of these assumptions – and this was probably what attracted Sloan's comment – the JIC claimed that the Soviets had the technical ability to wage war with the Commonwealth *within* the next ten years, thus seriously modifying the reconstruction axiom to a factor only in Soviet intentions, not capabilities. Weak points in the Soviet war machine, which the PHPS were rarely prepared to acknowledge, were seen to be the concentration of oil resources in the Caucasus, and availability of foodstuffs, raw materials and motor transport. Little consideration was paid to war damage, such as population depletion or destruction of facilities such as the Donbas mines or the Dnepropetrovsk dam, for it was predicted that losses would not only be made good in 'ten years, if not in five', but industry and transport would be *stronger* than in June 1941. Some indication of the remarkable transformation in services' thought about the USSR is shown by the comment that there were no weaknesses or bottlenecks in the transport and communications system. In 1940–42, this system was regarded as a disaster area. Factory dispersal had greatly impressed and seemed to render the USSR less vulnerable to strategic bombing than Japan or Germany had been.

The detailed section on the Navy did not back up the opening statement, for it acknowledged that the Soviets had no expertise in

building capital ships or aircraft carriers, though it praised their
light units (contrary to many reports by BNLOs), and noted that
the Red Navy would not be able seriously to challenge the Commonwealth at sea. Military equipment was praised; it was crude in
finish, but often innovatory and fit for purpose. The deficiencies
in motor transport (the Red Army largely travelled in US-made
vehicles) were acknowledged, but no comment was made on how
they would be made up. The Air Force was described as a 'rough
and ready affair'; it had plenty of aircraft and got its assigned
job done, usually by improvisation and at great cost. The Soviets
could acquire a strategic bomber force given time to produce the
aircraft. The present technical lag behind Britain, the USA and
Germany could be made up; the main limiting factor would be
technical education and limitations in the Russian character (the
ethnic stereotype died hard!). All in all, the body of the report did
not really support the summarising statements, for it showed the
Soviets with plenty of deficiencies to overcome in all three services. While clearly well-placed defensively, the offensive capabilities
that were part of the inherent assumptions of the PHPS papers were
not supported, or indeed discussed. The key issues of replacing over
20 million people, and of whether workers would be deployed in
developing the Navy and Air Force or rebuilding other parts of the
economy, which were crucial for assessing Soviet capabilities, and
about which the FO and PHPS made conflicting assumptions, were
not resolved.[23]

The findings of the JIC made no impact, it seemed, on PHPS
deliberations. The latter's December 1944 revise of their paper on
the Middle East, for example, assumed baldly that the Soviets were
likely to increase the offensive capability of their Navy and Air Force,
with no consideration of the time this would take and the impact
on other military developments.[24] It is certainly noteworthy that
when it served military interests (in terms of maintaining postwar
British forces at a high level), previous criticism of Soviet forces
was overlooked; only a year earlier, Portal had voiced the opinions
of all the RAF that had come into contact with the Red Air Force
that it was poorly trained and even in ground support, its main
task, had achieved little. Soviet air superiority over the Germans
was ascribed to Allied strategic bombing having drawn the *Luftwaffe*
back to Germany, and to Soviet use of British and American aircraft.[25]

Initially, only Warner objected to the emphasis in the PHPS
papers on the USSR as a potential enemy, as directed by the COS,

seeing it to be typical of the 'rabidly anti-Soviet forces'. Others, such as Jebb, Roberts and Cavendish-Bentinck, at first felt such studies were appropriate, but as the COS sharpened their focus on Soviet enmity and as the shallowness of the papers became apparent, came to share Warner's misgivings.[26] There was no real disagreement between the FO and the services that the USSR could possibly become non-cooperative or hostile in time. Disagreement centred on views of likely Soviet responses, and here it is clear there was now complete cleavage between the FO view that the Soviet cooperative mood could be maintained by taking into account their aspirations and sensitivities, and the COS view that no cooperative spirit had been shown and that they had no such sensitivities as could be affected by being amenable.

The difference of opinion was clear in discussion of all the PHPS papers, but was most fierce over those on the western group and the dismemberment of Germany. On receipt of the PHPS paper on western Europe the COS directed a re-emphasis, stating categorically that Germany would be impotent and the US was not a potential enemy, so all military plans for postwar should be based on a potentially hostile USSR. They were sceptical of the possibility of a world organisation or of the US helping Britain in time. To the COS the whole point of both the western group and a dismembered Germany was their utility as a bulwark against the USSR.[27] They did concede that this should not be overt, and they and the PHPS continued to accept that cooperation was the preferred policy, while implying, by devoting so much space to the idea and by advocating such measures, that they felt the alternative of non-cooperation more likely to happen. The COS understood the group must have as its immediate objective holding down Germany, 'but the more remote, but more dangerous, possibility of a hostile Russia using the resources of Germany must not be lost sight of'.[28]

The PHPS did continue to accept that the Soviets would be occupied with internal reconstruction after the war. The revise of PHP(44)17(O) dated 15 September gave this period as five years, and explicitly endorsed the conclusion of WP(44)436 that an immediate threat was unlikely for ten years provided Britain and the US were giving reasonable consideration to Soviet views. However, the tone suggested that after this time there *would* be a danger: the USSR was 'the greatest potential danger we have ever faced'. Defence in depth was needed, including all or part of Germany, even if that country was disarmed.[29] Dismemberment of Germany was strongly advocated in the PHPS paper on Germany, PHP(44)15(O), because of its use against the USSR: it would reduce the chance of a centralised united Germany moving into the Soviet orbit.[30] The FO argued this conception should be 'avoided like the plague', for it would destroy any chance of an enduring Anglo-Soviet alliance. In a counter-proposal, APW(44)90, the FO argued in favour of a united Germany, which could be a factor in holding the Anglo-Soviet alliance and the western bloc together, so long as the Soviets were convinced that Britain was not hostile. The FO in any case believed that dismemberment had to come from within Germany; if it was imposed from outside, it would only create massive irredentist problems later on.[31]

Eden had a confrontational meeting with the COS on 4 October. Sargent briefed Eden that the FO did not deny the Soviet Union was a possible enemy – that was not the point. At worst this could only happen in a number of years. Every effort must be made without sacrificing major British interests to get on terms with the Soviet Government and accustom them if possible to the practice of frank and friendly relations. Soviet suspicions were a danger and if they felt the western bloc was anti-Soviet they would immediately work against it. Knowledge in the Kremlin that Britain was thinking of a war against the USSR was, he warned, the surest way of bringing one about. Julian Lewis scathingly dismisses Sargent's argument, saying it suggests that the Soviets would only act to negate a western bloc and woo Germany if provoked to do so by discovering about such papers. If one accepts, as Sargent did, that the Soviets were suspicious of the British military and sensitive about British intentions in central Europe and especially regarding the treatment of Germany, then the argument is not so absurd.[32] The basic problem was that the COS were not conforming to the guidelines laid down in WP(44)436 which the FO had become convinced could work, but only if applied wholeheartedly. Eden pointed out the problems of searching for an enemy to justify military policy. The USSR, he felt, was being used as a scarecrow.[33] The degree to which the COS rejected the idea that Soviet sensitivity was relevant in modifying British actions was clearly shown in the discussion on 4 October; Portal said that the British should not worry about breeding Soviet suspicions – they were just as entitled to take precautions as the Soviets, who undoubtedly were not bothered by such considerations in their own contingency planning.[34] The dispute cannot be understood unless one sees the centrality to the whole cooperative

USSR thesis of the idea of sensitivity on the German question and the FO perception that as Ward put it, the Soviets had a remarkable facility for nosing out hostile thoughts about the Soviet Union.[35] Moreover, the COS, as Jebb had observed, did not accept the Four Power thesis either. Their idea for the future was that Anglo-American cooperation should continue in the CCS, and the USSR would have its own sphere. They did not take China seriously as a world power.[36] There was no meeting of minds on 4 October, and the only concession the FO was able to gain was that the COS would place sections of papers dealing with a hostile USSR in separate annexes with limited circulation.[37]

Qualified Optimism

Within the FO the long debate with the services firmed up acceptance of elements of the cooperative thesis. Hopeful signs were identified despite problems on a number of specific topics, particularly Poland, while there also remained a disinclination to be too optimistic ahead of signs that Soviet day-to-day behaviour was becoming more cooperative and therefore a surer sign of their intentions. It was still felt that final decisions by the Soviets had yet to be made, and so they were open to influence either way. Warner doubted if the Soviet Government had been able to give much time to the matter – so their present actions were most likely based partly on short-term considerations in connection with the conduct of the war, and partly on the 'old outlook'. Even Molotov, he felt, followed the course dictated by the old Soviet habit of mind unless instructed to the contrary by Stalin. It was he who was the advocate of cooperation; Communist Party and Politburo leaders might need some convincing that cooperation should be followed to any extent which involved much modification of the old ideas.[38]

A similarly qualified view was presented by Clark Kerr in his response to WP(44)436. He warned that the lack of an independent public opinion in the USSR gave the leaders great freedom of action and the ability to change policies quickly. He also cautioned, as Wilson did, that one should not expect the Soviets always to behave in a cooperative manner, even if they did intend to follow a policy of postwar cooperation with Britain and the US. Soviet policy was 'Janus-like', and Communist Parties would continue to be used as instruments of Soviet policy. Cooperation was likely to be complicated by the Soviet blend of pride, sensitivity to criticism and the Slav capacity for suspecting others. The Soviets would try cooperation, Clark Kerr concluded, but one must expect recurring tensions deriving from these characteristics. Warner was unimpressed by this critique, and the Ambassador did simplify his case by ignoring other constraints on Soviet actions, but the fundamental point matched the mood in the Northern Department of cautious optimism, coupled with concern that the Soviet style of behaving would lead people outside the FO to hasty conclusions about Soviet cooperativeness.[39]

It was generally felt that the best way to restrain this behaviour and communicate to the Soviets what effect it had was to speak firmly. Lockhart warned Sargent that while the Soviets valued the postwar alliance, they were intoxicated with success. Britain, he argued, was no longer playing from weakness. Sargent agreed.[40] However, the perception of Soviet sensitivity continued to operate: it was difficult to make a change that did not run the risk of Soviet over-reaction – the temptation was thus not to take the risk on any given issue, while continuing to assert that frankness was the right policy, when the time was right. Sargent defended this approach subsequently, in April 1945, by saying that at the time, with the Soviets bearing so much of the brunt of the war and with the result still in the balance, the avoidance of contention was rightly the prime aim, and it had been worthwhile for the Prime Minister to continue his effusive messages to Stalin.[41] While suggesting that Soviet policy could not be divined from rudeness and lack of cooperative spirit, Wilson argued that the Soviets would do exactly the same for British policy and shape their own policy by it.[42] The logic of the premise of Soviet commitment to cooperation and the perception of Soviet hypersensitivity demanded no half-measures. Whatever individuals' varying degrees of commitment, in practice they found themselves acquiescing in conciliatory action as the safest course; not now to avoid upset to the war effort, but to secure postwar cooperation. Sargent argued strongly that no risk must be taken to break the partnership, or indeed to put it under any stress that was not strictly necessary:

we cannot afford to quarrel with Russia in present circumstances. . . . Such a quarrel might well endanger the security of this country . . . either by driving the Soviet Union back into isolation or, still worse, forcing her into collaboration with Germany as soon as occasion offers.[43]

Jebb and Wilson combined to produce the statement that the situation around 1950 might well be that the Soviets,

> who have during the war emerged as a world power, will exert a world-wide influence comparable to that of any other similar power but, on present form it seems unlikely that, whatever the continuing difficulties of working with Russia may be, the Russians will attempt to extend their controlling influence in Europe beyond a certain geographical line. They might only be tempted to do so in the event of complete chaos in Europe West of that line; and again on present form this is quite improbable.

Soviet influence would be paramount in Poland, Czechoslovakia, Hungary, Bulgaria and probably Yugoslavia, and possibly Austria too. This did not necessarily mean Communist Governments, but they would look to the USSR for arms and would not take a very different line from the USSR in international affairs. Whether Italy was pro-Soviet depended on how much help the western countries gave there. Much revolved around whether the three Powers could work together; there was reason for optimism, in that in Europe at any rate each would seem to have satisfied all possible legitimate ambitions. The kind of sphere of influence described was obviously not regarded at this time as a threat to British interests, nor a sign of sinister Soviet designs. A clash of views on the Straits seemed unlikely; northern Iran was the area where some Soviet expansion might be expected, and the Middle East generally was the area where it was most possible that interests would clash. In the Far East anarchy in China might tempt the Soviets into Manchuria and even Korea, and thus a clash with the Americans, into which Britain might be drawn. The tone was thus reasonably optimistic, seasoned by the awareness that this was all highly speculative.[44]

Despite the bitter dispute between the COS and the FO over the PHPS papers, there were many points on which they were willing to agree concerning the USSR. This is shown graphically in a paper produced by the JIC at the end of 1944, JIC(44)467(O) 'Russia's Strategic Interests and Intentions from the Point of View of Her Security'. This paper was largely written by Sir Arthur Noble of the FO Services Liaison Department and was approved by the JIC and by the COS.[45] It represents the closest that is available to a genuine agreed consensus between the services and the FO on future Soviet policy.

The JIC revisited the issue of actual Soviet military capabilities, concluding they would be able to deploy very large forces, though their technical efficiency was lower than those of more advanced Powers. This was likely to increase, as was the growth of a military tradition. Most of the resources they needed were within Soviet frontiers, so the USSR could with less risk than any other European Power follow an isolationist policy and rely on its own military power to protect itself. The only vulnerable point on the frontier was between the Baltic and the Carpathians, so they would concentrate defensive force there.

Two main assumptions were made. First, the Soviet Government's desire for absolute security would be very great. Second, and connected with the first, was the desire to raise the standard of living (many Soviet citizens having seen conditions in other countries), rebuild devastated areas and undertake fresh industrial and agricultural development. This would require a long period of peace, though the process could be speeded up by reparations from Germany and large imports from abroad. The JIC concluded that the USSR would not be prepared to take any chances, and however small the risk of aggression, it would seek to build a system of security *outside* its borders. They would want in these countries a position similar to that of the British in Egypt; they would allow independence so long as they could ensure these countries followed a policy that protected Soviet strategic interests. Outside this zone of protection, they would try their best to keep Germany and Japan incapable of aggression. They would look to the Western Powers to complete the ring. If the Western Powers accepted Soviet predominance in the border states, then the Soviet Union would have achieved the greatest possible security and could not hope to increase it further by territorial expansion, nor was it easy to see what else the USSR could under such conditions hope to gain from a policy of aggression (assuming Soviet realism). Problems were more likely to arise from Soviet 'tactlessness'. There are elements here of the viewpoint in the PHPS papers, but this largely followed WP(44)304 and 436, particularly the thesis of limited, security-driven objectives.[46]

The COS themselves were capable of expressing positive feelings about the alliance. Portal noted at Yalta;

We are all becoming very pro-Russian, as they really do seem to be nice people, kind and sincere, clean-looking and frightfully keen on their show, and with absolutely no 'bounce' or arrogance. . . . I am absolutely certain that we shall have to make friends with them and that we shan't find it difficult; also we shall have to be the bridge between them and the Americans, who really don't get on very well with them at present. Quite a job for the future![47]

Likewise, the Cabinet discussion of 25 January 1944 and the lack of recorded opposition to WP(44)436 indicate a qualified optimism among Ministers.[48] For Churchill himself, his geopolitical outlook meant that the rapid advances of the Red Army caused him to revise somewhat his preference to avoid contentious issues. His approach in 1944 was to try to pin the Soviets down to agreements, while he had something to negotiate with. Like Eden he believed agreements could be reached and that Stalin would adhere to them if they were negotiated properly. He was not susceptible to the 'ganging up' argument accepted in the FO and which led the Americans pointedly to avoid close consultation with the British at Teheran and Yalta, writing to Eden, 'Any division between Britain and the United States will make us powerless in this matter. Together we can probably control the situation.' While determined that the Anglo-American relationship should not be sacrificed to the niceties of Soviet feelings, however, he also wanted to prevent this raising Soviet suspicions; as he told Colville in October, by flying to Moscow (for the 'Tolstoy' meeting, where he proposed the 'percentages' arrangement to Stalin), he hoped to discourage the idea that Britain and the US were intimate to the exclusion of the Soviets.[49] In fact, what he seems to have desired was to act as the link between an Anglo-American collaboration and an Anglo-Soviet one. He was apprehensive that the three Powers approached each topic from a different angle and in a different mood: 'as we can meet only at intervals of six months, it is very hard for anyone to have a policy.' By 1944 he was seeking a *modus vivendi* with the Soviets. This was regarded as possible to achieve on a basis of the mutual and realistic recognition of power and interests.[50] Churchill believed it was needed because of the range of options that would be open to the Soviets should they defeat Germany and create a power vacuum in east and central Europe. The necessary restraints on Soviet freedom of action would be achieved through Stalin's realism. Hence, therefore, his high hopes when Stalin appeared to be reasonable and to grasp the situation, and why he could be, in Harriman's words, 'all for Joe' while still apprehensive about the possibilities open to the Soviets and determined to limit them where it was in his power to do so.[51]

Churchill's belief in the pressures exerted on Stalin by the 'grim thing behind him' gave a further incentive to grant some of Stalin's requests, while being strong and firm in all other respects. He was hopeful of cooperation with Stalin himself, on the basis of war-time comradeship, but believed he had to be handled a certain way or else the more dangerous side of Soviet policy might come to the fore.[52] The percentages idea must be seen in this light. Rather than simply a concession of Soviet interest in Bulgaria or Hungary, which was self-evident, it was an assertion that Britain had an interest in those countries too. In areas where Soviet actions were becoming, or seemed likely to become, a cause for concern, Churchill was anxious to reach the personal agreements which he rated so highly – as soon as possible – to limit the dangerous effects of the Soviets perceiving lack of interest on the Anglo-American side. Churchill's expectations regarding Greece, and pleasure with the Yugoslav percentage, reflected his concern to limit Soviet influence to the areas the Red Army was to occupy. Churchill told Attlee the percentages were the best possible, with Greece able to be saved and a 50–50 solution in Yugoslavia.[53] He believed a change in the attitude of the Soviet officers with EAM in Greece completely vindicated his diagnosis of the proper policy. Whatever the vagueness of what had actually been agreed upon in Moscow, Churchill's subsequent attitude showed he believed an arrangement had been made.[54]

It is frequently claimed that the Soviet–Polish issue was a major influence in shaping the British Government's attitude to the USSR, but the influence the Polish imbroglio played on perceptions of overall Soviet commitment to cooperation is in fact questionable. Having, in 1943, resisted the temptation to force the Poles to make a frontier concession, one of the consequences of the increased faith in Soviet cooperativeness that followed the Moscow and Teheran Conferences was that Churchill, Eden, the FO and the Labour ministers saw hopes for a reasonable settlement of the Polish problem if the Poles *did* make a concession. Their great fear, now that it was certain that the Soviets would liberate Poland from German occupation, was that the Soviets would set up their own regime in Warsaw. Stalin's statement that he wanted a strong, independent Poland seemed a good sign, but the frontier was still, as Eden had told Hull in August 1943, his 'main question'.[55] The security axiom was at the heart of this belief. Stalin was believed to be less concerned about who was in power in Poland than in securing the Curzon line frontier, provided any regime was friendly – and such a Polish concession would be a good sign of such an attitude. Stalin was believed to be more amenable on this issue than his colleagues.[56] Strong pressure was put on the London Poles at the start and end of 1944, and there was irritation at the lack of movement by them. The Soviet demands were widely seen in the FO and by Churchill as not unreasonable; the continued Soviet reference to a line drawn up by a British Foreign Secretary of course helped make this so. While some Labour Party figures felt that Stalin's security obsession was old-fashioned, most saw his point, and the ethnicity of the region was on his side too. Churchill even went so far as to state the Soviet right was 'inexpungeable', and to add as a further reason (and typically) that the Soviet sacrifices of blood had strengthened this right.[57]

The Poles refused to budge and British irritation shifted to the Soviets for their refusal to compromise. What irritated most was the harsh tone of Molotov and Stalin's messages, for the mood eased when Stalin changed that tone. Differences over Romania and the crisis among the Greeks added to the tension.[58] Then came the Warsaw rising. Churchill, the FO and the Labour leaders came to accept that the Soviets were genuinely unable to aid the Poles on the ground, and anger and frustration were focused on Stalin's refusal to help them by air, or to allow the Allies to do so.[59] This has been seen as a crucial episode for attitudes to the USSR. This is actually hard to substantiate. It certainly confirmed the fear of many that whatever overall Soviet cooperativeness, their requirements in the states bordering them would be taken regardless of Allied susceptibilities. Churchill said the Soviet behaviour was 'strange and sinister', and the issue one of 'profound gravity', but he still hoped an appeal to Stalin, backed by the increase in prestige brought by victories in Normandy, would bring success.[60] It was felt that the firmness eventually displayed to the Soviets at the start of September had paid off, an exaggeration of what had been achieved.[61] These events may well have driven Churchill to Moscow, but the 'percentages' arrangement he proposed there was already foreshadowed in the May discussions of Romania and Greece, and Poland, like Italy, was not included in the percentages. In Moscow, he was once again very forceful in trying to get the London Poles to make concessions to Stalin, and continued to support the Soviet claims. It still seemed to him and Eden that it was the frontiers that mattered to Stalin, not installing his own set of Poles, the Union of Polish Patriots. The latter made a bad impression on all – and were clearly a puppet government-in-waiting – but it was noted that Stalin himself described them as a nuisance and did not seem very attached to them.[62]

The Polish situation did not drastically alter perceptions of the USSR and of Stalin and his policy during 1944; instead, British handling of the issue was shaped by those perceptions (especially the security axiom and views of Stalin), and Poland was seen in terms of larger Anglo-Soviet relations, rather than as the great test case. Many sharp words were written about the USSR's Polish policy (strangely, often not specifically criticising Stalin), but there was also much sympathy with Soviet attitudes, which were seen as cold-bloodedly realistic but not grossly unreasonable, and since not unexpected, not operating to undermine the cooperative assumptions. Thus the Yalta agreement could be made in good faith. The Soviets sacrificed some of this evident goodwill by the insensitivity of their handling of the issue. It was understood that for security reasons Poland was an area of acute interest and sensitivity for Stalin; opinions differed as to whether Stalin should be expected in return to understand and take account of British interest in Poland – he obviously found it easier to understand British interest in Yugoslavia or Greece. Some argued that if the Soviets wanted western friendship they had to acknowledge western interest in the question and accommodate their actions to it if they wanted to secure the wider goal of cooperation. The general inclination was not in 1944 to regard the Soviet attitude on Poland as an absolute indication of their policy to their allies.

Churchill's satisfaction with coming to an arrangement with Stalin in Moscow outweighed his concern about the Polish question. In the period between 'Tolstoy' and Yalta, Churchill was in a positive mood, largely because of the apparent adherence by the Soviets to the agreement not to interfere in Greece.[63] He cannot thus be seen to be out of line with the FO, nor the general thrust of opinion through his government, though he had reached this state of qualified optimism by a somewhat different route, and it was more dependent on a view of Stalin than on more complex theorizations and assumptions.

Churchill's oft-voiced enthusiasm for treating the Soviets firmly did not sit very well with his own endeavour to build a personal relationship with Stalin by florid, sentimental messages, which he maintained while at the same time finding fault with the American viewpoint.[64] Churchill's attitude appears to veer wildly from one extreme to the other. Moran explained it in terms of his health.[65] A better explanation is that Churchill was torn between perceptions that had conflicting implications. On the one hand, he believed Stalin was a realist and was friendly within the bounds of that realism. On the other, he could not rid himself of the idea that these were still Bolsheviks.[66] He thus required continual confirmation that the Soviets were cooperative. His acid tests were daily and sometimes trivial; hence the pendulum swings, for the Soviets themselves were far from consistent in their day-to-day policy. The two schools theory could not completely smooth out the impression left by Soviet 'misbehaviour'. Unlike Eden and some of the FO, he was not comfortable with the idea of therapeutic trust, which promised long-term results from trusting them and treating them as if they were already respectable in the hopes they would then become so. Churchill was prepared to trust Stalin, but he expected immediate results in manifestations of trustworthiness, cooperativeness or at least politeness. When they failed to materialise, his awareness of the possibilities open to the Soviets in geopolitical terms made him apprehensive that the Soviets would revert to type.

Neither Churchill nor Eden was consistent as to British policy, but with Eden keen to build a structure of cooperation on his Anglo-Soviet Treaty and Churchill still concerned for the successful prosecution of the war and pinning his hopes on a personal relationship with Stalin there was no lead towards 'frankness' from these men who had both at times voiced a dislike for a soft policy.[67] Their fluctuations did not please any of those in the FO, who if they differed on degrees of 'firmness' or 'softness' were united in agreeing that the worst way to handle the Soviets was to give them conflicting, contradictory signals. These would only strengthen their suspicions and uncertainty of British policy, thereby compromising their commitment to collaboration and driving them to reinsurance.[68]

Enthusiasm for firmness might have been expected from Attlee and Bevin, given their reservations about the frontier issue in 1942. However, it is remarkably difficult to state categorically what the attitudes of the Labour Ministers were on the issue of Soviet cooperativeness. While it is true that the nexus of foreign policy-making was Churchill–Eden/FO–COS, and that Churchill's style of government did not involve the extended examination of foreign policy issues by the War Cabinet, the Labour Ministers were certainly not totally excluded from discussion of these issues. Yet their views on them have to be gathered from inference and occasional (but unfortunately infrequent) comments recorded officially or informally.[69] After the discussion of Soviet frontiers in February–March 1942, they were not moved to dissent from Churchill's handling of relations with Stalin, nor with the FO recommendations that came to Cabinet. Attlee's chairmanship of the major Cabinet foreign policy committee, the Armistice and Post-War Committee, allowed him, he said, to get his own way, but no strong views on Soviet issues were demonstrated by him there.[70]

While, however, supportive of the aims of Churchill and the FO, in terms of securing, if possible, Soviet friendship, and voicing no opposition to the price to be paid, the Labour Ministers for whom there is evidence show no sign of having taken on board a number of the central perceptions comprising the wartime 'cooperative' image. They do not appear to have been impressed by the internal changes in the wartime Soviet Union. They were certainly suspicious of the dissolution of the Comintern; this indicated they had little readiness to see fundamental changes in the nature of the USSR and had a continued suspicion of its association with domestic Communist Parties. No Labour Minister attended a wartime conference until Attlee went to San Francisco in 1945. They did not therefore undergo any of the modifying effects that personal contact with Stalin had. Instead Attlee, Bevin and Morrison formed their view from 'Stalin-on-paper'; a much less attractive figure.[71] There was much less mention by the Labour leaders of the key terms suspicion and realism, and none of Soviet sensitivity. Attlee, for one, felt the Soviet heritage was essentially Asiatic. Their European ambitions were imperialistic, whether ideological or territorial. The Soviets, like the Americans, he thought, were 'immature' and not swayed by idealistic considerations.[72] He was convinced that Britain needed to be involved in Europe to balance Soviet influence, as part of a policy of being both tough on Germany and 'realistic' to the USSR.[73] To Attlee the western bloc would insure against a German or Soviet threat and be useful if the US returned to isolationism. It would prevent a power vacuum in Europe, which Attlee and Bevin, like FO officials, feared the Soviets would try to fill.[74] Bevin too favoured a western group, based on Britain, and was prepared for a similar set-up in the east, based on the USSR (and did not see them to be in competition), and has been seen by Rothwell to be less harshly minded towards the USSR at this stage than Attlee, though the evidence is not strong.[75] Unlike Attlee, Dalton was by no means convinced of the need or desirability of a German buffer against the USSR, any more than he was of the need for a buffer between the USSR and Germany. Dalton was convinced of the centrality of a continuing Anglo-American-Soviet alliance, and before San Francisco this was an attitude he shared with Bevin and Attlee.[76] Thus, while uneasy about Soviet actions in eastern Europe – described by Morrison as 'harsh and imperialistic' – the Labour leaders were happy to follow the policies laid down in WP(44)436 and by Churchill.[77]

While the Labour Party leaders looked forward to a constructive part being played by the Soviets in the postwar world, they shared the feelings of those who were concerned that the Soviets' inability or unwillingness to act as allies, in the way understood in Britain, might prevent full cooperation.[78] Allied policy should be aimed at both seeking to ensure they still saw international cooperation as profitable (providing the security they needed) and also binding them closely into the machinery so that it would be difficult for them to withdraw. Cooperation might well be difficult, but by no means impossible, since it did not have to mean full confidence. This was an attitude which was to persist in the Government after Attlee became Prime Minister, until 1947.[79] Attlee himself was later to prove willing to see legitimacy in Soviet security aspirations and to be cautious about seeing them as irrevocably hostile.[80]

By the beginning of 1945, there had thus developed an image of the USSR that gave rise to the belief that future cooperation was the most likely Soviet policy option, at least in the immediate postwar period. The perceptions that made up this image were formulated as the result of contributions from various sectors of the Government, though it was the FO which drew them together and formulated the concept of a cooperative Soviet Union most fully. The idea of Stalin's interest in cooperation with the West to provide security, his sensitivity about being treated as an equal and the importance of his reconstruction needs were all central to this concept. On this basis, the FO argued that the Soviet Union, for reasons of national interest, would follow a policy of cooperation within the world organisation for at least ten years. This interest was the need for security while continuing internal development of State Socialism and repairing war damage to the Soviet economy. Unless Stalin was convinced by British or American actions that they would be soft on Germany, or conversely that Europe was going to subside into chaos and disorder again, then collaboration would be tried.

He would seek to ensure friendly governments on his borders, and would probably prefer state Socialist or popular front governments following his foreign policy lead. He was not expected to want to communise these areas, though Communist Parties could be expected to continue to be used as instruments of Soviet national policy. None of this need impinge on Britain's vital interests, which should be clearly stated, though in a non-threatening manner.

Those who approved the FO's conclusions – including Eden, Churchill, Attlee and Bevin – did so because they shared, or at least conceded the possibility of, the interpretations involving Soviet cooperativeness, security-seeking and sensitivity and some of the perceptions that strengthened these beliefs, such as Soviet reconstruction needs and the personal amenability of Stalin, and therefore accepted the logic of working on that basis. This applied also to the JIC and COS, with the significant exception of the sensitivity theory, which the military did not accept. There was a wide range of views as to the importance to be attached to Soviet behaviour as an indication of their attachment to long-term cooperation. The central point is that appraisal of Soviet cooperativeness was based on assessments of how the Soviets viewed their interests, and attempts to reach conclusions about what factors shaped Soviet responses.

6
Towards Postwar Cooperation: 'Difficult, but not Impossible'

The months following the Yalta Conference have been seen as a period of rapid disillusionment in British Government attitudes to the Soviet Union. This process is taken as starting soon after the end of the Conference, in response to Soviet actions in Romania, and then in Poland and other countries, and reaching such a stage at VE Day, 8 May, that Martin Gilbert can describe the breakdown in relations as complete.[1] The Soviets acted unilaterally in the countries the Red Army overran, denied their allies access to information about what was going on there and obstructed their representatives. At the same time, the war situation for the Allies improved – the temporary setback in the Ardennes had passed and the advance on the Western Front was rapid. The environment in which policies were formulated therefore changed, and policy-makers had to face a new set of challenges. However, disillusionment is probably too strong a term to apply to this period. Many of the central assumptions that supported the cooperative theory were still taken to hold good, or at the least were not categorically discredited. British attitudes underwent some changes, but virtually all in the Government at the end of Churchill's premiership continued to see cooperation as a realistic policy target; difficult to achieve, and not necessarily smooth and intimate, but cooperation none the less, based on a fundamental commonality of interests.

At the same time, confusion and uncertainty were increasing and new questions were being asked. To describe this process as a decline in optimism is a little simplistic. What was happening was that some of the key assumptions were being subjected to new tests: particularly the issue of Soviet prioritisation of cooperation over unilateral security measures in eastern Europe (their reinsurance policy), the actual limits of the supposedly limited objectives, and the connection between Soviet methods and aims.

Images of Stalin and the Internal Political Situation

The development of the wartime image of Stalin reached its culmination at the Yalta Conference. Even those who can be regarded as sceptics about the USSR on many subjects, such as Cadogan and Portal, expressed admiration for the way Stalin conducted his affairs at the Conference and the skill with which he handled the other two leaders. Stalin's sagacity and sense of direction were never questioned. Instead his willingness to make concessions reinforced the impression made by his personal demeanour; once again marked in its contrast to the tone that they had become used to in telegraphic communication and contacts with lesser officials, including Molotov. His willingness to accommodate the susceptibilities of his allies made an impression, so that the Polish agreement, on which he gave little ground, did not seem so great a concession in return, and part of a statesmanlike pattern of give-and-take.[2]

The perception of Stalin did not depend solely on such passing events and persisted though the euphoria of Yalta was quick to pass away. Such hopes as there were of the arrangements depended greatly on the image of Stalin. Churchill was undoubtedly apprehensive, thinking of the geopolitical situation and the opportunities open to the Soviets; as he said to Sir Arthur Harris, once Bomber Command had finished its work, 'What will lie between the white snows of Russia and the white cliffs of Dover?' However, amid all the pessimism, his attitude towards Stalin remained a strong qualifying factor. Churchill had been impressed once again by Stalin at Yalta, saying to Moran that he did not think the USSR would move to a hostile stance while Stalin was alive: 'I do not believe he is unfriendly to us.' Churchill continued to distinguish strongly between Stalin and the other leaders, whom he regarded still as 'Bolsheviks'. Churchill saw Stalin to be amenable to personal appeals, should the Prime Minister choose to make them. In private, Churchill's remarks reflected the dependence of his view of Soviet policy on his image of Stalin. His remarks to Dalton indicate how important this was to him:

The PM spoke very warmly of Stalin. He was sure – and Sir Charles Portal had said the same thing to me . . . that, as long as Stalin lasted, Anglo-Russian friendship could be maintained. . . . [marginal comment;] PM said, 'Poor Neville Chamberlain believed he could trust Hitler. He was wrong. But I don't think I'm wrong about Stalin.'

Similarly, Churchill said to Colville that 'Chamberlain had trusted Hitler as he was now trusting Stalin (though he thought in different circumstances), but taking comfort, as far as Russia went, in the proverb about the trees not growing up to the sky.' Whatever Churchill's tactical shifts and attempts to use what means he had to improve Britain's geopolitical situation, this aspect of Churchill's attitude was to remain in place until the end of his premiership, and represents an underlying consistency in his attitude from at least August 1942, which can be overlooked, as it was obscured by tactical shifts and moodswings.[3]

The fundamental elements of the Stalin image remained in place across the Government. The most significant was the attribution of sagacious realism. There was no serious revision of this concept. Even if Stalin had not entirely rejected the Marxist viewpoint, as Balfour wrote, the central assumption was that he was a shrewd realist with no desire to overreach himself. His realism would thus be a limiting factor on his assumed desire to achieve absolute security.[4] Since he was driven by assessment of realities, not ideological assumptions, and his assessment was essentially a rational and intelligent (and therefore predictable) one, then he would respond to the logic of power.

There continued to be discussion, however, on the extent to which Stalin was free to impress this vision on the Soviet policy-making machine. While the war in Europe continued, the idea that Stalin was not entirely his own master persisted. Balfour, in January 1945, had rejected the theory, finding Stalin to be of the Kremlin, not against it. However, his replacement, Roberts, asserted that the Politburo could influence, even change, Stalin's decisions. The idea was also being advanced in the American Embassy, within which Roberts had close contacts. Harriman, now Ambassador, felt that after Yalta the Politburo had disapproved of the concessions Stalin had made there, and that furthermore the Red Army marshals were now also a force with viewpoints of their own that Stalin had to consider.[5] Clark Kerr, who had a low opinion of Harriman at this point, disagreed, and was never a prominent proponent of the idea.[6] In Whitehall, however, this explanation of the uncooperative actions by the Soviets, which so quickly followed the end of the Conference, was quite plausible. For it to be acceptable depended in the first instance on a favourable view of Stalin, and this continued despite the doubts and suspicions about aspects of Soviet policy that developed after Yalta.

Sargent picked up on ideas that were floating around about the power of the marshals, and put them together into a minute for the Prime Minister, dated 2 May 1945. Sargent endorsed the cooperative view of Stalin, writing that Stalin tended to take a 'broad and statesmanlike line'. The difficulties with Soviet policy had then, however, to be explained. The prevailing image in the FO of the nature of the Soviet policy-making process allowed for this. It had become acceptable that in the Byzantine central power structure of the USSR, any individual or group that had a power-base could be influential. Sargent's minute depended on this assumption, for it was not built on much information about the marshals themselves, but upon assumptions about what their position would be if this model of the Soviet machine held good. Sargent thus argued that problems of cooperation in the areas now controlled by the Red Army might be explicable in terms of the attitudes of the marshals, newly powerful, antagonistic to the West and probably fearful of its power. Sargent ended by suggesting that Allied Commanders try to open contacts with their opposite numbers. Churchill agreed with Sargent's minute.[7]

At the same time, Roberts, trying to service the FO's desire for more information, attempted an assessment of the figures in the background. He found the Politburo to be 'full of tough, tricky and untrustworthy personalities'. He suggested that they gave Molotov his orders, from which he could not shift one inch and that they could modify or reverse decisions of Stalin himself, or at least his communications to foreign statesmen. This implied, of course, that the brusquer of Stalin's messages need not necessarily herald a change of heart on his part and was a caution against reading too much into the tone of such messages. Roberts observed the leaders at the opening of the Supreme Soviet. Only two, he wrote, were normal (Shvernik and Andreyev). The rest were tough, fat, prosperous individuals like the leaders of any other ruthless totalitarian society. Zhdanov might be a plumper and perhaps more human version of Hitler. Beria and Malenkov gave the impression of being at worst perverts and sadists and at best reincarnations of medieval inquisitors.[8] In addition to Harriman, the leading State Department experts

Charles Bohlen and George Kennan were voicing similar views; Kennan in September 1944 in a paper passed to the FO had identified a 'xenophobic group' along lines mirrored by Roberts' later report.[9]

Roberts adhered to this interpretation as the war in Europe ended. He noted that the Soviets were being educated to adulate those figures in Russian history who were power politicians, like Peter the Great, Catherine the Great and even Ivan the Terrible. It was a mistake, he felt (agreeing with his predecessor), to see the Soviet leaders as anything but orthodox Marxists, but he concluded that this did not necessarily make them uncooperative. It is notable of Roberts' contributions at this time that though he had been critical of Clark Kerr when in the FO, he now endorsed the Ambassador's fundamental conclusion that the Soviets, though inclined to unco-operative *behaviour*, were not in their *intentions* uncooperative.[10]

In the Northern Department, a new arrival, John Galsworthy, agreed that the Politburo was increasingly willing to let Stalin feel the reins now and again, as the war in Europe came to an end. However, in response to Bohlen's comment that the 'boys in the backroom' were becoming increasingly vocal, Galsworthy also suggested that the Molotov/Stalin dichotomy was deliberately set up to allow withdrawal from an untenable position without loss of face. Thomas Brimelow, fresh from the Moscow Embassy, went further and questioned the whole theory, commenting as Dew had in 1941 that Stalin was very much of the Politburo. He found no evidence that the influence of that body had risen or fallen, and pointed out that recent speculation on that score seemed to be without solid foundation – he might have added that it always had been, though there may actually have been some truth in the basic concept.[11]

Notwithstanding these doubts in some quarters that Stalin could be excused from the authorship of unfavourable turns in Soviet policy by reference to the 'two schools' theory, the image of Stalin as statesman proved remarkably resilient. Errors and inconsistencies in his conduct of the war and of diplomacy were rarely recognised. Instead, in July, in a paper that was not notable for its optimism, Sargent could still write of Stalin's 'statesmanlike qualities'. Churchill's description of Stalin in August as a 'wise man' was not mere hyperbole for public consumption, but reflected truly the enduring image of the sagacious Stalin that was the central aspect of the Churchill Coalition's own Stalin cult.[12]

Views of Internal Developments and Reconstruction Needs

The FO had encouraged the view in other departments of the Government, through the widely circulated Weekly Political Intelligence Summaries, that a certain degree of liberalisation had been taking place in the USSR in the war, though themselves cautious about how far this would go, and by no means as definite about this as some British newspapers. Both Wilson and Dew had stressed that these changes should not be taken to mean an abandonment of Communism or a rejection of Marx, and had placed the changes in the context of the policy of 'Socialism in one country'. There was concern that outside the FO, and among the public, there was a tendency to misread these changes. As we have seen, the Northern Department had been clear that alongside wholesale social reforms which departed from classic Marxist-Leninist practice, the Communist Party's position in the USSR had been greatly strengthened. Its hold had been regarded as tenuous before the war, but victory had rendered it internally secure. There was interest as to whether this would then lead to a relaxation of the tyranny, but the general conclusion was that this certainly would not come before the regime was confident it had achieved external security as well. It was in reaction to over-optimism produced by exaggerated press stories that it was increasingly pointed out within the FO that Communism had not been abandoned. The truth was that there was some uncertainty exactly what the relationship could be between Marxism and the intense nationalism that had been generated by the war and energetically fostered by the regime.

Roberts warned that whereas there had been a tendency in the FO to ignore the ideological as distinct from the purely nationalist elements in the Soviet state, they should be noted carefully and watched for. Roberts stressed that Soviet leaders were still mainly guided by considerations of national self-interest, but added that the combination of intense nationalism and Marxist orthodoxy, which represented a fundamental difference between Soviet political philosophy and totalitarian practices and the outside world, meant it would be difficult to have normal and easy relations with the USSR. However, there was still no clash of interests – this was, he wrote, a fundamental truth. In essence Roberts was repeating and endorsing Clark Kerr's line that it was the Soviet manner of acting, their methods, that caused the problems, not their fundamental aims.

Roberts placed greater emphasis than the Ambassador on 'orthodoxy', whatever that meant in a Stalinist context, but it had not brought him into any disagreement with that nostrum. Roberts' letters in late April 1945 in fact demonstrate very clearly the particular nature of British official attitudes at this time; while to later commentators aware of subsequent events there are signs of what would become Cold War attitudes, the use of the words 'Marxism' and 'ideology' should not obscure the fact that these attitudes had not yet been reached, whatever the growing sense of confusion and unease. A month later, Roberts reiterated the view that though there would be difficulties and hard words, the Soviet attitude to Britain was likely to remain at bottom defensive rather than aggressive, and thus remain based on the alliance.[13]

The belief that the USSR would have massive reconstruction and rehabilitation needs in the postwar era and that these would be a primary influence on the shape of its foreign policy continued to be a fundamental component of the British Government's view of the USSR up to the end of the Coalition. Most of the minutes and memoranda that attempted to forecast Soviet policy made reference to reconstruction needs, without the authors feeling the need to prove the validity of this assertion, so much of an accepted assumption had this become. Roberts did so in his despatch of 25 April, adding that the Soviets now had a further economic problem in the need to consolidate their new zone of influence and rebuild it.[14] Ward looked at the issue slightly differently, seeing it as increasing the possibility of isolationism, since the Soviets might be distracted internally. They might, he thought, have to withdraw their resources from parts of eastern Europe, except the direct line of communication to Germany, and demobilise their armed forces because of the manpower shortages at home.[15] Ward and Wilson stressed the Soviet need to recuperate and to raise the populace's standard of living in discussions with the PHPS of drafts of the overall survey of Britain's postwar strategic position, PHP(45)29(O).[16] The PHPS themselves continued to accept that a minimum of five years would be required by the Soviets for reconstruction.[17] In his paper 'Stocktaking after VE Day', Sargent reached a similar conclusion, asserting that the Soviet Union was weakened by war and certainly could not afford another war in Europe in the immediate future.[18]

Bruce Lockhart still hoped on 11 April 1945 that these Soviet economic needs would offer a lever to influence their policy.[19]

However, by July 1945 it seemed more likely that the Soviets would rather go short than make themselves dependent on outside economic aid. As Warner had argued earlier, they could if necessary suppress consumer demand without incurring serious domestic problems, given their continued control over their populace, and this gave them considerable scope to refuse unfavourable terms. Thus Pierson Dixon of the Southern Department wrote that though reconstruction needs would shape Soviet foreign policy, this did not give much scope for Britain to shape that policy; the Soviets would aim for self-sufficiency as they had always done, and would not forgo security or political aims in order to get economic assistance. The Northern Department agreed, stating:

We doubt whether the Soviets would allow any major aim of their policy to be deflected by our use of the financial lever. A much more potent influence on Soviet policy is likely to be the need for demobilisation rehabilitation and internal development in Russia as elsewhere.[20]

Roberts was more optimistic, building on his point that their occupation of eastern Europe was a considerable burden to them. He wrote that the Americans in particular could make effective use of the financial lever. He thought that though the Soviets could restore their own economy alone (with delays and hardship) they could not cope single-handed with their new and heavy responsibilities in Europe. They would however find them difficult to drop without immense loss of prestige. Here was a suggestion of what was to be an important component of the later containment theory, namely that the Soviets had actually become over-stretched in taking over eastern, south-eastern and part of central Europe, and that this would impose all sorts of pressures upon the Soviet economy, particularly if it entailed a high level of military mobilisation.[21]

As with the 'two schools' theory, once the war in Europe ended questions began to be asked about the factual basis of this enduring assumption. This time it was Cadogan who asked the pertinent question whether Britain had any evidence about actual Soviet reconstruction needs. He felt dubious now about the whole assumption, and Eden agreed with him, though neither of them had voiced such doubts earlier; indeed they had endorsed it both in internal FO discussion and by making it a central element of WP(44)436 in August 1944. Lockhart had written that Stalin was faced with reconstruction problems he could not solve without Anglo-American aid, on which Cadogan commented:

> I have often heard this said but I have never heard it argued in any detail. Can it be accepted as true, without any qualification? [Eden: 'I fear not.']

He went on to state that while the USSR had received enormous military aid from the Allies in the war, it was also a fact that its own production was proof of an astonishing rate of development which, if maintained, might lead it almost anywhere, a point the JIC had made in JIC(44)366(O). Cadogan failed to take into account the unevenness of this development, which meant the USSR had been able to achieve such miracles of munitions production in some areas by depending on the Allies for others (such as soft-skinned vehicles, medical supplies and to a certain extent, food).[22] Cadogan's comment reflected the fact that Britain's own economic weakness meant that she could not hope to have much of an economic lever at her disposal. The actual scope of Soviet reconstruction needs was backed by a fair amount of data and observation about the destruction of the Soviet economic infrastructure in the war. However, as the postwar period approached, the precise effect of this on Soviet foreign policy was becoming, if anything, more uncertain.

Views of Soviet Foreign Policy: Security and Limited Objectives

The events of early 1945 necessarily renewed the debate on the issue of limited objectives and focused attention particularly on whether there should as a consequence be a revision of views of the ways the Soviets defined 'security'. The JIC, under FO prompting, had established that these limited objectives were not threatening to Britain's own vital, non-negotiable interests.[23] The crucial area, where the 'acid tests' of most individuals were to be applied, was eastern Europe. It was here, it was felt, that Soviet motivations would be revealed, and in their cooperativeness clear evidence given of their commitment to postwar collaboration. It was Soviet actions here that generated most doubts and pessimism about that collaboration. However the cooperative thesis was held too strongly, and corresponded too much to British interests, to be thrown away lightly. The inclination was to keep a sense of proportion in terms of wider interests and to see Soviet actions in the light of existing interpretations.

Thus, it was pointed out in the FO on a number of occasions that Stalin would regard himself as having been granted the right to make his own dispositions in the region by the October 1944 percentages agreement, which after all had been Churchill's suggestion, not his own. Churchill was not alone in reading the continued (if grudging) passivity of the Greek Communists to be a sign that Stalin regarded that agreement as still in operation. Stalin, furthermore, had been assured that he had a right to friendly governments on his borders.[24]

It had already become clear to most Government observers that the Soviets were organising some kind of eastern bloc. The apparently amenable Soviet attitude to a western bloc, for instance, had been taken to derive from the idea that it would give justification for their own. Of itself this was not considered a problem in 1944; although earlier there had been concern to avoid this, and there was still anxiety about dividing Europe too rigidly into two camps. It all depended on how this bloc was constituted. It seemed likely to be held together by bilateral treaties and some bases arrangements; this does not appear to have generated much British concern in early 1945. Duggald Stewart of the Southern Department commented: 'they have shown that they fully understand the principle of spheres of influence and are willing to play by the rules.'[25] Stewart saw Poland to be of the greatest importance, and Yugoslavia also to be more important than Romania or Bulgaria, justifying the acceptance of these *de facto* spheres.

The key question was whether this undoubted sphere was going to be an 'open' one or one totally closed to outside contacts, especially economic. The developing friction with the Soviets after Yalta on examination can be seen to centre on this issue, as the British met with Soviet obstructionism when they tried to regain control of economic assets in Romania, and to send military missions into Bulgaria, Poland, Hungary and finally Austria. When Eden, Sargent and others complained of 'abominable' Soviet behaviour, it was this exclusion that was uppermost in their minds. An FO paper, 'Examples of Russian Bad Faith', of 20 July, commented,

The majority of our complaints in these countries [Romania and Bulgaria] arise not from violation of agreements, but from complete failure to accord us the co-operation to which we are entitled.[26]

Beginning with Romania, the Soviets were characterised as setting up puppets in the countries they occupied, and using ruthless methods to deal with those they regarded as unsound in their attitude towards their 'liberators'. The central issues were, however, whether these actions were consistent with their security aim, and whether they indicated the activation of the 'reinsurance' policy. Representatives on the spot, like Houstoun-Boswall in Sofia, were affected by their treatment by the Soviets and by their knowledge of what had been agreed at Yalta, and equally by their ignorance of the percentages agreement (though word of it reached Maclean in Yugoslavia).[27] It is clear that these diplomats' critical stance was not entirely mirrored in Whitehall, where there was a reluctance to spring to the idea immediately that wholesale Sovietisation was taking place. These actions in establishing their own governments, while regrettable, were not seen necessarily as an indication of wholesale Soviet expansionism. In considering this issue, the Northern and Southern Departments were prepared to draw a clear distinction between Soviet actions in their sphere of interest and those outside; however unpleasant they were, actions within the Soviet sphere were not to be regarded as tests of cooperativeness.[28] This was to prove to be increasingly difficult to sustain, as the Soviets showed less and less concern even to keep up appearances.

While there were mentions of Soviet (and historical Russian) expansionism, these actions could be fitted into a security interpretation, which still seemed entirely plausible. On the issue of Soviet motivations, fear of Germany still featured as the main ascribed motive. Galsworthy saw the Soviet aim as the establishment of permanent security by a belt of closely knit satellites. Stewart agreed in July 1945 that security in this area was still the dominant motive, with the propagation of Communism a long way second. Part of the problem in Anglo-Soviet relations that this issue raised was that the Yalta Declaration on Liberated Europe effectively established a new yardstick for Soviet cooperativeness, particularly for those who looked to Soviet behaviour for confirmation of their overall commitment to cooperation. Stewart for his part believed it was not at all clear the Soviets were rushing to remodel the former Axis satellites:

They have had to balance the disadvantages of installing Governments which could be trusted to be completely pro-Russian, but were not representative, and of permitting the establishment of Governments which were sufficiently representative to keep order without any expenditure of Russian effort, but were not so 'trustworthy' as a completely Communist-controlled Government.

A scare about the degree of German secret service penetration, he believed, impelled them to install a puppet government in Romania, but in Hungary they installed a comparatively bourgeois government with no sign they were encouraging Communist attempts to gain predominance:

we were before Yalta perfectly prepared to allow the Russians the predominance in the ex-satellite Balkan countries to which we agreed in Moscow last October, but it has unfortunately been quite impossible to persuade them to realise that the Yalta Declaration on Liberated Territories altered this and not only entitled us, but even obliged us, to interest ourselves in what the Russians were doing.[29]

Sargent put the matter a little differently, believing the Soviets feared a coalition of liberal democracies and the revival of Germany, and were responding by seeking security by *lebensraum*. They were, however driven by fear of Germany, not a desire for further territorial expansion beyond satisfaction of their long-standing frontier demands.[30] Sargent had already argued on 13 March that democracy had never flourished in central and south-eastern Europe, except in Czechoslovakia. It was no surprise that the peoples of these states might be more interested in gaining security and stable governments than political liberties. The Soviets took the line that what they were doing was part of their general war policy; a *cordon sanitaire* against Germany which would require governments to be modelled along totalitarian lines. They would consider this an essential part of their security system.[31]

The Moscow Embassy agreed with Sargent's stress on the significance of the German question in interpreting these Soviet actions; to Roberts, the fear of Germany still meant that for the Soviets British treatment of that country was their touchstone. The Soviets were genuinely very worried about Germany, so would value the

Anglo-Soviet alliance and the World Organisation. Roberts stressed the fundamentally defensive orientation of these Soviet actions. He attributed recent signs of Soviet doubts about a western bloc to their fears that Germany would be included in it.[32] Clark Kerr and the Southern Department agreed in June that security was still the main Soviet motive.[33] Sargent himself conceded that the Soviets appeared genuinely to believe Britain had no right to interfere with their paramount interest in Romania, Bulgaria and probably Hungary.[34]

Some of Eden's comments revealed a more pessimistic attitude. In March he asserted that Anglo-Soviet relations were now completely lacking in all confidence.[35] In the US, he was influential, as Wilson Miscamble has shown, on President Truman's famous demonstration of pique to Molotov.[36] He was in fact either absent in the US, ill or preoccupied with House of Commons business (as Leader of the House) through most of April, May and June, so that expressions of his opinion on Soviet questions are infrequent. The views he did express, particularly in comments to Churchill prior to the Potsdam Conference, were very much on the lines of the more pessimistic of his comments during 1944. Eden certainly appears among the more disillusioned of the British policy-makers. On the eve of the Potsdam Conference, he wrote:

> on any and every point, Russia tries to seize all that she can and she uses these meetings to grab as much as she can get.... I am deeply concerned at the pattern of Russian policy, which becomes clearer as they become more brazen every day.[37]

Conclusions from Soviet Behaviour and the Decline of the Hypersensitivity Model

The aspect of the 1944 thesis that showed most change was the doctrine of Soviet hypersensitivity. Whereas in 1944 this had been significant, as shown in the debate between the FO and the COS on the treatment of the German question, now even its keenest advocates had grown sceptical or impatient. In his contacts with British diplomats, Maisky (now a Vice-Commissar for Foreign Affairs) continued to excuse Soviet misconduct by referring to their inferiority complex and lack of manners. He asked for patience, but this was becoming in increasing short supply. Even Clark Kerr contested Maisky's apologia, claiming that the British had been at pains to be circumspect, frank and honest, and 'all we had got in return was a series of affronts'.[38]

Kollontai – described by Clark Kerr as 'an old and warm friend of mine' – was franker than Maisky, but pressed the same idea. She claimed the Soviets were at the same stage of development as the English in Cromwell's time. They were also bad psychologists, who went blundering into situations without thinking. They were conscious of their success and wanted the world to pat them on the back and feel their strength. They were children and should be treated as such – in time their weakness would pass. They knew they must cooperate with Britain, she said; the latter should 'practise patience, patience, and more patience'. Kollontai's image of clumsy Soviet diplomacy, Maisky's comments about the bad psychology of members of his Government and Litvinov's similar criticisms make an interesting contrast to the tendency within the British Government to exaggerated respect for the skill and sagacious realism of the Soviets, and their single-minded and well-planned pursuit of goals. Clark Kerr's view of these comments was: 'The truth is that the Russians are in a hurry to be great and that is uncomfortable.' The FO instructed him to reply stiffly to Maisky that he of all people should know ample allowances had been made for the 'peculiarities of the Russian mentality'. There was frustration that contacts with Stalin and Molotov and Soviet victories had not removed the suspiciousness.[39]

Maisky's fundamental point, which was that Soviet behaviour and demeanour were not an indication of the overall direction of their policy, remained an issue of debate.[40] Clark Kerr still argued that Soviet methods were not sure guides to their policy intentions, but he felt that their behaviour was now shaped less by a morbid sense of inferiority than by an exaggerated sense of confidence and power brought on by the magnitude of their victories, and also in some part by the adulation of the western press and political leaders. This was just an adolescent phase, however, which would be followed by settled collaboration.[41] Clark Kerr found the idea borne out in Soviet behaviour in subsequent months. The Soviets, he wrote on 10 July, were 'rejoicing in the impulsions of early manhood'. They were giddy with success and a sense of 'boundless strength', feeling there was little or nothing to stop them making their greatness felt and not disposed to take much account of others' views along the way.[42]

Clark Kerr did feel, however, that this did not betoken a fundamental rejection on Stalin's part of the policy of cooperation. This still corresponded to Soviet interests, and Britain should be careful not to react to the clumsy way they did things. He found no sign in the actual policy content to suggest they had become hostile; like Wilson in 1944 he was prepared to overlook Soviet 'bloodiness', to accept that the Soviets viewed Poland as matter of vital security, and to try to look at the totality of policy. Thus he argued that the Soviets were still cooperative, but there would certainly be difficulties in cooperating with them. He conceded that Anglo-Soviet relations would never be intimate or always easy. However, there were solid reasons, most particularly mutual fears of Germany, why the Anglo-Soviet alliance would endure; sentiment and common cultural ties aside, mutual interests would provide the firm foundation for postwar cooperation:

> While memories of German aggression and fears of its revival linger in Russian minds, as they must for some years to come, these fears, together with the need for help in shouldering the heavy burden of reconstruction, should provide a solid basis for Anglo-Soviet co-operation in the major tasks of European reconstruction.[43]

Others were less disposed to overlook bad Soviet behaviour. They believed that if the Soviets wanted cooperation they should act in a fashion that took account of their allies' susceptibilities, particularly now that the military burden was being equally shared. There was definitely less preparedness all round to put up with what Roberts described as the Soviet 'dog-in-the-manger attitude'. Some emphasised that the over-confident Soviets were not perhaps weighing forces as carefully as in the past. Others introduced a new explanation of Soviet truculence: the Soviets had assessed the realities of power and had realised that their position would never be stronger, and so were securing as many bargaining counters as they could. This was opportunistic, reflective of defects in their cooperative spirit and a confirmation of their continuing suspiciousness, but fell short of being irreversibly uncooperative.[44]

Frank, Firm, but not Unfriendly: the Continuing Debate on How to Handle the Soviets

The movement in perceptions of Soviet policy, while more confused and less definite than is sometimes asserted for this time, was sufficient to shift the balance somewhat in the running debate on what the best British policy would be. The Allied advances in the west and then victory in Europe also provided a strong impetus to review the policy alternatives: the time appeared ripe for the kind of policies that had long been advocated but had never come into operation; for the military 'strict reciprocity', for the diplomatists 'firm and frank exchange of views' and for some in addition, including Eden and Churchill, what they called showdowns. None of these involved a rejection of the thesis of a cooperative USSR. There was a sense from April 1945 that the situation offered an opportunity, but one which had to be exploited immediately, for it could not be assumed that it would last. The main elements of this position were the military strength of the British and Americans, their physical occupation of a large part of the occupation zone in Germany assigned to the USSR, and the Soviets' own exhaustion. The key factor making these diminishing assets was the declared US policy of early withdrawal, not only from the Soviet zone, but from Europe as a whole. This sense of opportunity brought forth a widespread advocacy of active and more confrontational tactics. This was intended to build a better basis for cooperation, and was not envisaged to be a new non-cooperative policy, though that is how it appears on a superficial reading of the evidence and a failure to identify the elements of continuity both in the underlying images of the USSR behind policy formulations, and in the policy debate. The catchphrases of 'firmness' and 'frankness' did not represent a dramatic break with the established parameters of discussion.

That this was so was demonstrated in the contributions from the Moscow Embassy. Clark Kerr and Roberts emerged as articulate advocates of a modification in British policy, which fell, however, well short of a reversal of that previously practised. Moving on in his despatch of 27 March from his remarks about Soviet over-confidence and immaturity, the Ambassador put forward almost a definitive statement of the 'frankness' line. Britain, he argued, should stop the popular adulation that only fed the dangerous Soviet sense of strength:

> we need not, I think, be over nice in our approach to her. When we are shocked we may say so in all frankness. . . . they will judge their partners and conduct their policy towards them by their own realistic standards.

Britain should stand up for her vital interests, at the same time recognising that it was fruitless to argue over Romania and Bulgaria. The Soviets, he argued, respected the British and valued their cooperation if they stood up for what the Soviets recognised were British vital interests; Turkey, Greece, Iran, for instance. Even then there might be some 'squalls', but this should be taken in proportion and overall the alliance would 'serve us well and pay a steady, though not spectacular, dividend'.[45]

A month later, Roberts expanded upon the theme. It was possible, he argued, to forge a useful working relationship with the Soviets, if Britain was 'tough and realistic', the qualities he ascribed to the Soviets. These realists must be shown that Britain was determined and strong enough to defend her own interests and that there was a limit beyond which the Soviets could not safely go. He followed up Clark Kerr's comment on Romania and Bulgaria by advocating a recognition that Soviet action had divided Europe. Britain should concentrate on organising the Allies' half. This was not, however, an argument for building up the West in a Cold War-style confrontation. Roberts argued on the contrary that this recognition of the facts was, far from being a policy of despair, the best way to avoid either a sudden or a gradual deterioration in Anglo-Soviet relations. It involved a middle course; and as such was in essence the 'frankness' approach. On the one hand, the exaggerated adulation of the Red Army and the Soviet system should be cut back. On the other hand, policy-makers should not follow the advice of those 'who see a Prussian in every Russian'. This was, he made quite clear, a tactical change, while keeping in place the long-term strategy based upon the Anglo-Soviet alliance and the avoidance of conflict, which would be achieved by ensuring the Soviets did not make misjudgements on the basis of underestimating Britain's strength and willingness to protect its interests and friends. Then the Anglo-Soviet alliance, Roberts believed, 'should continue to serve us well'.[46]

In the FO there was a matching sense that the precepts of the frankness approach could now at last be applied with a freedom that was not possible before. This was not a new idea, of course, and previously it had effectively been rendered toothless by the fear that the Soviets would misperceive it as a complete rejection of cooperation by the British. The notable feature of the post-Yalta period was that this aspect of the Soviet sensitivity thesis simply ceased to operate. The Soviet arrogance that appeared so much in evidence largely negated it. As a consequence, there was a tendency to speak in terms of showdowns with the Soviets as an immediate way of altering the relationship from what was expedient in wartime to what was more appropriate in peace, and at the same time attempt to modify Soviet behaviour in eastern Europe. This attitude was primarily advocated within the FO by Sargent. Both Eden and Churchill were to voice their approval of it. In parallel with his views on Soviet policy, Sargent's views on handling the Soviets underwent some development in this period. Two weeks before Clark Kerr's despatch, on 13 March, he too argued that Britain should limit its complaints about Soviet behaviour. He wrote that it was out of all proportion that Britain should endanger its fundamental policy of postwar cooperation with the Soviet Union for the sake of an issue which, even if it was not entirely academic or quixotic, was not vital to British interests in Europe. He based himself on the Soviet security thesis. By criticising the regimes set up in Romania and Bulgaria, Britain was attacking what the Soviet Government considered an essential part of its security system. Poland was a separate and special case, but, he argued, it was important not to weaken the case by treating on the same lines other countries where Britain was not so committed. Effectively, Sargent was arguing for a concentration on British vital interests, and a realistic approach to the situation in eastern Europe, which was not a vital area to Britain, and where Britain could in any event not influence what happened, and would be sacrificing its larger aim in pursuit of a chimera.[47] He expressed some sympathy for the Soviet pursuit of security.[48] However, he did not stick to this fatalistic realist line. On 31 March, Lockhart suggested a heart to heart with the Soviets, involving his ideal of 'plain but not unfriendly speaking on both sides'. Britain's approach, he felt, was all wrong. It had misled the Soviets so that it was possible that even Stalin believed they were very strong and Britain was weak, which was not in fact the case. To keep them sweet the Soviets had been allowed to believe this, but the effects of Allied air power would be plain to see in Germany, and Stalin would certainly not wish to push the USSR into another war.[49]

Sargent agreed that the Soviets underestimated Allied strength; hence their suspicions about the nature of the victories in the west. Lockhart warned that unless the USSR curbed what he saw as its 'present policy of sovietization and studied contempt of U.S. and Britain', or unless something was done to put a stop to Soviet unilateral action, Anglo-American hostility to the USSR would increase to a dangerous extent and we should lose the peace'. Lockhart recommended 'a much more vigorous policy towards Russia – not an unfriendly policy but a frank and firm clearing of views'. There should not therefore be a squabbling over incidents, but a heart-to-heart talk with the Soviets on their intentions, it being made clear to them that if they carried on the way they were going the Allies would go their own way and there would be no Anglo-American help for them. When Sargent reiterated that the Soviets were entitled to security, Lockhart argued that Soviet victory policy might exceed the limits of security if they were not faced with Allied firmness.[50]

Sargent was non-committal at the time, but this dialogue with Lockhart seems to have stiffened up his attitude, for his subsequent contributions were very similar to the ideas Lockhart advanced. He attributed the Soviet attitude since Yalta – their truculence and their determination to give nothing away – to the improvement in the Allied strength and position. He now, in contrast to his 13 March paper, suggested a showdown. Stalin would simply suspect cunning if Britain continued to propitiate from a position of strength (which assumed Stalin perceived that strength). Soviet reactions to a showdown were difficult to gauge, but the situation could not be worse than the present state of drift as Sargent saw it. The aim was a frank, realistic and plain-speaking approach, not to bring a break, but to develop Anglo-American-Soviet cooperation along the right lines.[51] However, when O'Malley argued that it was now time to 'take the gloves off', Sargent felt such an approach was 'truly desperate' and 'unnecessary if we play our cards reasonably well', adding that the US would not in any case agree to such a policy at this time; a consideration that rendered the attempt at any kind of showdown, or even much of a frankness approach, still impossible to achieve.[52]

The response to Stalin's opportunism that Sargent recommended on the eve of the coming to power of the Attlee administration bore some surface similarities to the classic Cold War stance. He now argued that Britain should take a stand to prevent the situation crystallising to her permanent detriment. Britain should maintain her interests in Finland, Poland, Czechoslovakia, Austria, Yugoslavia and Bulgaria, though she might have to acquiesce in Soviet domination of Romania and Hungary. If a trial of strength was to take place it should be now, instead of waiting for it to take place further west after Stalin had pocketed for good those six states that he now controlled by political pressure and military force. Britain must be anti-totalitarian and at times live beyond her means. She should take the offensive and challenge Communist penetration in as many eastern European countries as possible, and counteract every attempt by the Soviet Government to communise or control Germany, Italy, Greece or Turkey. He saw the idea of concentrating on western Europe, put forward by Roberts and Jebb, as a 'policy of despair'. However, Sargent was not positing any kind of grand design on Stalin's part. Such a strategy was designed to get better cooperation in the long term, just as the frankness approach had always been intended to do. It was not impossible to achieve the double task of holding the Soviets in check and amicably cooperating with the United States and Soviet Union in the resettlement of Europe. Collaboration with the Soviet Union, and even the United States, he concluded, was not going to be easy; neither, however, was it impossible.[53]

The approach that won most favour in the FO was clearly based on the continuing assumption that Soviet aims had their limits and that the quest for security was at the heart of the measures they were taking to secure friendly governments in the states the Red Army occupied. It fell short of a direct confrontation, and was close to the established 'frankness' approach. Most agreed that, as Wilson put it, 'we need never be frightened of standing up to the Russians where our vital interests are concerned.'[54] It was felt that while some Soviet behaviour could only be worsened by protest, Britain should stand up for its interests, and should not overestimate Soviet strength.[55]

Churchill was right in line with the general inclination towards the 'frankness' approach. On 5 April he wired to Roosevelt that the tone of the Soviet messages suggested they were vexed or jealous, and the Anglo-American response should be a firm and blunt stand. The aim would be to clear the air and bring the Soviets to realise that there was a point 'beyond which we will not tolerate insult'. This was the 'best chance of saving the future'; again a frank approach was to bring relations back onto a good footing, not to force a break. The Soviets had to be forcibly made aware of the consequences of their treating Allied interests and views with such scant regard.[56] Sharing the sense that Allied strength offered opportunities, but that it would not last, Churchill continued to press such an approach on Roosevelt and then Truman, with little effect.[57]

By 1945, Churchill believed cooperation with Stalin was possible but that the Allies must respond firmly or the Soviets would be tempted to take advantage of the opportunities offered to them by their military advances. Military necessities had changed: if the Soviets wanted cooperation, then they would have to pay a price, and behave. If they wanted to be treated like a civilised power, they had to act like one and rein in their tendency to act like a bully. The 'Russians', as he preferred to call them, were patriots when fighting the common foe, but their methods towards neighbouring states showed their usual Communist techniques, to which Churchill was opposed as he was to Communists in Britain.[58]

Churchill felt the American attempt to pretend the special relationship did not exist and to deal with the Soviets without prior agreement on tactics with the British weakened the Allied position and encouraged Stalin to be truculent. This was a point he particularly pressed on the new President, Truman, over the Polish question and the issue of the withdrawal of Allied armies to demarcated zones, with limited success.[59] He was frustrated by what he saw as a US failure to understand the dynamics of the situation almost as much as he was by Stalin, who was behaving as would be expected when faced with such tactics as Roosevelt's in his last months, which appeared to signal Allied disinterest in Soviet actions. Indeed there was admiration for the adroit way Stalin played Roosevelt alongside annoyance that the opportunity to exert influence on Soviet policy was being lost. A Stalin faced by a united Allied front would, Churchill believed, have been far different than when confronted by this apparent disunity and an unwillingness to state bluntly what the Allies wanted and what the Soviets could not do without harming relations. Thus he, like many FO officials, though quite independently, had come to want a 'frankness' approach; also based on the hopes it would improve cooperation, not as an alternative to it.[60] Churchill's pessimism, which Gilbert describes as 'despair', following Colville's description, was real and well documented, but we should be careful lest we allow awareness of this to obscure the nature and basis of Churchill's attitude on how to handle the Soviets in the last months of his administration.[61] He did not reject the idea of postwar cooperation, and clearly regarded a bargaining policy as likely to bear fruit. Soviet power impressed him, indeed sometimes he exaggerated it for effect, but he still saw there to be means available of effective behaviour modification.

The consequence of not having followed a 'frankness' approach earlier – of which he was at least as guilty as the Americans – and thus giving Stalin the wrong signals, was that Churchill believed a tougher policy was now required. The show of diplomatic strength had not been made and it was for the Allies now to resort to the realities of power. The Allied armies should press on to take politically important targets such as Prague, Berlin and Lübeck. The aim of this was twofold: first, to set limits on the Soviet sphere of influence, second, to acquire bargaining counters to secure better Soviet behaviour on Poland, Austria and other issues. Withdrawal to prearranged zones and the release of resources would be linked to satisfactory performance on the Soviet side and settlement of outstanding problems. The Soviets would appreciate the exercise of power and would respond. Reality of power was to Churchill by no means a bad basis for relations – indeed, in view of well-known Communist tendencies it was the only practical one and, in a world of conflict, hardly an inappropriate one. If Soviet preponderance of power made them so assertive in the absence of this policy, then Churchill saw another chance to try it and bring the Soviets to cooperate at Potsdam in the shape of the atomic bomb.[62] Stalin, with his assumed realistic appraisal of the balance of forces, would then see it as in his interest to collaborate better. He must be brought to realise that there was a price to pay for his reinsurance policy and that the easy option was easy no longer. Yalta had made this reinsurance policy potentially more attractive than the 'primary' one of cooperation because it appeared from the American attitude that he would get the benefits of the cooperative policy anyway. The task subsequently as Churchill saw it was to disabuse Stalin of this misunderstanding if cooperation was to be revived; a difficult, but not an impossible task.

Another bargaining counter was control of egress from the Baltic and Black Seas; however, when it came to the Big Three meeting at which Churchill had previously wanted such linkage to be made, he conceded on this question without securing a *quid pro quo*.[63] Churchill's actual handling of the Soviets continued, in fact, to be at variance with his words uttered both within the Government and to the US. More than for Eden, Churchill's ambivalence remained. He was not yet the fully-fledged Cold Warrior, and the breach with the USSR was not as total or irreversible as has been implied.[64] This is clear if the true meaning of 'frankness' and even the tougher approach that followed is understood. It was the question of the most appropriate strategy to bring cooperation that was still most hotly debated, rather than the question of whether cooperation was possible at all. The frankness approach was based on the belief that the right method could bring cooperation about. To be sure, Churchill was quite prepared in the last months of the war to talk sharply to the Soviets where previously he had restrained himself. He made it quite clear that he disapproved of Soviet actions in the territories they had liberated – doing so most forcefully in an epic *tour d'horizon* with Ambassador Gusev on 18 May.[65] He always maintained that he would have had a showdown over the western border of Poland had he returned to Potsdam. In fact his attitude in the first sessions at Potsdam had hardly been uncompromising. His willingness to look objectively at Soviet claims persisted, to alarm Eden that he was being too felicitous. He accepted the Soviets had a legitimate claim for a warm water port and access to the oceans; the USSR was 'like a giant with her nostrils pinched'.[66] If Stalin's image had become a little tarnished, gratitude at his attitude over Greece in accordance with the Moscow percentages agreement remained. As with the FO, Churchill's main gripe seems to have been that the percentages were not being observed, because the Soviets were obstructing British activity in the liberated countries, rather than concern about the Declaration on Liberated Europe. The effect of Stalin's Greek policy should not be underestimated; Churchill kept referring to it as a point on the credit side of the ledger – this was clearly a major acid test for him and satisfactory Soviet performance there was a powerful balancing factor to offset against actions elsewhere.[67]

Perceptions of the USSR at the End of the Churchill Coalition

It has been argued that by the time of the Potsdam Conference, British attitudes had developed to a point where there were two extremes, with the FO still seeking cooperation by concessions, and the military, on the other hand, already wishing to plan for the inevitable conflict, with people like Churchill in the middle moving uncertainly and uneasily.[68] In this interpretation, by July 1945 the balance was shifting in favour of military views as the outlines of the Cold War were beginning to form. This is something of a misrepresentation of both 'extremes', which actually were not so far apart as this simple dichotomy suggests, for it ignores the frankness school into which many fell and involves a misinterpretation of the meaning of the often-used word 'toughness'. It is the result of focusing on the discussion of British policy and passing over the actual perceptions of the USSR that gave particular meaning to words like 'toughness' and 'firmness'. Moreover, the PHPS argued that the USSR had the capability and was in a geographical position to be a major threat to the Empire at many points. They did not say that this threat was imminent. They argued that it was the worst case that had to be guarded against. This cannot be said in itself to be a movement to the Cold War attitude that held that the Soviets definitely had the intentions, and indeed a timetable of action, as well as the capacity. The PHPS papers continued to suggest that in the reconstruction period Soviet interests would point them in the direction of cooperation, so long as certain security desiderata were met. This is some way from a doctrine of an irrevocably hostile USSR, of the kind Maclean had advanced in 1940.[69]

There was certainly some movement in policy recommendations, particularly from the beginning of April 1945; a product as much of a sense of Allied strength and optimism as of despair about the Soviets. This brought a belief that now was a good time for the long-touted change in strategy, not to non-cooperation but to firmness; toughness in negotiation, but not toughness in the sense of confrontation.[70] It is only after study of the preceding years, and knowledge of the nature of the Government debate on the USSR that this becomes evident. British policy was still, up to the end of the Churchill Coalition, geared towards finding a way of getting on with the Soviets, within the context of some kind of meaningful cooperation and educating them to be civilised members of the community of nations. In spring and summer 1945 this was still seen as a realisable goal if diplomacy was skilful and backed by the newfound strength, and there was a fairly realistic idea of what cooperation would mean. It would not be the joint military staffs or cultural exchanges favoured by Wilson, nor the close economic collaboration advocated by Skaife. It would be a relationship with its inbuilt tensions, involving a *de facto* division of Europe, but bound by solid interest. One of the problems was the inability to devise a policy on Germany that would perpetuate that bond; Germany had to be strong enough to be a latent threat, but the act of keeping it so would raise suspicions that would render cooperation impossible. Another problem was the perennial one now assuming greater prominence; even if the Soviets were cooperative in intention, it was becoming abundantly clear that their methods – what Lockhart called their 'unilateral malfeasances' – left much to be desired.[71] The problem was that behaviour was often the only guide to overall objectives; this was the source of most uncertainty and doubt in the summer of 1945.

In the period from Yalta to the end of Churchill's premiership, developments took place in some of the perceptions that have been identified as central. The sensitivity idea was transformed into an increasing awareness of Soviet over-confidence and arrogance. The three central ideas, realism as a driving force, the goodwill of Stalin and the significance of postwar reconstruction needs, remained remarkably unaltered in spite of the rocky path of relations. These were strongly held perceptions, not claims made out of the expediency of the moment in 1944. There was still a sense of a number of constraints on Soviet freedom of action, not least of which was seen to be a consciousness, at least on Stalin's part, of the military strength of the Allies. This might explain some of his present actions, as attempts to pick up bargaining counters while he was strong (before he had to begin reconstruction), but also suggested to all those who believed Stalin to be a realist, that he would not want to risk a breakdown in relations, since he could not afford a situation of armed tension, let alone war. The principal Soviet motivation was still identified as the search for security, though the definition of security seemed to be getting drawn very wide, and to involve crude methods of control in the limitrophe states. Britain's response continued to be based on the assumption that it was possible to find a method to modify Soviet behaviour, and that this could be achieved within the context of continued cooperation. There was certainly a lower level of certainty about some areas of the thesis and estimates of what cooperation would mean were necessarily changing, but it was not yet regarded in the policy-making elite, across the spectrum from the military to Wilson and Clark Kerr, as impossible or undesirable.[72]

That British attitudes were by no means yet in Cold War mode is apparent when we approach the 1945 period from the earlier time and can see the limited nature of developments and changes that had taken place and in particular understand what specific meaning attached to words like 'frankness' and 'firmness'. These changes were more often than not responses to the new situation within the context and framework of the 1944 assumptions. They are understood best in terms of their relation to the past rather than with our knowledge of the events and attitudes that were to come.

7
Conclusion

The commitment to long-term cooperation with the Soviet Union that developed in the Churchill Coalition was founded upon a certain set of images of the USSR. Understanding the core assumptions that were made is necessary for comprehending the particular course of British policy. The thesis of a cooperative Soviet Union conceded that the USSR was a difficult power at times to deal with, but its leader had decided on a policy of collaboration. Failure to identify both this preparedness to envisage difficulties within the overall assumption of collaboration and the significance of the image of Stalin has led to the strength of this thesis being underestimated and the effects of an image of the USSR on the shape of British policy during the Second World War being largely overlooked. The fact that they later changed completely must not be allowed to obscure the evidence that these attitudes were genuinely held. Nor must the rational basis for them be underestimated. It is clear, from careful examination of the documentary record from the period of the wartime Churchill Coalition, that there was a sincere belief that it was possible to build long-term cooperation with Stalin's Soviet Union; indeed, that this was an unprecedented opportunity to bring the USSR in from the cold, into the community of nations. This was founded on a certain set of images of the USSR. The thesis was built upon a group of interrelated perceptions of Soviet internal developments, of the personality and motivations of Stalin, Soviet approach to their position in the world, and Soviet susceptibilities and sensitivities.

There were three basic assumptions that sustained the belief in future Soviet collaboration. These were neither insincere windowdressing nor 'planted', which is not to say that they were not open to reinterpretation in the light of events and fresh intelligence, and all were developed in debate, with a demonstrable range of views and emphases. The first assumption was that Soviet aims were limited, largely defensive and not likely to impinge upon areas of vital British interest. Far from desiring to propagate world revolution, Stalin simply wanted protection, particularly against a resurgent Germany, in order to continue the internal development of industrialisation and State Socialism interrupted by the war and preparation for war. He assessed these factors with stern realism. The second assumption was that the destruction of the already weak economic infrastructure of the country was colossal, and that the cost of reconstruction would be immense; and even if Stalin sought to do this without foreign help, he would seek the cheapest possible foreign policy to enable him to concentrate on this task. Collective security with Britain and possibly the USA if it did not return to isolationism, would provide this cheap option. It was taken as axiomatic that this would exercise a strong leverage on Soviet foreign policy and that the Soviets would be anxious to avoid external conflict or the need to maintain large armed forces. In effect there would now be a limit to the dangerous freedom of action perceived in 1940. Third, Stalin was a wise statesman, a sagacious realist, who was trustworthy where it could be seen that his interests were clearly engaged in his entering into undertakings, who had become persuaded of the wisdom of a cooperation policy with the West.

Linked with these assumptions were conclusions drawn from the changes in the USSR during the war, especially the revival of nationalism and religion, and from the sensitivity of Soviet leaders and officials to being treated in a way commensurate with their status as the government of a Great Power and the leading protagonist in the war against Germany. The changes towards a class-based, socially conservative society were seen to have inevitable consequences regarding Soviet conduct on the international scene. Obviously it made a difference if it was true that the country was now run by managers not revolutionaries. Stalin was assumed to be behind most of these changes; and since he was also viewed as prime mover behind the Soviet cooperation policy with Britain, then the linkage seemed clear.

These were not unreasonable assumptions, and the irrationality of Stalin's postwar policies was by no means foreshadowed in wartime internal developments.[1] Some of these perceptions were also in evidence in the US Government. There is no indication that the

Americans were the source of such ideas for the British, though there was some sharing of viewpoints, principally between the Moscow Embassies. The fact that American observers arrived at similar views about Soviet reconstruction needs, security motives and the character of Stalin is noteworthy, in so much as it supports the conclusion that these theories were based on observation of real developments, not conjured out of the imagination.[2] They sometimes put a different emphasis on such ideas, for instance on the Soviet inclination to 'unilateralism' and the implications of reconstruction needs, and they often did not agree on policy responses. They too wished to avoid 'ganging up' and were conscious of Soviet sensitivities – and like the British found a firm approach preferable, but in practice elusive.[3]

In both the US and British governments there continued to be debate as to whether it was better to treat the Soviets robustly because they suspected gestures of goodwill, or conversely to bring them to act like civilised allies by treating them as respected equals.[4] An assumption based ultimately on self-evident Soviet suspicions and shared alike by those advocating concessions or tough bargaining, was that Soviet policy was susceptible of modification by outside influence. None of the interpretations suggested that Soviet cooperation could be achieved without a correctly formulated British policy: this was believed as strongly by the COS as it was in the FO. Agreement on this basic precept did not lead to consensus on method. Different emphases on different elements of the wartime image of the USSR brought a range of opinions on how to secure Soviet cooperation. The problem was that the security, realism and sensitivity assumptions did not produce a clear and unambiguous conclusion on what was actually the best method of doing this. 'Firmness' and 'frankness' were easier to advocate in theory than to put into practice. If cooperation was assumed, therefore, questions remained on the proper strategy to secure and encourage it.

How British policy-makers translated such perceptions into British policy depended on their outlook on world affairs, and Britain's role. Undoubtedly they assumed that Britain should, and could, remain a World Power.[5] Their estimates of British 'vital interests' were framed on the assumption that the Empire and Britain's other worldwide commitments would continue. British policy to the USSR has been seen as 'pragmatic', and indeed Eden and others liked to see it that way.[6] However, assessments of interests and practicality are shaped by appraisal of other powers' intentions and capabilities. British policy cannot simply be seen as 'pragmatic' without reference to the perceptions that informed that pragmatism.

Lord Bullock has pointed out that Grand Alliances rarely last beyond the defeat of the mutual enemy.[7] It is usually a feat of skill, with some fortune, that they remain together that long. The Grand Alliance of the Second World War, like other such alliances before it, was certainly the result of a coincidence of interests.[8] However, these interests were not believed by the protagonists to be completely served by the defeat of Germany. All were conscious that Germany had been defeated 20 years before, yet the problem had reappeared. So long as attitudes were still dominated by the scale of effort required to defeat Hitler it seemed imperative that this situation not be allowed to happen again. To the members of the alliance, this coincidence of interest did not appear so short-term as it has to subsequent writers, with the benefit of hindsight. As this study has shown, it was the belief that there was a shared fundamental interest in common action to prevent German resurgence that was at the heart of the assumption that the alliance could last beyond the war that had created it.[9] For British policymakers, while they viewed the USSR with continued uncertainty and the suspicions that scholars continue to focus upon, there also seemed, from observation and interpretation, a logical basis for believing that cooperation was a real possibility.[10]

Moreover, in the present course of Soviet foreign policy and the imperatives that seemed to be operating in the Kremlin, it appeared that there was now an unprecedented chance to address the problem of the Soviet Union as a rogue player in world politics: to bring to an end that dangerous situation where the USSR had been isolated and had pursued policy objectives by subversive and irregular methods. This sense of opportunity to modify Soviet behaviour has often been overlooked, yet it is clearly evident in the British documentary sources for the period, as we have seen.[11] It is worth reiterating that this did not mean that it was believed that the USSR would become 'civilised' overnight, even by the most enthusiastic for cooperation: as Clark Kerr had warned, one could expect 'recurring tension'.[12] There were, after all, plenty of tensions in relationships with other allies, such as the French, and even the Americans. This would all, however, be within acceptable limits, and interests would continue to bind the Anglo-Soviet alliance. It was after the war ended that these acceptable limits and the attitudes that went with them changed.

A final point can be made. While this study is not concerned with judging whether British mistakes or ill-will in this period caused the Cold War, it is clear that for all the concern to secure postwar collaboration some of the seeds of later conflict were planted in the war. This was not because the British were totally wrong about the USSR – many of their assumptions were astute (though some, such as Stalin's military wisdom, were wide of the mark). However, both British and Soviet policy-makers had many acid tests of each others' attitudes, most of which remained in operation at the end of the war. In a position of some uncertainty – indeed as Churchill had predicted, 'deepening confusion' – both were unprepared to forgo entirely their reinsurance policies, but could not unambiguously convince the other that these were not primary policies, for 'frank' communication never really took place.[13] The existence of policy debate within the British Government was well known to a Soviet leadership whose tendency was to think the worst of the British establishment (they knew all about the PHPS views on dismemberment for instance, through Donald Maclean), so that while there was a broad consensus on cooperation, the existence of those with doubts or reservations was probably ultimately of greater significance, not for wartime policy, but for subsequent events; a result of Soviet perceptions of the British, however, more than a result of the most widespread perceptions of the USSR within the Churchill Coalition.[14] At the end of that Coalition, despite all the difficulties of the final period of the war, the prospects did not seem overwhelmingly bleak, even from the Moscow Embassy, never a posting that encouraged flights of optimism. Frank Roberts wrote on 30 June 1945 of 'a very welcome *détente*' since the troubles preceding and following victory in Europe, and that there was 'no reason for undue despondency over the future of Anglo-Soviet relations'.[15]

Notes and References

Chapter 1

1 Eden minute 2 July 1944 PRO FO371/40696/U5407 (documents are at the Public Record Office, London, unless stated otherwise); War Cabinet Paper (44)436 'Soviet Policy in Europe' 9 August 1944 CAB66/53 (hereafter cited as WP with year, number and date); Stettinius report of mission to Britain, 7–29 April 1944 *Foreign Relations of the United States 1944* (hereafter *FRUS* with year) vol. III, 10–11; K.G. Ross, 'Foreign Office Attitudes to the Soviet Union 1941–45', *Journal of Contemporary History,*16 (1981), 538.
2 W.S. Churchill, *The Second World War* (London, 1948–54) vol. 3, 346, vol. 6, 250, 367–74.
3 D.C. Watt, 'Britain and the Historiography of the Yalta Conference and the Cold War', *Diplomatic History*, 13 (1989), 89; F.M. Carroll, 'Anglo-American Relations and the Origins of the Cold War: The New Perspective', *Canadian Journal of History*, 24 (1989), 206; G. Gorodetsky, *Stafford Cripps' Mission to Moscow 1940–42* (Cambridge, 1984), idem, 'The Origins of the Cold War: Stalin, Churchill and the Formation of the Grand Alliance', *The Russian Review*, 47 (1988), 145–70.
4 Gorodetsky, *Stafford Cripps*, 96, 138–9, 164.
5 N. Tolstoy, *Stalin's Secret War* (London, 1983), 287–8, 338; S. de Mowbray, 'Soviet Deception & the Onset of the Cold War. British Documents for 1943 – A Lesson in Manipulation', *Encounter*, 63 (1984), 16; J. Charmley, *Churchill. The End of Glory* (London, 1993), 455, 467, 612; A. Glees, *The Secrets of the Service: British Intelligence and Communist Subversion 1939–51* (London, 1987), 51.
6 L. Kettenacker, 'The Anglo-Soviet Alliance and the Problem of Germany, 1941–45', *Journal of Contemporary History*, 17 (1982), 446; J.M. Lewis, *Changing Direction. British Military Planning for Post-war Strategic Defence, 1942–47* (London, 1988), 337; D. Fraser, *Alanbrooke* (London, 1982), 450.
7 E. Barker, *Churchill and Eden at War* (London, 1978), 221, 287, 291; W.M. McNeill, *America, Britain and Russia. Their Cooperation and Conflict 1941–46* (London, 1953), 536; M. Kitchen, *British Policy Towards the Soviet Union during the Second World War* (London, 1986), 271; V. Rothwell, *Britain and the Cold War, 1941–47* (London, 1982), 4.
8 R. Cecil, review of Glees, *Secrets*, in *Intelligence and National Security*, 3 (1988), 342; T.H. Anderson, *The United States, Great Britain and the Cold War, 1944–47* (Columbia, MO, 1981), 182.
9 Lewis, *Changing Direction*, 139 note 95; Ross, 'Foreign Office', 528; Rothwell, *Britain*, 14.
10 M. Kitchen, 'Winston Churchill and the Soviet Union during the Second World War', *Historical Journal*, 30 (1987), 424–5; L. Aronsen and

M. Kitchen, *The Origins of the Cold War in Comparative Perspective* (London, 1988), 86; Charmley, *Churchill*, 507–8; Rothwell, *Britain*, 104.

11 Warner minutes 17 February 1942 FO371/32876/N927, 30 August 1943 FO954/26A.

12 J.M. Lee, *The Churchill Coalition* (London, 1980), 169.

13 The Government was anxious to prevent the left reaping any benefit from having been correct about the resilience of the USSR, but the 'stealing the thunder' campaign, which involved taking over the organisation of pro-Soviet events, also served the purpose of making the Government (especially its Conservative members) appear supportive of the USSR and thereby quieten criticism. The FO often regretted the uncritical pro-Soviet fervour, but there was no doubt that it was orchestrated by the Ministry of Information, MI5 and Special Branch, who checked the credentials of all pro-Soviet organisations and ensured the non-Communist ones were favoured, Parker to Monckton 15 July 1941, Home Policy Committee (HPC) meeting 4 September 1941, INF1/676; P.M.H. Bell, *John Bull and the Bear. British Public Opinion, Foreign Policy and the Soviet Union, 1941–45* (London, 1990), 42–5, 56–66; M. Balfour, *Propaganda in War 1939–45: Organisations, Policies and Politics in Britain and Germany* (London, 1979), 228–30.

14 D. Yergin, *Shattered Peace. The Origins of the Cold War and the National Security State* (Boston, 1977), Chapters 1 and 2.

Chapter 2

1 F.S. Northedge and A. Wells, *Britain and Soviet Communism. The Impact of a Revolution* (London, 1982), 50–3, 62–73; R. Manne, 'The Foreign Office and the Failure of Anglo-Soviet Rapprochement', *Journal of Contemporary History*, 16 (1981), 736–7.

2 D. Lammers, 'Fascism, Communism and the Foreign Office 1937–39', *Journal of Contemporary History*, 6/3 (1971), 68; F. McLynn, *Fitzroy Maclean* (London, 1992), 26, 41–3, 51.

3 Neither of these important officials has been subject to biographical study. They were both born in 1884, and had been in the FO since before the First World War. Charles Webster described Sargent as having the views of the FO of around 1910, Webster diary 3 February 1946, BLPES. Roderick Barclay found him 'cynical, pessimistic and unconstructive, though very likeable'. Jebb thought him brilliant, but pessimistic and inclined to debunk theorisations. He had not served overseas since 1919. Cadogan was, again according to Jebb, cautious, conventional, 'clearly shy and repressed emotionally', and a methodical worker not given to the more passionate viewpoints of his predecessor, Vansittart. R. Barclay, *Ernest Bevin and the Foreign Office* (London, 1975), 83; Lord Gladwyn, *The Memoirs of Lord Gladwyn* (London, 1972), 70, 73; Bruce Lockhart diary 13 April 1943, in K. Young, ed., *The Diaries of Sir Robert Bruce Lockhart, 1939–65* (London, 1980).

4 K. Feiling, *The Life of Neville Chamberlain* (London, 1970), 425; Halifax comments to Dominions Ministers 1 November 1939 CAB 99/1; War

Cabinet Minutes (hereafter cited as WM with the year, meeting number and date) WM(39)43rd 9 October 1939 CAB 65/2.

5 Collier memorandum 31 January 1940 FO371/24845/N1360; Sargent minute 24 March 1940 FO371/24843/N3363; Maclean paper, 'Possibilities of Allied Action Against the Caucasus' (draft) ud(undated) March 1940 FO371/24846/N3698; Kirkman and Hammond minutes 6 March 1940 WO208/1754; WM(40)66th 12 March 1940 CAB65/6.

6 Sargent memorandum 'The future direction of Soviet policy' 14 March 1940 FO371/24843/N3538; M. Gilbert, *Finest Hour. Winston Churchill 1939–41* (London, 1983), 49, 98, 100–1; Churchill conversation with Welles 12 March 1940 *FRUS1940*:I, 84.

7 Seeds to Halifax 21 March 1939 FO371/23061/C3968; J. Haslam, *The Soviet Union and the Struggle for Collective Security in Europe 1933–39* (London, 1984), 230. Gottfried Niedhart makes the important point that for the British the USSR occupied a peripheral position; there was underlying anti-Bolshevism, but no policy-makers built their policy around it; indeed the USSR was usually ignored, at least until 1939, 'British Attitudes and Policies towards the Soviet Union and International Communism, 1933–9', in W. Mommsen and L. Kettenacker, eds, *The Fascist Challenge and the Policy of Appeasement* (London, 1983), 291; C. Keeble, *Britain and the Soviet Union, 1917–1989* (London, 1990), Chapter 6.

8 Collier to Butler 18 March 1940 FO371/24846/N3313; Halifax, *Fulness of Days* (London, 1957), 207; cf. Gorodetsky, *Stafford Cripps*, 96.

9 Sargent memorandum 14 March 1940 FO371/24843/N3538.

10 Sargent memorandum 'Possibilities of further Soviet–German collaboration' 17 July 1940 FO371/24852/N6029; circular to HM Representatives (HMRR), South-Eastern Europe 5 September 1940 FO371/24902/R7463; Sargent minute 28 June 1940 FO371/24844/N5853. Lothian, Ambassador to the US, told Welles that the British Government supported Cripps' view that the Soviets were increasingly apprehensive regarding German victories, 18 June 1940 State Department Papers, US National Archives, College Park, Maryland, Record Group 59 (hereafter RG59) 711.61/739.

11 Maclean minute 25 May 1940, NID report 'Soviet Intentions in North East Europe' 20 June 1940, FO to Cripps 14 June 1940 FO371/24844/N5701, N5808; Halifax conversation with Ambassador Kennedy 21 June 1940 FO371/24761/N5862; Rose minute 26 July 1940 FO371/24968/R6751.

12 FO to Cripps 14 June 1940 FO371/24844/N5808.

13 Clutton minute 22 February 1941 FO371/29778/R1452; FO to HMRR S. E. Europe 28 February 1941 FO371/29779/R2110.

14 Dominions Office to Smuts 1 November 1940 FO371/24845/N7046.

15 FO to Cripps 2 December 1940 FO371/24848/N7348; Maclean summary 24 November 1940 FO371/24853/N7279; 2 Collier minutes 31 January 1941 FO371/29463/N373; comments on Cripps despatch 26 January 1941 FO371/29500/N947; WM(41)20th Confidential Annexe (CA) 24 February 1941 CAB65/21.

16 The belief that Germany would not attack the USSR was built more on estimates of German aims and interests, and the Soviet desire to

avoid war, than on concepts of the natural affinity of Germany and the USSR: see Cavendish-Bentinck minute 27 March 1941 FO371/26518/ C2919, cf. Gorodetsky, *Stafford Cripps*, 112–14, and idem, 'Churchill's Warning', 981.

17 Maclean minute 12 October 1940 FO371/24852/N6922; Halifax to Cripps 27 November 1940 FO371/24848/N7323; Burgin memorandum 5 March 1941 FO371/29498/N951.

18 Report by Wavell AIR2/1911; Martel conversation with Liddell Hart 6 October 1936 Liddell Hart papers, Liddell Hart Centre (LHC) LHII/1936; J. Herndon, 'British Perceptions of Soviet Military Capability, 1935–9' in Kettenacker and Mommsen, eds, *Fascist Challenge*, 301–2; K. Neilson, '"Pursued By A Bear": British Estimates of Soviet Military Strength and Anglo-Soviet Relations, 1922–1939', *Canadian Journal of History*, 28 (1993), 209–11.

19 COS283rd meeting 18 March 1939 CAB53/10; FP(36)82 'Report on the Military Value of Russia' 24 April 1939 CAB27/627; Neilson, 'Pursued By A Bear', 203.

20 Weekly Résumé 5 October 1939 CAB80/1; WP(39)101 28 October 1939 CAB66/3. Soviet performance against the Japanese in 1938 had been noted as poor, Herndon, 'British Perceptions', 347; WM(40)10thCA 12 January 1940 CAB65/11; WP(39)179 31 December 1939 CAB66/4.

21 MI2 paper, 'The Foreign Relations of the USSR' 2 November 1940 FO371/ 24845/N7310.

22 Greer to DMI 6 January 1941, Sillem minute 8 January 1941 WO208/ 1758.

23 Tamplin minute 8 January 1941, Mackenzie paper 'Will Stalin Fight?' 8 January 1941, Tamplin minute 17 January 1941, MI2b paper 'Strategy of the Red Army in a War against Germany' 27 January 1941 WO208/1758.

24 JIC(41)218(F) 23 May 1941 'German Intentions Against the USSR', MI2 comments 22 May 1941, JIC(41)234 'The Possible Outcome of German–Soviet Relations' 31 May 1941, Barclay (MI14) comments 1 June 1941 WO208/1761.

25 Cadogan minute 21 June 1940 FO371/24849/N5788.

26 WM(40)123rd 15 May 1940, 127th 18 May 1940, 149th 31 May 1940 CAB65/7; Lockhart diary 4 May 1940, 21 May 1940; Dalton diary 17 May 1940 in B. Pimlott, ed., *The Second World War Diary of Hugh Dalton 1940–45* (London, 1986); Cripps conversation with Halifax 20 May 1940 FO371/24847/N5648; H. Hanak, 'Sir Stafford Cripps as British Ambassador in Moscow, May 1940–June 1941', *English Historical Review*, 94 (1979), 56.

27 C. Cooke, *The Life of Richard Stafford Cripps* (London, 1957), 242–3, W. Jones, *The Russia Complex* (Manchester, 1977), 46, *Tribune* 1 December 1939, T.D. Burridge, *British Labour and Hitler's War* (London, 1976), 38.

28 E. Estorick, *Stafford Cripps. A Biography* (London, 1949), 243.

29 Cripps to FO 27 July 1940 FO371/24844/N6072.

30 Cripps to Halifax 10 October 1940 FO371/24848/N7323.

31 Cripps to FO 2 August 1940 FO371/24845/N6243; Earle to Hull 10 June 1940 *FRUS1940*:I, 606.

32 Cripps to FO 20 November 1940 FO371/24848/N7238.

33 Cripps to FO 11 October 1940, 13 October 1941 FO371/24845/N6881, N6875.

34 Cripps to FO 11 October 1940 FO371/24848/N6838, to Monckton 31 August 1940 and Halifax 2 September 1940 FO800/322.

35 Cripps to FO 8 August 1940 FO371/24847/N6105, 2 July 1940 FO371/24844/N5937; Steinhardt to Hull 22 September 1940 RG59 741.61/899.

36 Maclean minute 9 August 1940 FO371/24847/N6105.

37 Maclean minutes 3 July 1940, 10 July 1940 FO371/24844/N5937; Halifax to Alexander 19 August 1940 FO371/24847/N6105.

38 *Daily Herald* 1 December 1939; Burridge, *British Labour*, 21, 38; B. Donoghue and W. Jones, *Herbert Morrison. Portrait of a Politician* (London, 1973), 255.

39 B. Pimlott, *Hugh Dalton* (London, 1985), 284–6, 294; Hall to Dalton 19 August 1940, Ward and Lucas minutes 3 September 1940 FO837/1082.

40 Dalton minute 18 May 1940, Palairet to MEW 5 June 1940, Gaitskell to Herbertson 26 June 1940 FO837/1127.

41 Postan note on FO to Athens 2 April 1941 FO837/1098.

42 Hall to Baxter 23 July 1940, and to Sargent 23 July 1940, Trench minute 27 July 1940, Baxter minute 1 August 1940, Postan minute 20 August 1940 FO837/1130.

43 Postan note 6 September 1940 FO837/1082; Maclean minute 26 August 1940, Collier conversation with Postan 6 September 1940 FO371/24852/N6359.

44 Halifax letter to Knatchbull-Hugessen (Ankara) 21 February 1940 FO800/323; Baggallay minute 9 February 1940 FO371/24581/E573; HMRR mtg 8 April 1940 FO371/24902/R4832; MI2b note on South Caucasus 31 January 1940 WO208/1753.

45 Cadogan minute 2 June 1940 FO371/24847/N5689.

46 Sargent draft of Halifax to Cripps 13 August 1940 FO371/24847/N6105.

47 Cadogan minute 12 November 1940 FO371/24852/N7163.

48 Maclean minute 9 August 1940 FO371/24847/N6105.

49 Eden to Cripps 17 January 1941 FO954/24B.

50 Butler minutes 16 April 1940 FO371/24843/N3363, 12 March 1940, 29 March 1940 FO371/24846/N2779, N3313.

51 Cripps to Eden 9 March 1941 FO954/24B.

52 Postan note on Sargent paper 20 August 1940 FO837/1130.

53 WM(40)185th 28 June 1940 CAB65/7; Collier minute 10 November 1940 FO371/24845/N7148.

54 Cripps to FO 8 December 1940 FO371/24849/N7387.

55 Cripps to FO 11 November 1940, 20 November 1940, Maclean minute 5 December 1940 FO371/24848/N7173, N7238, N7366.

56 Sargent minutes 11 December 1940, 3 January 1941 FO371/24849/N7387, N7548.

57 Cripps to FO 29 December 1940 FO371/24849/N7548, 31 December 1940 FO371/29463/N29; Steinhardt to Hull 8 February 1941 RG59 741.61/920; Cripps to Eden 9 March 1941 FO954/24B.

58 Sargent minutes 6 February 1941 FO371/28563/N502, 28 March 1941

FO371/29464/N1229; Maclean minute 15 March 1941, Collier minute 27 March 1941 FO371/29500/N947, N1164.

59 Churchill, *Second World War* vol. 2, 118; FO to Cripps 13 June 1940 FO371/24844/N5808; Hanak, 'Cripps', 61; Dalton to Halifax 24 June 1940 FO837/1127.

60 Cf. Hanak, 'Cripps', 54.

61 WM(40)271st 15 October 1940 CAB65/9; FO to Cripps 15 October 1940 FO371/24845/N6875, Halifax to Cripps 27 November 1940 FO371/24848/N7323; Atherton to Welles 26 November 1940 RG59 711.61/768.

62 Cripps to FO 2 tels 11 November 1940 FO371/24848/N7165, N7163.

63 Cripps to Eden 9 March 1941 FO371/29500/N1164; Cripps to Eden 28 March 1941 Eden to Cadogan 29 March 1941 FO371/29464/N1289, N1360.

64 Eden had told Cripps, 'I share with you a keen desire to improve our relations with the Soviet Government and I have also had my share of disappointment in these endeavours . . . it is . . . an advantage that the Russians profess to regard me as one who has no prejudices against them . . .', letter 17 January 1941 FO954/24B.

65 FO to Eden 2 April 1941 FO371/29271/N1323; Cadogan to Eden 2 April 1941 FO371/29464/N1360.

66 Sargent minute 9 April 1941, Eden minute 15 April 1941, Sargent draft of Eden to Cripps 16 April 1941 cf. Sargent's 28 March 1941 minute FO371/29464/N1386, N1229; Sargent note on Halifax to Collier 26 April 1941, Eden conversation with Maisky 16 April 1941, Sargent to N. Dept 18 April 1941, FO to Halifax 19 April 1941 FO371/29465/N1806, N1658, N1667.

67 Churchill to Cadogan 3 April 1941, 5 April 1941 FO371/29271/N1323; Defence Committee meeting DO(40)39th 31 October 1940 CAB69/l, WM(41)20thCA 24 February 1941 CAB65/21, F.H. Hinsley, *British Intelligence in the Second World War: Its Influence on Strategy and Operations* (London, 1979) vol. 1, 432, 437, 440.

68 Churchill to Stalin 3 April 1941 FO371/29479/N1366.

69 FO to Cripps 4 April 1941 FO371/29479/N1366.

70 Cripps to FO 2 tels 19 April 1941 FO371/29465/N1725; Cripps to FO 23 April 1941 FO371/29480/N1761, N1762.

71 Cadogan minute 19 April 1941, Collier minute 22 April 1941 FO371/29465/N1667, N1725; Sargent minute 26 April 1941 FO800/279.

72 Churchill to Eden 22 April 1941 PREM3/395/16.

73 Warner memorandum 14 May 1941 FO371/29465/N2233; Cripps to FO 9 May 1941 FO371/29500/N2102; Eden minute 9 May 1941 FO371/29498/N2050; JIC(41)234 'The Possible Outcome of German-Soviet Relations' 31 May 1941 WO208/1761.

74 Butler minute 26 May 1941, FO meeting 28 May 1941 FO371/29465/N2565, N2566; FO to Halifax 17 June 1941 FO371/29501/N2840.

75 Butler minute 30 April 1941 FO371/29465/N1801; Sargent minute 1 June 1941 FO954/24B; 17 June 1941 meeting on propaganda should Germany attack the USSR FO371/29483/N2904.

76 Johnson to Hull 13 June 1941 *FRUS1941*:I, 170–2; Avon, *The Reckoning* (London, 1965), 269; WM(41)61st 19 June 1941 CAB65/18; HPC meeting 18 June 1941 INF1/913.

77 WM(41)58thCA 9 June 1941, 59thCA 12 June 1941 CAB65/22; Warner minute 8 June 1941 FO371/29466/N2889.

78 J. Kennedy, *The Business of War* (London, 1957), 147; B. Bond, ed., *Chief of Staff: The Diaries of Lieutenant-General Sir Henry Pownall* (London, 1974) vol. 2 1940–44, diary 29 June 1941.

79 JIC(41)234(F) 9 June 1941 FO371/29483/N2906; JIC(41)247 10 June 1941 CAB79/12; Nicolson diary 24 June 1941 in N. Nicolson, ed., *Harold Nicolson. Diaries and Letters* (London, 1967) vol. 2 1939–45; Kennedy, *Business*, 147, 149; Ismay, *Memoirs of General the Lord Ismay* (London, 1960), 225; T. Barman, *Diplomatic Correspondent* (London, 1968), 99.

80 Churchill to Roosevelt 14 June 1941 (sent on 15 June 1941) PREM3/230/1.

81 Colville diary 22 June 1941 in J. Colville, *The Fringes of Power. Downing Street Diaries* (London, 1985) vol. 1 1939–October 1941.

82 Colville diary 21 June 1941; Duff Cooper to Eden 28 June 1941 INF1/913; WM(41)64th 30 June 1941 CAB65/18.

83 S. Lawlor, 'Britain and the Russian entry into the war' in R. Langhorne, ed., *Diplomacy and Intelligence during the Second World War* (Cambridge, 1985), 171–2.

84 WM(41)62nd 23 June 1941 CAB65/18; Morton to Churchill 31 August 1941 PREM4/64/5 and 12 November 1941 INF1/913.

85 Colville diary 21 June 1941, cf. his account in J. Wheeler-Bennett ed., *Action This Day. Working with Churchill* (London, 1968), 89.

86 Gilbert, *Finest Hour*, 1123; COS to Macfarlane 14 July 1941 FO371/29486/N3729.

87 Macfarlane article on service in the USSR, Macfarlane papers 31, Imperial War Museum (IWM); Instructions to Naval Mission ADM223/506; Hinsley, *British Intelligence*, vol. 1, 483.

88 Nicolson note for HPC 17 June 1941 INF1/913 cf. FO/Information meeting 17 June 1941 FO371/29483/N2904, where it was agreed, 'There would probably be strong pressure in some circles to treat Russia as an ally. This should be resisted. Our attitude would however depend on that of the Russians, who would probably not wish to regard themselves as our allies.' Eden conversations with Maisky 26 June 1941, 30 June 1941, Cripps to FO 27 June 1941 FO371/29466/N3226, N3304, N3231.

89 Sargent minute 9 July 1941, Eden talk with Winant 9 July 1941 and to Cripps FO371/29467/N3561, N3603; WM(41)64th 30 June 1941 CAB65/19; Steinhardt to Hull 9 July 1941 *FRUS1941*:I, 179–81.

90 Harvey diary 21 March 1942, J. Harvey, ed., *The War Diaries of Sir Oliver Harvey* (London, 1978).

91 A.J.P. Taylor, *Beaverbrook* (London, 1972), 165; A. Foster, 'The Beaverbrook Press and Appeasement: The Second Phase', *European History Quarterly*, 21 (1991), 7, 10–11.

92 A. Chisholm and M. Davie, *Beaverbrook. A Life* (London, 1992), 282, 322, 326. On Beaverbrook's isolationism, see Beaverbrook to Liddell Hart 3 September 1939 LHI/52; Beaverbrook to Churchill 30 September 1940 Beaverbrook papers, House of Lords (BBK), D/425; Foster, 'Beaverbrook Press', 8–9.

93 'Apologia for *Evening Standard*', BBK D/494. Generally, the Beaverbrook press was isolationist on eastern Europe, friendly and indulgent to the USSR, guided by Stalin's foreign policy not his domestic activities, Foster, 'Beaverbrook Press', 21.

94 Gorodetsky, *Stafford Cripps*, 200–4.

95 DO(41)22 19 October 1941 CAB69/3, DO(41)67th 20 October 1941 CAB69/2.

96 Poster for 'Tanks for Russia', INF13/123.

97 DO(41)62nd 19 September 1941 CAB69/2.

98 Churchill to Beaverbrook 30 August 1941 BBK D/94, H. Balfour diary 26 September 1941, Inchrye papers, House of Lords.

99 Cripps despatch 15 September 1941 FO371/29490/N5447; Cripps to Eden 20 September 1941 FO954/24B.

100 Beaverbrook to Eden 15 September 1941 BBK D/338; His secretary's notes on Cripps' despatches show the genesis of Beaverbrook's tactics; to counter the Soviet 'inferiority complex' as to their status as an ally by building up Soviet prestige in private and public. Beaverbrook's personal relationship with Stalin was to be the key to the success of the mission, Farrer notes BBK D/90; Balfour diary 21 September 1941; Beaverbrook, 'Russian Narrative' 25 June 1945 BBK D/100; A. Harriman and E. Abel, *Special Envoy to Churchill and Stalin* (London, 1976), Chapter 4; D. Farrer, *G For God Almighty* (London, 1969), 75; J.D. Langer, 'The Harriman–Beaverbrook Mission and the Debate over Unconditional Aid for the Soviet Union, 1941', *Journal of Contemporary History*, 14 (1979), 469.

101 Balfour diary 30 September 1941, 9 October 1941; WP(41)238 8 October 1941 CAB66/19.

102 DO(41)64th 15 October 1941 CAB69/2; DO(41)22 'Assistance to Russia' 19 October 1941 CAB69/3.

103 DO(41)71st 3 December 1941 CAB69/2 cf. Beaverbrook at DO(41)67thSS 20 October 1941 CAB69/8; J.E. Beaumont, *Comrades in Arms* (London, 1980), 76–9.

104 Sinclair to Beaverbrook 20 October 1941, Air Staff paper 27 November 1941 BBK D/327; WM(41)111thCA 11 November 1941 CAB65/24; Beaumont, *Comrades*, 67–9.

105 JP(41)104th 15 August 1941 CAB84/3; COS(41)155(O) 31 July 1941 CAB80/59; Brooke diary 14 July 1941, 28 October 1941 Alanbrooke papers 2/4, LHC; DO(41)62nd 19 September 1941 CAB69/2.

106 DO(41)71st 3 December 1941 CAB69/2; Brooke diary 4 December 1941, 25 February 1942 Alanbrooke 2/5; COS(41)41st(O) 2 December 1941 CAB79/55; JP(41)1038 15 December 1941 CAB84/38.

107 Warner minute 3 December 1941, Cavendish-Bentinck minute 4 December 1941. FO371/29501/N7081; Whitcfoord (DDMI(I)) to VCIGS 12 August 1941, Tamplin minute 1 October 1941 WO208/1776; Sillem minute 19 September 1941 WO208/1777; MI3c appreciation 13 September 1941 Martel papers, IWM, GQM4/3.

108 Kennedy, *Business*, 149; Dalton diary 18 November 1941. For Russian-speaking officers, see notes on Theakstone and Martin FO371/29574/N5882, A. Birse, *Memoirs of an Interpreter* (London, 1967), 80.

109 Cadogan diary 22 May 1942 in D. Dilks, ed., *The Diaries of Sir Alexander*

Cadogan, 1938–46 (London, 1971); Charmley, *Churchill*, 456–7; D. Carlton, *Anthony Eden* (London, 1982), 183–4.

110 McLynn, *Maclean*, 63.
111 FO to Cripps 21 October 1941 FO371/29470/N6267; Eden to Cripps 10 November 1941 FO371/29493/N6544. In a draft telegram to Cripps, Cadogan wrote, 'our prime need of cooperation with the Soviet must override all other considerations' 2 October 1941 FO371/29491/N5679.
112 Dew minute 15 November 1941, Maisky conversation with Eden 12 November 1941 FO371/29470/N6288. Soviet sympathisers in Britain made great play of speeches by Halifax, Page Croft and Moore Brabazon as indications of such feelings among the British ruling class, Brabazon to Blackburn 7 August 1941 and Churchill 3 September 1941, Brabazon papers, RAF Museum, Croft to Maisky 25 October 1941 Croft papers, Churchill College, 1/16.
113 Cripps to Eden 29 July 1941 FO954/24B.
114 WP(41)238 8 October 1941 CAB66/19; Peirson to Harvey 29 October 1941 FO371/29470/N6312.
115 WM(41)102nd 13 October 1941 CAB65/19.
116 Maisky conversations with Eden 17 October 1941, 27 October 1941 FO371/29469/N6059, N6228.
117 WM(41)104th 20 October 1941 CAB65/19, 123rdCA 3 December 1941 CAB65/24; Churchill to Cripps 28 October 1941 FO371/29471/N6583.
118 Cripps to FO 25 October 1941 FO371/29492/N6169; Cripps warned of the danger of a growth of a feeling of isolation in Moscow, and an obsession there that 'we were sitting back and watching'.
119 Cripps to Churchill 29 October 1941 FO371/29471/N6584. Churchill was of the opinion that the Soviets were more dependent on Britain than *vice versa* and reacted strongly to assertions of this kind by Cripps, Churchill draft to Cripps 3 October 1941 FO371/29491/N5679.
120 Stalin to Churchill 8 November 1941 FO954/24B. Churchill was disgruntled by Stalin's tone. It took a mollification by Maisky, prearranged with Eden, to bring him round; he then wrote to Stalin that he wished for a personal correspondence with him, as with Roosevelt, and stated Britain's desire for postwar collaboration with the USSR, WM(41)111thCA 11 November 1941 CAB65/24, Eden conversation with Maisky 20 November 1941 FO371/29471/N6704, Harvey diary 21 November 1941; Churchill to Stalin 21 November 1941 FO371/29472/N6750.
121 Skaife minutes 2 November 1941 FO371/29493/N6364, 9 November 1941 FO371/29470/N6490; Maisky to Leith-Ross 15 October 1941, Leith-Ross to Greenwood 29 October 1941 T188/253.
122 Warner minute 23 November 1941 FO371/29422/N7503.
123 Churchill minute 1 November 1941 FO954/24B; Sargent minute 18 November 1941 FO371/29470/N6288.
124 Sargent minute 26 October 1941 FO371/29493/N6514.
125 Dew and Cadogan minutes 17 November 1941 FO371/29494/N6801.
126 Harvey diary 14 November 1941.
127 The phrase was Sargent's, minute on Stalin's speech 12 November 1941 FO371/29494/N6631; Maisky conversation with Eden 26 August 1941 FO371/29489/N4840.

128 Warner minute 17 November 1941 FO371/29470/N6288, minute on Stalin's message 12 November 1941 FO371/29471/N6540, minute 23 November 1941 FO371/29422/N7503.

129 Harvey diary 14 November 1941; Eden minute 13 November 1941 FO371/29494/N6631.

130 Dew minute of FO meeting 18 November 1941 FO371/29472/N5839; Cripps to Eden 5 November 1941 FO371/29493/N6544. Harvey noted, 'We felt the important thing is to convince Stalin that we mean to work with him during and after the peace. If we can convince him of this, then the fact that our ideas for post-war are still nebulous needn't matter – all that should be studied properly later', diary 18 November 1941.

131 FO meeting 19 November 1941 FO371/29015/W13829.

132 Dew minute 3 November 1941 FO371/29470/N6312.

133 Eden to Cripps 10 November 1941 FO371/29493/N6544.

134 Eden Memorandum 'Forthcoming Discussions with the Soviet Government' 26 November 1941 WP(41)288 FO371/29472/N6835; WM(41)120thCA 27 November 1941, 124thCA 4 December 1941 CAB65/24; Eden conversations with Maisky 1 December 1941, and Winant 4 December 1941 FO371/29472/N6893, N7013; Winant to Hull 4 December 1941 RG59 740.0011/17085.

Chapter 3

1 Title of account of conversations between Major Magnus and Major-General Solovodnik 20 May 1944 FO371/43315/N3353.

2 Churchill to Eden 16 January 1944 PREM3/399/6.

3 Rothwell, *Britain*, 90–2; Kitchen, *British Policy*, 157–8, 177–8.

4 Clark Kerr to FO 17 April 1943, to Sargent 12 July 1943 FO371/37001/N2366, N4002; D. Gillies, *Radical Diplomat. The Life of Archibald Clark Kerr, Lord Inverchapel, 1882–1951* (London, 1999), 23, 81, 167; Barman, *Correspondent*, 170–1.

5 Clark Kerr despatch 30 September 1942 FO181/964/4; Balfour to Warner 17 March 1944 FO371/43304/N2068; Clark Kerr to Warner 24 May 1944 FO800/302; Barman, *Correspondent*, 149–51.

6 Churchill to Eden 14 July 1944, Cadogan minute 17 July 1944 FO954/26B.

7 Blunden to MacNulty 6 August 1942 FO371/32922/N5000; Warner minute 10 November 1942 FO371/32923/N5832; A. Foşter, 'The Times and Appeasement: the Second Phase', *Journal of Contemporary History*, 16 (1981), 460–1.

8 Kitchen, *British Policy*, 61; Hill paper 15 April 1943 FO371/36948/N2364; Barman, *Correspondent*, 151–4; Ismay diary 25 October 1943, Ismay papers/III/5/la, LHC.

9 The FO came to conclude when Polish pessimism proved unfounded that the Poles were jealous of the Soviets and of losing their position as Britain's major ally: Clarke minute 7 October 1941 FO371/29491/N5751; Dew minute 11 May 1942, Sargent minute 12 May 1942 FO371/32921/N2405, N2488. As the Poles' reputation fell, so Pika's rose, Pika

report 20 October 1941 FO371/29492/N6068, Lockhart minute 8 December 1941 FO371/29494/N6891.

10 Macfarlane to DMI 2 August 1941 FO371/29488/N4281; Exham to DMI 23 September 1942 AIR40/2344; Turner to DDMI(I) (Kirkman) 3 August 1943 WO208/1833; Fawkes report 7 October 1941 ADM223/248; B.F. Smith, *Sharing Secrets with Stalin. How the Allies Traded Intelligence, 1941–1945* (Kansas, 1996), 151, 171.

11 Ismay to Hollis 14 January 1944 PREM3/396/10; NID report 17 November 1943 ADM223/506; Hinsley, *British Intelligence*, vol. 2, 41, 618.

12 e.g. JIC(44)21(F) 20 January 1944 'The Situation on the Russian Front' AIR40/2344.

13 'Report by a British Officer of a visit to Leningrad' 29 January 1944–5 February 1944 FO371/43312/N1122; report of tour of White Russia, 2–10 August 1944 FO371/43316/N5774; SBNO Black Sea diary September 1941 ADM223/506.

14 Haigh minute 24 September 1944 FO371/43336/N5598; O Malley despatch 30 April 1943 FO371/35261/U2011; M. Gilbert, *Road to Victory* (London, 1986) 239; Lockhart minute 11 April 1945 FO371/47860/N4102; Martel drafts for *The Russian Outlook*, 1947, GQM6/1; Miles to DNI 26 November 1942 ADM223/248; Rear-Admiral Archer described 'this suspicious and semi-civilized ally', Naval Mission report, 1943–45 ADM223/506; SOE D/P.1 to D/HV 30 May 1942 HS4/327.

15 Clark Kerr to Eden 8 June 1943, 24 June 1943 FO371/36949/N3673, N3934; Skaife minute 7 December 1943 FO371/36952/N6777; Baggallay to Eden 25 February 1942 FO371/32906/N1585.

16 SBNO Murmansk to DNI 20 September 1941, 29 January 1942 ADM223/249; Cripps to FO 20 September 1941 FO371/29469/N5585.

17 Dew minute 19 July 1941 FO371/29487/N3826; Lockhart memoranda 20 February 1942 FO371/32876/N927, 23 February 1942 BBK D/96.

18 Dew minute 27 December 1941 FO371/29499/N7355; SO2 paper 25 June 1941 HS4/327.

19 Baggallay to Sargent 18 January 1943 FO371/36944/N583.

20 Preston minute 11 February 1941, Collier minute 10 March 1941 FO371/29498/N841; Lambert memorandum 5 August 1942 FO181/966/13.

21 Balfour paper 19 March 1942, Inchrye papers; Strang minute 2 November 1941 FO371/29471/N6774.

22 Collier to Butler 7 September 1940 FO371/24841/N6488; Lambert memorandum 5 August 1942 FO181/966/13.

23 Haigh minute 24 September 1944 FO371/43336/N5598.

24 Cripps to FO 24 July 1941, 3 August 1941 FO371/29488/N4043, N4260; Dew minutes 24 July 1941 FO371/29488/N4004, 20 September 1941 FO371/29499/N5448. Sumner (FRPS) predicted a 'Suvorov spirit' that the regime had been cultivating for five years, and that a 'Chungking' was more likely than a 'Brest-Litovsk' minutes 1 July 1941, 20 July 1941 FO371/29499/N3476, N4702.

25 WO to Macfarlane 5 July 1941 ADM223/506; MI3b appreciation of the Romanian situation 13 August 1941 WO208/4616; JIC(41)376(F) 23 September 1941 FO371/29491/N5649; Political Review 9 March 1942 FO371/33026/N3996.

26 Baggallay to Eden 25 February 1942 FO371/32906/N1585.
27 Stalin Order of the Day 1 May 1942 FO371/37032/N3670; Clark Kerr despatch 10 October 1942 FO181/964/8.
28 JIC(42)200(F) 1 June 1942 AIR40/2344; COS(42)169th 4 June 1942 CAB79/21; Exham to Reed 4 September 1942 FO181/964/8; MI3c notes on Hungarian reports 1 September 1942 WO208/1805; Davidson minute 11 September 1942 WO208/1815; MI3c summary 4 November 1942 WO208/1820; Baggallay to FO 13 January 1943 FO371/36944/N582. In fact, Stalin went to the front only once, after the battle of Kursk, R. Overy, *Russia's War. Blood upon the Snow* (New York, 1997), 254.
29 Skaife memorandum 19 December 1942 FO371/32924/N6633.
30 Food and transport went to maintaining the Red Army and industrial workers, together with Government officials, the NKVD and party functionaries. Those classified as 'useless mouths' – dependants, especially the elderly, and those in non-essential occupations, had to fend as best they could, JIC(42)459(F) 2 December 1942 AIR40/2344; MEW report on Soviet rations 31 March 1944 FO371/43329/N2032.
31 2 Clark Kerr despatches 10 October 1942 FO181/964/8.
32 JIC(41)290 31 July 1941 WO208/1777.
33 Sillem note 19 September 1941 WO208/1777; MI3c comments 1 September 1942 WO208/1805; Berthoud to Warner 4 February 1942 FO371/32920/N1235; Baggallay to Sargent 18 January 1943 FO371/36944/N583.
34 Skaife memorandum 24 February 1944 FO371/43313/N1547.
35 Warner comment on Stalin speech 7 November 1942, minute 1 December 1942 FO371/32923/N5782, N6068; Cheshire to ACAS(I) 6 October 1942 AIR40/2344; Thornton minute 24 July 1943 WO208/1833; Eden conversation with Maisky 8 August 1943 PREM3/396/13; M. Harrison, 'The Soviet Economy and Relations with the United States and Britain, 1941–45', in A. Lane and H. Temperley, eds, *The Rise and Fall of the Grand Alliance* (Basingstoke, 1995), 75, 77–8, 86.
36 Wilson minute 12 August 1943 FO371/37033/N4506; Dew minute 13 August 1943 FO371/36950/N4893; Balfour to FO 10 September 1943 FO371/37057/N5805.
37 Whitefoord to Dew 2 October 1941 FO371/29491/N5751; Warner minute 28 September 1944 FO371/43336/N5598.
38 Firebrace note, 'British Military Relations with the USSR' 24 November 1943 FO371/36970/N7241; Clark Kerr to Warner 3 August 1944 FO800/302.
39 MI3b appreciation 13 August 1941 WO208/4616; MI3c notes 1 September 1942 WO208/1850; JIC(42)200(F) 1 June 1942 AIR40/2344; Baggallay despatch 25 February 1942 FO371/32906/N1585.
40 Tamplin to MI3 Colonel 15 July 1942 WO208/1777; JIC(42)459(F) 2 December 1942 'Russian Strength during the Winter 1942–43' AIR40/2344.
41 Aircraftman Clague note 19 March 1942 AIR46/21; COS(42)178th 13 June 1942 CAB79/21; Boseley report 11 May 1942 FO371/32921/N2547.
42 Ignatieff note 4 September 1942 WO208/1815; Fawkes report 10 November 1941 FO371/29499/N6539.
43 Clark Kerr to Eden 13 October 1942 FO371/32922/N5267; Exham

to Clark Kerr 12 October 1942 FO181/964/4; SBNO Black Sea report 4 March 1943 WO208/1750.

44 Dew minute 13 October 1942 FO371/32922/N5267; Exham to DMI 14 October 1943 FO181/964/4.

45 Clark Kerr despatch 3 November 1943 FO371/36952/N7539; SBNO North Russia report, 15 December 1942 FO371/32924/N6354; Penn report 22–31 October 1943 FO371/43310/N295; Babington memorandum 12 August 1943 FO371/36960/N6227; SBNO Black Sea note 26 October 1943 WO208/1761.

46 Dew minute 18 April 1943, MEW note 1 May 1943 FO371/36948/N2337, N2637.

47 JIC(42)459(F) 2 December 1942 AIR40/2344; Tamplin note 24 October 1942 WO208/1805; Noble note 22 May 1943 FO371/36959/N3026.

48 JIC(42)200(F) 1 June 1942, JIC(42)459(F) 2 December 1942, JIC(43)409(O) 2 October 1943, JIC(42)298(O) 2 August 1942 AIR40/2344; Naval Mission Diary 5 May 1942 ADM199/1102; Ambrose report ud. December 1941 ADM223/248.

49 e.g. PHP(44)17(O) Revise 15 September 1944 'Security of Western Europe and the North Atlantic' FO371/40741A/U7618.

50 Dew minute 21 November 1942 FO371/32923/N5858.

51 Baggallay despatch 25 November 1942 FO371/36944/N55; Dew minute 20 April 1943 FO371/36948/N2335; Hill report 29 January 1944–5 February 1944 FO371/43316/N1122.

52 Lambert to FO 3 December 1942 FO371/36944/N275; *Krasnaya Zvezda* 7 January 1943, Lambert despatch 14 January 1943 FO371/36945/N1243, N1251.

53 The press advocated dancing and other 'social graces' for officers, Clark Kerr despatch 3 November 1943 FO371/36952/N7539.

54 Lambert despatch 14 January 1943 FO371/36945/N1251; NID16 view 8 March 1943 FO371/36946/N1464.

55 Balfour to FO 21 December 1943 FO371/36952/N7626. Stalin hoped Churchill 'would set about learning the new tune and whistling it to the members of the Conservative party', Clark Kerr to Churchill 3 February 1944 FO800/302.

56 Baggallay despatch 25 February 1942 FO371/32906/N1585.

57 Skaife memorandum, 'The Future of the USSR in the Post-War Years' 19 December 1942 FO371/32924/N6633; Clark Kerr despatches 30 September 1942 FO181/964/4, 2 August 1943 FO371/36950/N4533. He commented on the use of the word *Russki* rather than *Sovietski*, and Lambert speculated how long it would be before *Rossiiski* (Great Russian) came back into use, Lambert minute 15 April 1943 FO371/36947/N2234.

58 Dew minutes 30 July 1943 FO371/36950/N4309, 6 May 1943 FO371/37001/N2896.

59 Kuibyshev Embassy to FO 28 July 1942 FO371/32949/N4525.

60 Balfour to Warner 15 August 1944 FO371/43316/N5186.

61 Skaife minute 5 October 1943, Dew minute 5 October 1943 FO371/37052/N5523.

62 Dew minute 15 September 1943 FO371/36951/N5175.

63 Skaife minute 13 September 1943 FO371/36951/N5715; Sargent minute 5 July 1944 FO371/43315/N3816.
64 Clark Kerr to FO 27 July 1944 FO371/43316/N5009.
65 Clark Kerr to FO 16 September 1943 FO371/36951/N5807; NID note on Soviet Naval Officers 23 August 1942 ADM223/506.
66 Skaife memorandum 19 December 1942 FO371/32924/N6633.
67 Wilson minute 14 May 1944 FO371/43335/N2833.
68 Dew minute 15 August 1943 FO371/36950/N4893; Wilson minute 26 December 1943 FO371/36952/N7539.
69 Balfour to Warner 17 July 1944 FO371/43336/N5415.
70 Clark Kerr despatch 3 November 1943 FO371/36952/N7539.
71 Lockhart memorandum 11 April 1945 FO371/47860/N4102.
72 Political Review 4 December 1944 FO371/43449/N7946; Ministry of Information paper ud. October 1943 FO371/36951/N6150; Wheeler-Bennett memorandum 10 April 1944 FO371/40691/U3704; Hill report 2–10 August 1944 FO371/43316/N5774, Magnus report 20 May 1944 FO371/43315/N3353.
73 Penn report of visit to Destroyer *Baku* 31 October 1943 FO371/43310/N295.
74 Dew minute 16 January 1942 FO371/36920/N302.
75 Maisky statement 23 September 1941 FO371/29490/N5565; Randall note 18 December 1941 FO371/29549/N7356; Waddams to Warner 18 November 1942, citing a survey of the 'more intelligent' members of the populace: 72 per cent of those feeling there were obstacles to proper understanding between Britain and the USSR named the Soviet treatment of religion as the chief difficulty, FO371/32950/N5912.
76 Dew minute 23 July 1941 FO371/29486/N3462; Wilson minute 8 April 1942 FO371/32949/N1800.
77 Cripps to FO 11 October 1941 FO371/29470/N6317; Dew minutes 15 January 1942, 15 June 1942 FO371/32949/N284, N3366; Naval Mission diary 4 October 1941, 'God appears quite popular here at present, Stalin having referred to Him favourably in his speech', ADM199/1102.
78 Clark Kerr despatch 13 May 1942 FO371/32949/N3538; additional rations were provided for making traditional Easter cakes, Naval Mission Diary 5 April 1942 ADM199/1102.
79 Clark Kerr despatch 20 September 1942 FO371/32950/N5328.
80 Minutes by Wilson 21 September 1942, Dew 25 September 1942, Warner 25 September 1942, Sargent 25 September 1942, Cadogan 28 September 1942 FO371/32949/N4838; Eden minute 7 February 1943 FO371/36961/N508; Wilcox to Warner 10 August 1943 FO371/36962/N4560.
81 Clark Kerr report of Pan-Slavonic meeting 9 May 1943 FO371/36961/N4356; Dew minute 7 October 1943 FO371/36962/N5604.
82 Warner minute 19 May 1943 FO371/36961/N3047.
83 Clark Kerr despatch 1 October 1943 FO371/36963/N6710.
84 Clark Kerr noted that the CPSU had been told religion 'corresponds with the moral needs of the people.' to FO 10 September 1943, Skaife minute 15 September 1943 FO371/36962/N5264, N5253. There was some truth in Skaife's view, W.C. Fletcher, 'The Soviet Bible Belt: World War II's Effects on Religion', in S.J. Linz, ed., *The Impact of World War II on the Soviet Union* (New Jersey, 1985), 91.

85 Bell, *John Bull*, 70.
86 Winant to Hull 24 May 1943 *FRUS1943*:III, 532–3; Lambert to Sargent 23 May 1943, Clark Kerr to FO 24 May 1943 FO371/37019/N3086, N3082; Political Review 4 December 1944 FO371/43449/N7946.
87 Warner letter to Clark Kerr 28 May 1943 FO800/301.
88 Dew minutes 4 June 1943 FO371/37019/N3082, 4 May 1943 FO371/36948/N2658; Warner minute 5 May 1944 FO371/43335/N2652. NID stressed the danger from the Communist Party, and its eagerness to gather secrets for the Soviet Union, probably with the Springhall/Uren case in mind, Rushbrooke to VCNS 13 June 1943 ADM223/506.
89 Warner minute 29 October 1941 FO371/29471/N6215; Cripps to FO 6 October 1941, FO371/29491/N5813; Skaife minute 2 November 1941 FO371/29493/N6364.
90 MEW papers 'The Economic Effects of the Russian Advance during the Period July–October 1943' 20 October 1943 FO371/36951/N6487, 'Report on Economic Resources of Eastern Russia' 28 July 1944 FO371/43329/N4864.
91 Baggallay despatch 26 February 1942 FO371/32921/N1598, to Sargent 18 January 1943 FO371/36944/N583.
92 Warner minute 21 November 1942 FO371/32923/N5858; Sargent minute 23 April 1943 FO371/36948/N2364; Sargent wanted 'a small Standing Inter-departmental Committee to deal with Russian questions, so as to make certain that they are all being handled on the lines laid down by the Foreign Office'.
93 MEW paper 'Conditions in Russia' 12 October 1943 FO371/36951/N6382; Skaife to Wilson 28 July 1944, Radice (Head, Enemy Branch) to Warner 28 July 1944 FO371/43329/N4286, N4864.
94 Cripps to FO 25 October 1941 FO371/29492/N6169; Berthoud report 9 March 1942, Macfarlane to DMI 26 March 1942, Clark Kerr to FO 3 July 1942 FO371/32921/N1911, N1690, N3485; Overy, *Russia's War*, 273.
95 Cadogan and Eden minutes 29 July 1942 FO371/32989/N4140; Clark Kerr to FO 1 October 1942 FO371/32990/N5066.
96 MEW reports 23 March 1942, 11 April 1942 FO371/32988/N1901, WP(42)309 21 July 1942 CAB66/26.
97 Enemy Branch Report 5 September 1942, Minister's Conference 8 October 1942 FO837/32; MEW report 22 October 1942, JIC(42)58th 1 December 1942 FO371/32990/N4561, N6195; Baggallay to Sargent 18 January 1943 FO371/36944/N583; MEW paper 20 October 1943 FO371/36951/N6487; COS(43)346th 15 December 1943 CAB79/87; Dalton diary 8 February 1944.
98 MI14 had concluded that in wartime, Soviet railways were incapable of additional efforts and the rail system was the weakest link in the conduct of military operations, MI14 Report on Soviet railways 9 May 1940; MI6 report from French source 'Beaune' 30 August 1941 WO208/1750. While oil and manpower shortages reduced agricultural productivity, the real problem was seen to be getting what was produced to where it was needed, JIC(41)376(F) 23 September 1941 FO371/29491/N5649; MEW paper 'Food Position in Russia' 23 March 1942 FO371/

32988/N1901. The situation was actually better than the British assumed, H. Hunter, 'Successful Spatial Management', in Linz, ed., *Impact*, 51.

99 MI3c report 5 March 1943 FO371/36958/N1539; JIC(42)459(F) 2 December 1942 AIR40/2344; Wilson visit to Chelyabinsk 30 April 1943 FO371/36948/N3268.

100 Gifford note 12 March 1943 FO371/36948/N2658.

101 Enemy Branch note 1 May 1943, MEW paper 'The Economic Effects of the Russian Advance, November 1942–March 1943' 29 April 1943 FO371/36948/N2637, N2887; Balfour to FO 4 November 1943 FO371/36952/N7542.

102 MEW paper 20 October 1943 FO371/36951/N6487.

103 JIC(43)409(O) 2 October 1943 AIR40/2344; Clark Kerr to FO 14 October 1943 FO371/36960/N6687.

104 MEW paper 20 October 1943 FO371/36951/N6487; Clark Kerr to FO 25 August 1943 FO371/37052/N5508; Balfour to FO 4 November 1943 FO371/36952/N7542.

105 Baggallay despatch 25 November 1942, Warner minute 18 March 1943: 'I don't believe the Soviet Govt. will lightly abandon their idea of being self-sufficing. I hope I'm wrong.' FO371/35338/U67, U1725; Nichols paper, 'Russian Shipping Position after the War' 15 March 1943 ADM223/506; Churchill to Attlee 1 February 1943 FO954/22A.

106 MEW paper 20 October 1943 FO371/36951/N6487.

107 Wilgress despatch 23 June 1944 (suggesting the standard of living could be returned to the 1938–40 level in three years, with German help) and Enemy Branch comments (replacement of livestock and repair of capital depreciation would take much longer) 21 September 1944 FO371/43329/N5080.

108 PHP(44)13(O)(F) 6 June 1944 CAB81/45.

109 JIC(44)366(O)(F) 22 August 1944 'Russian Capabilities in Relation to the Strategic Interests of the British Commonwealth' CAB81/124.

110 Wilson to FO 28 February 1943 FO371/36946/N1514; SBNO Black Sea report 4 January 1943 WO208/1750; J. Barber and M. Harrison, *The Soviet Home Front 1941–1945* (London, 1991), 172–3.

111 Lambert minute 3 February 1943, Wilson to Dew 22 February 1943 FO371/36946/N1418, N1516; Hubbard (Bank of England) to Skaife 19 January 1943 FO371/36944/N504.

112 Skaife minute 12 August 1942 FO371/32989/N3820; Clanchy (NID16), by contrast saw the Soviet Government to be skilful in keeping the people ignorant of high standards of living and freedom in the outside world, brief for Waldock c20 February 1943 ADM199/604.

113 Skaife paper 5 July 1942 FO371/32989/N3515; Lockhart memorandum 'Russia and the Allied Governments' 9 August 1943 FO371/36992/N4531: Stalin's aim was 'to give every Russian a dinner jacket and a white shirt'.

114 Skaife minute 12 August 1942 FO371/32989/N3820.

115 Warner to Vickers 10 July 1942, Vickers to Warner 20 July 1942 FO371/32989/N3515, N3820.

116 Wilson minute that the USSR would try to get what it wanted from Germany, free of charge 27 July 1942, Jebb minute 31 July 1942 FO371/32989/N3820.

117 Wilson draft telegram 27 August 1942, Warner to Dew 10 September 1942 FO371/32989/N3820. Warner found the discussion 'interesting', but allowed it to lapse.

118 Committee on Post-War Trade With Russia, 1st meeting 15 September 1943 FO371/36983/N5470; Ismay to Casey 14 March 1944 Ismay/IV/Cas.

119 Wilgress despatches 9 March 1944 FO371/43413/N398, 23 June 1944, Warner minutes 10 September 1944 FO371/43329/N5080 and 29 July 1944 FO371/40741A/U6792; K.G. Ross, *The Foreign Office and the Kremlin* (Cambridge, 1984), 43.

120 WP(44)436 (CAB66/53) described an 'ardent desire to resume rapidly their interrupted programme of internal development'. Rehabilitation/ development would take at least five years.

121 Hill report 13 February 1944 FO371/43314/N1910; Political Review 4 December 1944 FO371/43449/N7946; British personnel's experiences with the NKVD reinforced the impression given from occasional glimpses of the Soviet penal system, Reed to Dew 17 March 1943 FO371/36945/ N1840; Dew minute 12 April 1943 FO371/36946/N2172. Berthoud estimated there were between 7 and 15 million in labour camps, to Warner 4 February 1942 FO371/32920/N1235.

Chapter 4

1 'We live in a world of wolves – and bears', Churchill said, Colville diary 4 March 1944; Clark Kerr despatch 27 March 1945 FO371/47941/ N3934.

2 Archer diary 23 January 1945, Archer papers, IWM; Cadogan diary 11 February 1945; Eden to Cadogan 5 January 1945 FO954/22B.

3 Warner minute 12 November 1941 FO371/29471/N6540; Jebb minute 5 February 1943 FO371/35396/U2329; Eden to Halifax 2 tels 10 February 1942 FO371/32875/N798.

4 Birse, *Memoirs*, 103; Q. Reynolds, *Only the Stars Are Neutral* (London, 1943), 76; Kitchen, *British Policy*, 77, 235; Harriman and Abel, *Special Envoy*, 266.

5 Churchill statement, 8 September 1942 Hansard, *House of Commons Debates* vol. 383 col. 95; Jones, *Russia Complex*, 68; Macfarlane recollected 'my admiration for his amazing and unusual qualities grew with every month I spent in the Soviet Union', paper 'Russian Artillery 1941–45', Macfarlane/1,22; Brooke 'Notes On My Life' on diary, 28 November 1943.

6 Baggallay to FO 28 February 1942 FO371/32876/N1155; Clark Kerr to FO 14 June 1943 FO954/26A; Balfour to Warner 16 January 1945 FO371/ 47860/N3013.

7 Eden to Churchill 8 November 1943 Ismay/IV/Avo; J. Haslam, 'Stalin's Fears of a Separate Peace, 1942', *Intelligence and National Security*, 8 (1993), 98–9; C. Andrew and O. Gordievsky, *KGB. The Inside Story of its Foreign Operations from Lenin to Gorbachev* (London, 1990), 239.

8 Eden to Halifax 22 January 1942 FO954/29; Lockhart memorandum 23 February 1942 BBK D/96; Cripps speech, Grand Hotel, Bristol in

The Times 10 February 1942. Eden wrote in 1941 that Stalin was 'the true lineal descendant of Chenghiz [*sic*] Khan and the early Tsars', minute 24 January 1941 FO371/29500/N367.

9 Churchill to Eden 16 January 1944 PREM3/399/6; Clark Kerr to Warner 14 August 1943 FO800/301.

10 Warner minute 2 December 1944 FO371/43336/N7650; Eden to Churchill 29 October 1943, Clark Kerr to FO 8 November 1943 FO371/36957/ N6353, N6646.

11 Stalin remarks to Eden on propaganda role of Free German Committee 21 October 1943 FO371/37030/N6262; Clark Kerr to FO 11 August 1944 PREM3/355; Warner minute 31 May 1944 FO371/43305/N3246.

12 Dalton diary 13 January 1942. O'Malley tried to link the domestic tyranny with foreign policy, but received short shrift in the FO, despatch 30 April 1943 and minutes thereon FO371/35261/U2011.

13 Churchill statement, 8 September 1942 Hansard, *Debates* 383/95. Attlee wrote, 'Molotov's smile never seemed to go beyond his lips, but Stalin had a lively sense of humour', Attlee, *As It Happened* (London, 1964), 147; Dalton diary 13 January 1942; Ismay diary 27 October 1943 Ismay/ III/5; Clark Kerr to Cripps 26 April 1942 FO800/300; W. Strang, *Home and Abroad* (London, 1956), 159, 165.

14 Rendel to Warner 17 October 1944 FO371/43317/N6589; Clark Kerr to Cadogan 21 August 1942 PREM3/76A/10; Eden to Churchill 31 January 1944 PREM3/396/11.

15 Clark Kerr to FO 29 February 1942 FO181/964/10; Clark Kerr 'Bracelet' diary 16 August 1942 FO800/300.

16 T. Paterson, *On Every Front* (New York, 1979), 162–8.

17 Collier minute 6 February 1941 FO371/29498/N426; Cripps to FO 26 January 1941 FO954/24B.

18 Churchill to Roosevelt 5 November 1944 FO954/26B; Macfarlane to DMI 22 September 1941 BBK D/90; Clark Kerr to FO 29 June 1942 FO371/32883/N3403; Cadogan minute 6 January 1942 FO371/32920/ N80.

19 Clark Kerr to FO 13 September 1943 FO954/26A; H. Macmillan, *War Diaries. The Mediterranean 1943–1945* (London, 1984), diary 29 November 1943, 26 March 1944.

20 Dew minute 15 May 1943 FO371/36948/N2791; Baggallay to FO 13 February 1942 FO371/32920/N899.

21 Warner minute 31 January 1942 FO371/32920/N500; Skaife to Embassy 26 January 1944 FO371/43310/N575; J. Balfour, *Not Too Correct an Aureole* (Salisbury, 1983), 93–4.

22 Postan to Cavendish-Bentinck 4 November 1941 FO371/29493/N6465; Naval Mission diary 8 December 1941 ADM199/1102; Baggallay to FO 13 February 1942 FO371/32920/N899, N900.

23 Nichols to Warner 8 March 1943, Clark Kerr despatch 16 March 1943 FO371/36946/N1464, N1862; Warner minute 2 December 1944 FO371/ 43336/N7650.

24 Cripps to FO 30 June 1941, FO to Cripps 1 July 1941 FO371/29485/ N3279, N3301.

25 Stalin said to Cripps on the completion of the mutual assistance

agreement that 'some Communist speakers in this country were speaking in a pro-German sense and this would enable him to put a stop to it', Cripps to FO 10 July 1941 FO371/29467/N3565.

26   Macfarlane to Dill 22 November 1941 FO371/29471/N6749; Macfarlane to Brooke 22 December 1941 WO216/124.

27   Cripps to FO 23 September 1941 FO371/29490/N5542.

28   Eden to FO 18 December 1941 FO371/29472/N7013.

29   Clark Kerr 'Bracelet' diary 14 August 1942 FO800/300.

30   Churchill to Attlee 14 August 1942 FO800/300; Colville diary 11 September 1941; Jacob diary 13 August 1942 in C. Richardson, *From Churchill's Secret Circle to the BBC* (London, 1991).

31   Churchill to Roosevelt 24 October 1942 FO954/25B, wondering if anything had occurred 'inside the Soviet animal to make it impossible for Stalin to give an effective reply', and whether the Red Army had gained a more powerful position in the Soviet machine.

32   Original Warner minute (pasted over) 1 December 1942 FO371/32923/N6068; Dew minute 11 November 1942 FO371/32918/N5882.

33   FO memorandum 29 December 1942 FO371/36954/N66.

34   Wilson conversation with Maisky 4 February 1943, Dew minute 4 February 1943, Clark Kerr to FO 12 April 1943 and 16 April 1943 FO371/36954/N872, N2227.

35   JIC(42)58th 1 December 1942 FO371/32990/N6195. Clark Kerr said, 'Stalin was our friend, Molotov our enemy.' COS(42)346th 15 December 1942 CAB79/87.

36   Churchill to Eden 18 March 1943 FO954/26A. Later in the year, Churchill wrote to Roosevelt regarding an insulting telegram from Stalin; 'I think, or at least hope, that this message came from the machine rather than Stalin as it took twelve days to prepare. The Soviet machine is quite convinced it can get everything by bullying.' Clark Kerr had suggested this: 'I fancy I see more of Molotov's hand than of his in the reply . . .' Clark Kerr to FO 14 October 1943, Churchill to Roosevelt 16 October 1943 FO954/26A.

37   Reed to Dew 2 April 1943 FO371/36954/N2135.

38   Clanchy to Waldock c20 February 1943, Rushbrooke minute 15 September 1943 ADM199/604.

39   Wilson memorandum (revise) 26 May 1944 FO371/43305/N3554.

40   Churchill to Attlee 17 October 1944 PREM3/355/13.

41   S.R. Lieberman, 'Crisis Management in the USSR: the Wartime System of Administration and Control', in Linz, ed., *Impact*, 62–3, M. Djilas, *Conversations with Stalin* (London, 1962), 69; A. Filitov, 'The Soviet Union and the Grand Alliance: the Internal Dimension of Foreign Policy', in G. Gorodetsky, ed., *Soviet Foreign Policy, 1917–1991. A Retrospective* (London, 1994), 99.

42   WP(42)48 28 January 1942 'Policy Towards Russia' FO371/32875/N563; FO aide mémoire for Winant 25 February 1942 CAB127/75; FO paper 'The Four Power Plan' 8 November 1942 FO371/31525/U742.

43   MSC memo 'The United Nations Plan' 10 March 1943 FO371/35396/U1158; Wilson minute 29 May 1944 FO371/43305/N3246; Lockhart memo 9 August 1943 FO371/36992/N4531.

44 Dew minute 30 April 1942 FO371/32880/N2221; British plans centred on the self-denying ordinance first suggested by Eden to Molotov, 7th meeting with Soviet delegation 9 June 1942 FO371/32882/N3000. For a summary of developments on this subject, see Eden to Clark Kerr 11 July 1943. FO371/36955/N4006.

45 Eden to Clark Kerr 4 February 1943, Clark Kerr to FO 25 February 1943, Churchill to Eden 26 February 1943, Eden to Churchill 1 March 1943 FO371/35338/U321, U888.

46 Jebb minute 10 May 1943 FO371/35261/U2011; Warner minute 24 September 1943 FO371/36992/N6007; Dew minute 15 October 1943 FO371/37031/N6851.

47 Dixon memorandum 30 March 1942 FO371/32879/N1946; minutes in FO371/35261/U2011; Rothwell, *Britain*, 194.

48 Eden note 10 February 1944 FO371/35396/U867, minute 3 April 1944 FO371/43304/N1908; Cadogan minute 20 October 1943 FO371/37031/N6851.

49 Baggallay to Warner 25 November 1942 FO181/966/21; Warner minute 5 April 1944 FO371/43335/N2652; Sumner paper 'The USSR and the Principles of the Atlantic Charter and of the Four Freedoms' 3 February 1944 FO371/43332/N744.

50 Political Review 9 March 1942 FO371/33026/N3996; FRPS paper 'The USSR and the European Powers' 10 May 1943 FO371/37017/N2979; WP(42)516 8 November 1942 FO371/31525/U742; Eden to Churchill 19 August 1943 FO371/36992/N5060.

51 Harvey diary 11 November 1941; Baggallay despatch 11 February 1942; FO490/1; Memorandum on Soviet Frontiers 23 August 1943 FO371/36992/N5060; Eden conversation with Stalin 21 October 1943, Eden to Churchill 22 October 1944 FO371/37030/N6262; Sargent minute 19 October 1943 FO371/37031/N6851.

52 Cripps to FO 15 November 1941 FO371/29471/N6605; Lockhart memorandum 16 March 1942 BBK D/96; Lambert memorandum 5 August 1942 FO181/966/13; Baggallay to Cadogan 14 December 1942 FO954/25B; Cadogan minute 19 January 1943 FO371/36958/N250.

53 Sargent minute 14 November 1941, Warner minute 23 November 1941 FO371/29422/N6510, N7503.

54 SOE AD/3 to AD 10 May 1942 HS4/327; Warner to Clark Kerr 5 February 1943 FO371/36954/N872; Maisky conversation with Eden 31 August 1943 FO371/36956/N4977. The left-wing press gave support to such views, e.g. *Tribune*'s open letter to Stalin 23 October 1942.

55 WM(42)lstCA 1 January 1942 CAB65/29; Dalton diary 13 January 1942; Eden to Churchill 6 March 1942 FO371/32877/N1174; Winant to Hull 10 January 1942 *FRUS1942*:III, 492.

56 Churchill to Eden 8 January 1942 FO371/32874/N108; Halifax conversation with Welles 18 February 1942 RG59 741.6111/5 1/7.

57 Beaverbrook papers 'Controversy Over Russia' 3 March 1942 FO954/25A and WP(42)71 'Russia' 18 February 1942 CABl27/329; WM(42)l7thCA 6 February 1942 CAB65/29, WM(42)18th 9 February 1942 CAB65/25.

58 Brooke diary 12 October 1941.

59 Attlee at the 6 February 1942 Cabinet meeting described recognition

as 'wrong and inexpedient' WM(42)17thCA CAB65/29. Biddle memorandum of Bevin views 20 February 1942 RG59 740.00119/1047; K. Harris, *Attlee* (London, 1982), 197.

60 Cadogan diary 24 February 1942, minute 7 February 1942 FO371/32905/ N885; Cavendish-Bentinck minute 6 May 1942 FO371/32881/N2524.

61 Dew minute 14 March 1942 FO371/32877/N1364; WM(42)24thCA 25 February 1942 CAB65/29: 'there was no doubt that Russia regarded the United Kingdom as of greatest importance from the point of view of the post-war settlement in Europe and wanted to work with us after the war'.

62 Harvey diary 18 December 1941; Wilson minute 14 January 1943 FO371/ 36958/N250.

63 Eden minute 11 November 1942 FO371/32884/N5608. Emphasis in original.

64 Sargent minute 4 March 1942 FO371/32876/N1155; Warner minute 28 February 1942 FO371/32877/N1226; Harvey diary 16 May 1942.

65 Wilson to Clark Kerr 15 May 1944 FO800/302; Standley account of Clark Kerr views 8 August 1943 *FRUS1943*:II, 347; Birse, *Memoirs*, 138; cf. Rothwell, *Britain*, 104.

66 FO meeting 19 November 1941 FO371/29015/W13829; Eden to Churchill 12 July 1942 FO954/25B; Eden to Churchill 2 November 1943 FO954/ 26A; Cavendish-Bentinck minute 16 December 1943 FO371/36970/N7241; Kitchen, *British Policy*, 163.

67 Cripps to FO 19 April 1941 FO371/29465/N1725.

68 WP(42)48 28 January 1942 FO371/32875/N563; Warner minute 16 February 1942 FO371/32876/N827.

69 Lockhart memorandum 23 February 1942 BBK D/96, diary 10 March 1942, 4 April 1942. Similarly, SOE's Soviet section noted the Soviet desire for acceptance as a civilised country, D/P.1 to D/HV 26 May 1942 HS4/327.

70 FO to Halifax 26 March 1942 FO371/32878/N1653.

71 Clark Kerr to Warner 10 August 1943 FO800/301; Clark Kerr to Warner 28 August 1943 FO371/36956/N4929.

72 Eden conversation with Maisky 31 August 1943 FO371/36956/N4977.

73 Dew minute 30 August 1943, Warner minute 30 August 1943 FO371/ 36956/N4929.

74 Clark Kerr to Warner 10 August 1943 FO800/301; Clark Kerr to FO 5 November 1943 FO371/37031/N6575.

75 Dew minute 15 October 1943 FO371/37031/N6851.

76 Clark Kerr to FO 5 November 1943 FO371/37031/N6575; Eden to Churchill 2 November 1943 FO954/26A.

77 Wilson letter to Clark Kerr 19 March 1944 FO800/302. Earlier, Pownall had noted the importance of remembering the Soviets were 'Oriental not old Etonians', diary 17 August 1941: the phrase was a useful shorthand to distinguish the two cultures.

78 Wilson paper 24 April 1944, to Clark Kerr 15 May 1944 FO800/302.

79 Sargent minute 1 April 1944, Eden minute 3 April 1944 FO371/43304/ N1908; Eden to Churchill 9 May 1944 FO371/43636/R7380.

80 Clark Kerr despatch 31 August 1944 FO371/43336/N5598.

81 Clark Kerr to FO 15 September 1944 FO371/44713/U7393.

82 Clark Kerr to Eden 25 September 1944 FO800/302.

83 Sargent to Eden 30 August 1944, 26 September 1944 FO371/43306/ N5126, N6124; Political Review 4 December 1944 FO371/43449/N7946.

84 Dew minute 9 November 1942 FO371/32884/N5608.

85 Lockhart memorandum 23 February 1942 BBK D/96, Stalin Order 23 February 1942 FO371/32920/N1121.

86 Baggallay to FO 28 February 1942 FO371/32876/N1155.

87 Sargent minute 4 March 1942 FO371/32876/N1155, memorandum 5 February 1942 FO371/32905/N885.

88 FO to Halifax 10 February 1942 FO371/32875/N798; FO to Halifax 7 March 1942 FO371/32877/N1174.

89 Sargent minute 9 March 1942 FO371/32877/N1279; Roberts minute 28 March 1942 FO371/32879/N1910; Harvey diary 26 May 1942.

90 Sargent minute 14 May 1942 FO371/32881/N2152; WM(42)134th 6 October 1942 CAB65/28; JIC(42)58th 1 December 1942 FO371/32920/ N6195; Lockhart diary 10 December 1942; Dew minute 14 August 1943 FO371/36955/N4591; Cripps to Eden 10 August 1943 FO371/36992/N4717.

91 Jebb minute 13 June 1943 FO371/36983/N3547; Warner to Clark Kerr 28 September 1943 FO800/301; Dew minute 15 October 1943 FO371/ 37031/N6851.

92 Roberts minute 20 May 1944, Jebb minute 28 May 1944 FO371/40691/ U3704.

93 Sargent minute 1 April 1944 FO371/43304/N1908; Hull to Harriman 15 January 1944, 22 January 1944 *FRUS1944*:III, 1229, 1234.

94 Warner minute 24 May 1943, Strang minute 29 May 1943 FO371/ 35261/U2011; Eden memorandum 23 August 1943 FO371/36992/N5060; FO-MSC meeting 23 June 1943 FO371/35407/N2937.

95 JP(42)354 3 April 1942 CAB84/44 considered North Atlantic security in terms only of a German threat, because of the imminent treaty; the N. Dept requested that they consider a Soviet threat too, Somers Cocks minute 7 April 1942, to Howkins 14 April 1942 FO371/32832/ N1806, Howkins to Scott 13 May 1942 CAB119/65.

96 Ronald minute 23 April 1942 FO371/32482/W5996; Payne to Ronald 19 February 1942 FO371/32423/W3003; Howkins to Ismay 4 June 1942 CAB119/64. The MSC comprised Brigadier van Cutsem, Rear-Admiral Bellairs and Spaight (Air Ministry official).

97 The three from the MSC were joined by Air Vice-Marshal Longmore, Major-General Grove-White and Waldock (Naval Secretary, Admiralty) to form the PHPS/c. Jebb was Chairman, partly because none of the services would accept a member of another as Chairman, and partly because the FO were anxious to influence proceedings: Le Mesurier note 25 June 1943 CAB119/64; COS(43)199(F) 25 July 1943, DoP meeting 9 April 1943, Jebb to Cadogan 12 May 1943 FO371/35449/U3151, U2232, U2235.

98 Hollis to Sargent 23 September 1943 FO371/36992/N6007.

99 COS(43)364(O) 5 July 1943 CAB80/71; COS(43)569(O) 22 September 1943 CAB80/75; Lambert note of PHP(43)4th 16 August 1943 FO371/ 35449/U3151; JP(43)283(F) 24 August 1943 CAB84/55.

100 FO-MSC meeting 23 June 1943 FO371/35407/U2937.
101 Sargent minute 31 January 1944 FO371/43335/N1008; JIC(44)105(O) 20 March 1944 CAB81/121.
102 Ward minute 25 February 1944, Le Mesurier to Ward 5 April 1944 FO371/43384/N2292, N2293.
103 WP(42)48 28 January 1942 FO371/32874/N563; Dew minute 22 February 1942, Warner minute 2 March 1942 FO371/32876/N1023, N1156; Eden to Churchill 6 March 1942, Sargent minute 9 March 1942 FO371/ 32877/N1174; WM(42)lstCA 1 January 1942, 24thCA 25 February 1942 CAB65/29; Eden minute 8 February 1942 FO371/32905/N885.
104 Baggallay to FO (3 telegrams) 11 February 1942, 20 February 1942 FO371/ 32876/N927, N1023; D. Glantz and J. House, *When Titans Clashed. How the Red Army Stopped Hitler* (Kansas, 1995), 97, 106.
105 Warner minute 16 February 1942 FO371/32876/N927.
106 Lockhart memorandum 23 February 1942 BBK D/96; Lockhart diary 10 March 1942, 4 April 1942. Few of the secondary sources recognise Lockhart's influence: an exception (for 1945) is J. Zametica, 'Three Letters to Bevin: Frank Roberts at the Moscow Embassy, 1945–46', in idem, ed., *British Officials and British Foreign Policy, 1945–50* (Leicester, 1990), 45.
107 Sargent memorandum 'A Possible Development of the Russo-German War' 5 February 1942 FO371/32905/N885.
108 Lockhart minute 20 February 1942 FO371/32876/N927; Lockhart minute to Sargent 8 March 1942 FO371/32877/N1439; Lockhart paper 16 March 1942 BBK D/96. Differences between Sargent (who followed Lockhart) and Cadogan were shown in Cadogan's modifications of Sargent's draft telegrams to Halifax, Cadogan diary 23, 24, 25 March 1942. For Lockhart's view of the split in the FO between the Cadogan and Sargent approaches, see diary 13 April 1943.
109 The concession was described to Halifax as a timely gesture showing British sympathy, WM(42)37th 25 March 1942, FO to Halifax 26 March 1942 CAB65/29; Churchill to Roosevelt 7 March 1942 FO371/32877/ N1174.
110 Warner minute ud. March 1942 FO371/32876/N927.
111 Winant to Hull 23 June 1942 RG59 741.6111/29; Beaverbrook to Liddell Hart 11 June 1942 LHII/1942; FO to Halifax 29 May 1942 FO371/32881/ N2746; WM(42)68thCA 26 May 1942 CAB65/30. The Treaty was a shock to Molotov too. He told Stalin the British draft (which omitted any mention of frontiers) was 'unacceptable, as it is an empty declaration which the USSR does not need.' Stalin replied, 'We do not consider it an empty declaration but regard it as an important document. It lacks the question of the security of frontiers, but this is not bad perhaps, for it gives us a free hand. The question of frontiers, or to be more exact, of guarantees for the security of our frontiers ... will be decided by force.' Molotov to Moscow 24 May 1942, Stalin to Molotov 24 May 1942 in O.A. Rzheshevsky, *War and Diplomacy. The Making of the Grand Alliance. From Stalin's Archives* (trans. T. Sorokina, Amsterdam, 1996).
112 Harvey diary 26 October 1942; WM(42)145thCA 26 October 1942 CAB65/

32; Eden minute 11 November 1942 FO371/32884/N5608. The suspension of convoys to northern Russia was extended so that shipping could be diverted to the landings in North Africa in November 1942.

113 Dew minute 'New Soviet Party Line on Foreign Policy to Allies' 11 November 1942 FO371/32918/N5882.

114 FO circular, by Warner, 29 December 1942: even Cadogan saw this as an important moment, enjoining franker and closer cooperation by British representatives with Soviet colleagues, minute 23 December 1942 FO371/36954/N66.

115 FO paper 20 October 1942 FO371/31525/U742; WM(42)161st 27 November 1942 CAB65/28.

116 Gladwyn, *Memoirs*, 115.

117 Warner minute 9 May 1942 FO371/32880/N2221, paper 'Russian Participation in Allied Economic Machinery' 19 May 1942 FO371/32881/N2638, draft for interview with Ellis Smith MP, 8 November 1942 FO371/32885/N6539

118 Cavendish-Bentinck minute 16 October 1943, Sargent minute 19 October 1943, Cadogan minute 20 October 1943 FO371/37031/N6851, Eden to Churchill 19 August 1943 FO371/36992/N5060. Eden told Hull the Soviets had only two policy choices, one based on three-power cooperation, one on isolation, note 23 August 1943 FO371/36992/N5060.

119 Clark Kerr to FO 14 June 1943, Eden lunch with Winant and Maisky 2 September 1943 FO954/26A; Sargent minute 5 July 1943 FO371/37045/N4905; FO to Moscow 18 September 1943 FO371/37028/N5413; Lockhart diary 12 August 1943; Harvey diary 24, 30 August 1943.

120 Eden to Churchill 24 October 1943, Cadogan to Halifax 4 November 1943 FO371/37030/N6263, N6447; 5th Moscow meeting 23 October 1943 FO371/37031/N6921.

121 Churchill to Attlee 14 August 1942, Churchill to Stalin 24 November 1942 FO954/25B; Gilbert, *Road to Victory*, 639; Churchill to Clark Kerr 2 May 1943, Churchill to Eden 31 July 1943 FO954/26A; Churchill to Eden 15 February 1944 and meeting with Mikolajczyk 16 February 1944 FO954/20.

122 FO meeting 23 June 1943 FO371/35407/U2837.

123 Ronald minute 8 June 1942 FO371/32429/W8466; Bevin at Jowitt Committee 1st meeting 31 March 1942 CAB87/2; Wilson minute 13 June 1943 FO371/36983/N3547.

124 Warner to Clark Kerr 8 July 1943, 29 September 1943 FO800/301; Churchill to Clark Kerr 16 June 1943 FO954/26A; Warner to Balfour 25 January 1944 FO800/302.

125 Warner to Clark Kerr 9 April 1943: the choice was 'appeasement' or the 'frank exchange of views as between allies' FO800/301; Clark Kerr to FO 30 July 1943 FO954/26A.

126 Warner to Clark Kerr 12 May 1943 FO800/301.

127 Warner minute 16 December 1943, Eden minute ud. September 1943, Martel to COS 26 September 1943 FO371/36970/N7241, N5349, N5680.

128 WM(43)32nd 18 February 1943 CAB65/33; NID16 report on Soviet Naval Mission 1 May 1943 FO371/36969/N2782; Martel to Brooke 9 October 1943, COS(43)729(O) 24 November 1943 FO371/36970/N5930, N7241;

Brooke diary 13 August 1942, 17 February 1943; Beaumont, *Comrades*, 114; idem, 'A Question of Diplomacy: Military Missions to the USSR, 1941–45', *Journal of the Royal United Services Institute for Defence Studies*, 118/3, (1973), 76–7; Nelson to Sargent 6 June 1942 HS4/327; Gillies, *Radical Diplomat*, 145.

129 Wilson minute 11 July 1943 FO371/36969/N3968; Lockhart diary 11 February 1943, 4 December 1943; Warner to Clark Kerr 12 May 1943, Clark Kerr to Warner 31 July 1943 FO800/301.

130 Lockhart diary 12 August 1943; Cadogan diary 18 October 1943.

131 Churchill to Eden 13 August 1942 FO954/25A, 29 June 1943 CAB120/683; Churchill to Drummond 1 December 1942 FO954/25B; WM(43)42ndCA 18 March 1943 CAB65/36.

132 WM(43)135thCA 5 October 1943 CAB65/40; Lambert minute 27 July 1943 FO371/36991/N4514; Harvey diary 24 August 1943; K. Sainsbury, 'British Policy and German Unity at the End of the Second World War', *English Historical Review*, 94 (1979), 797, 801.

133 WM(43)59th 27 April 1943, 63rd 3 May 1943 CAB65/34; Warner to Clark Kerr 28 May 1943 FO800/301; Gilbert, *Road to Victory*, 390, 664.

134 Balfour to FO 2 January 1944 FO371/43310/N62; Harvey diary 25 October 1943; WM(43)169thCA 13 December 1943 CAB65/40; Eden to Churchill 29 October 1943 FO371/36957/N6353; Cadogan to Halifax 4 November 1943 FO371/37030/N6447.

135 Warner memorandum on Moscow Conference 29 October 1943 FO371/37035/N6789.

136 WM(44)11thCA 25 January 1944 CAB65/45; Churchill to Eden 16 January 1944 PREM3/399/6. For the *Pravda* story, Beaverbrook to Churchill 24 January 1944, Eden minute 28 January 1944, Churchill to Stalin 24 January 1944 PREM3/396/11; cf. Hull to Harriman 15 January 1944 *FRUS1944*:III, 1229.

137 C. Kennedy-Pipe, *Stalin's Cold War. Soviet Strategies in Europe, 1943 to 1956* (Manchester 1995), 27–9, 35–6, 39, 42; W. Kimball, 'Stalingrad: A Chance for Choices', *Journal of Military History*, 60 (1996), 109; J. Erickson, 'Stalin, Soviet Strategy and the Grand Alliance', in Lane and Temperley, eds, *Grand Alliance*, 150; information supplied by V. Batyuk, Russian Academy of US and Canadian Studies.

Chapter 5

1 Sargent minute 31 April 1944 FO371/43335/N2832.

2 FO paper 'Probable Post-War Tendencies in Soviet Foreign Policy as Affecting British Interests' 29 April 1944 FO371/43335/N1008.

3 Wilson memorandum (revise) 26 May 1944 FO371/43305/N3554.

4 Comments on Wilgress despatch 9 March 1944 FO371/43335/N2652.

5 Warner minute 16 June 1944 FO371/43335/N3742; Warner to Ward 11 August 1944 FO371/40741A/U6875.

6 Duff Cooper despatch 30 May 1944 FO371/40696/U5407, Eden to Duff Cooper 25 July 1944 FO371/40701/U6543.

7 Jebb minute 18 June 1944, Harvey minute 25 June 1944 FO371/40696/U5407.

8 Sargent minute 30 June 1944, Eden minute 2 July 1944 FO371/40696/U5407.
9 FO paper 'Western Europe' 9 May 1944 FO371/40698/U6139; Jebb to Ronald 7 April 1944 FO371/43384/N2293.
10 FO paper 'British Policy Towards Europe' 22 May 1944 CAB21/1614.
11 FO to COS 14 June 1944 FO371/40740/U5908; Warner to Squire 9 June 1944, Warner to Peel 9 June 1944 FO371/43335/N2833, N3091; cf. Kitchen, *British Policy*, 216.
12 WM(44)43rd 3 April 1944 CAB65/46; Eden minute 3 April 1944 FO371/43304/N1908; Churchill to Eden 4 May 1944, Eden to Churchill 9 May 1944 FO371/43636/R7380; Gilbert, *Road to Victory*, 648, 651–2; Churchill to Eden 8 May 1944 FO954/20.
13 WP(44)304 7 June 1944 CAB66/51.
14 Cranborne to Eden 12 June 1944, Cadogan minute 19 June 1944, Eden minute 20 June 1944 FO371/43335/N4956.
15 WP(44)436 9 August 1944 CAB66/53.
16 PHP(43)1(O) 8 March 1944 FO371/43384/N1120, revised as PHP(44)13(O)(F) 'Effect of Soviet Policy on British Strategic Interests' 6 June 1944 CAB81/45; JIC(44)105(O)(F) 'Soviet Policy after the War' 20 March 1944 CAB81/121.
17 PHP(44)12(O) 'Draft Assumptions for PHPS Strategic Studies' 26 May 1944 FO371/40740/U4379.
18 PHP(44)20 'Air Defence of Great Britain' 2 May 1944 – subsequent drafts were even less certain of a ten-year threat-free period, PHP(44)20(F) 19 May 1944 FO371/40791/U3978, U4584.
19 Separation from other parts of the planning machinery meant the PHPS could make no assessment of British capabilities, A. Gorst, 'British Military Planning for Postwar Defence, 1943–45', in A. Deighton, ed., *Britain and the First Cold War* (London, 1990), 92. The new PHPS were Captain Allen RN, Brigadier Curtis and Air-Commodore Warburton, each in his early forties. They lacked the broader experience in armistice and control matters, and the internationalist tendencies of their predecessors. Jebb note 2 May 1944, Ismay to Cadogan 2 August 1944, FO371/40736/U3498, U6770; COS(44)249th(O) 27 July 1944 CAB79/78.
20 PHP(44)17(O)3rd Rev 20 October 1944 FO371/40741B/U7975.
21 Sterndale-Bennett's criticism of the south-east Asia paper PHP(44)6(O) 1 October 1944 could have applied to many of them; it gave the impression of being thrown together merely from the study of a map, without regard to political difficulties and realities, minute 10 October 1944 FO371/40741A/U7658.
22 Sloan minute 18 September 1944 FO371/40741A/U6875.
23 JIC(44)366(O)(F) 22 August 1944 'Russian Capabilities in Relation to the Strategic Interests of the British Commonwealth' CAB81/124.
24 PHP(44)16(O) 'Strategic Interests in the Middle East' 14 December 1944 FO371/40741B/U8672.
25 JIC(43)409(O) 2 October 1943 AIR40/2344, Portal at CCS113th mtg, 20 August 1943 *FR Washington & Quebec 1943*, 911.
26 COS(44)248th(O)CA 26 July 1944 CAB79/78; Jebb minute 7 June 1944, Warner minute 23 May 1944 FO371/40740/U6253, U4379; Cavendish-

Bentinck minute 18 July 1944, Jebb minute 25 July 1944 FO371/40741A/
U6791, U6792.

27   Warner minute 12 July 1944, Jebb to Cadogan 18 July 1944,
PHP(44)17(O)(F) 20 July 1944 FO371/40741A/U6283, U6791, U6792.

28   Hollis to Jebb 27 July 1944 FO371/40703/U6772; Jebb note of COS views
28 July 1944 FO371/40741A/U6793; Sargent to Eden 18 August 1944
FO371/43306/N5126.

29   Warburton to PHPS 31 July 1944, PHP(44)17(O)Revise 15 September
1944 FO371/40741A/U6793, U7618; Davison to Redman (BJSM) 27 July
1944 CAB122/1566; PHP(44)20(O) 'USSR – Questionnaire to JIC' 11 August
1944 CAB81/45.

30   PHP(44)15(O) 'The Dismemberment of Germany' 25 August 1944, Jebb
minute 27 October 1944 FO371/39080/C11955, C14995.

31   APW(44)90 'The Dismemberment of Germany' 20 September 1944,
Troutbeck minute 6 September 1944 FO371/39080/C13517, C11631.

32   Sargent minutes 30 August 1944, 26 September 1944 FO371/43306/N5126,
N6124; Sargent memorandum 4 October 1944 FO371/39080/C13518;
Lewis, *Changing Direction*, 131–2.

33   Sargent note following COS-Eden meeting 4 October 1944 FO371/39080/
C13518.

34   Portal at 4 October 1944 meeting FO371/43336/N6177; COS letter
2 October 1944 FO371/39080/C13517.

35   Ward minute 13 December 1944 FO371/40397/U8520.

36   COS(44)51st 17 February 1944, Jebb minute 19 February 1944 FO371/
40740/U1751.

37   COS-Eden meeting 4 October 1944 FO371/43336/N6177; COS(44)346th
(O)CA 24 October 1944 CAB79/82.

38   Warner minute 2 December 1944 FO371/43336/N7650; Warner minute
13 November 1944, Eden minute 16 November 1944 FO371/43317/N7046;
Balfour to Warner 16 January 1945 FO371/47860/N3013.

39   Clark Kerr despatch 31 August 1944 FO371/43336/N5598.

40   Lockhart diary 7 October 1944.

41   Sargent memorandum 2 April 1945 FO371/47881/N4281.

42   Wilson to Clark Kerr 3 October 1944 FO800/302.

43   Sargent minute 1 April 1944 FO371/43304/N1908; Sargent minute 2
September 1944 FO371/39410/C11277.

44   Jebb notes for political background for PHPS world survey 18 December
1944 FO371/40741B/U8523.

45   Cavendish-Bentinck, Warner notes on JIC(44)467(O) 18 December 1944
FO371/47860/N678.

46   JIC(44)467(O) 18 December 1944 FO371/47860/N678. The COS found
this paper sound though designated it as a 'staff study', not a definitive
COS statement of opinion, COS(44)411th(O) 27 December 1944 CAB79/
84; COS(45)29th 26 January 1945 CAB79/29; JP(44)278(F), COS(45)6th
4 January 1945 CAB79/28.

47   D. Richards, *Lord Portal of Hungerford* (London, 1977), 289, 297; Dalton
diary 2 February 1945; Martel, whose spell in Moscow had not been a
happy one, wrote, 'I quite agree that there may be danger, but my
whole feeling from close contact with them is that they will be con-

tent with being a bally nuisance in European affairs and nothing more than certain demands for warm water access which is reasonable enough', to Liddell Hart 3 September 1944 LHI/492.

48 WM(44)11thCA 25 January 1944 CAB65/45; Churchill to Clark Kerr 10 March 1944 FO954/20; Jones, *Russia Complex*, 78, 85, 95; Lee, *Churchill Coalition*, 160. There is no recorded discussion of WP(44)436.

49 Gilbert, *Road to Victory*, 501, 723, Churchill to Eden 10 July 1944 FO371/43636/R7903; Colville diary 8 October 1944.

50 Churchill to Roosevelt 1 April 1944 FO954/26B; Churchill to Eden 1 April 1944 FO371/43304/N1908; Gilbert, *Road to Victory*, 859, 988; Charmley, *Churchill*, 543.

51 WM(45)22nd 19 February 1945 CAB65/51; Harriman and Abel, *Special Envoy*, 161.

52 Moran diary 14 October 1944, in Moran, *Churchill. The Struggle for Survival, 1940–65* (London, 1966); Jacob to Hollis 17 October 1944 CAB127/34; Churchill to Attlee 18 October 1944 CAB120/165; WM(44)157thCA 27 November 1944, WM(44)164thCA 11 December 1944 CAB65/48.

53 Churchill to Attlee 18 October 1944 CAB120/165; Laskey (Southern Department) noted the percentages assumed Britain would have *some* influence in all the countries, for these were not separate zones, minute 23 October 1944 FO371/43636/R17490; R. Garson, 'Churchill's "Spheres of Influence": Rumania and Bulgaria', *Survey*, 24 (1979), 151, 157. Kimball and Mark have suggested Roosevelt was amenable to 'open spheres': Soviet control but not exclusion of the Allies, with coalition governments of 'anti-fascist' elements, and this seems equally to apply to Churchill between Moscow and Yalta, E. Mark, 'American Policy Toward Eastern Europe and the Origins of the Cold War, 1941–46: An Alternative Interpretation' *Journal of American History*, 68 (1981), 313–16, W. Kimball, *The Juggler. Franklin Roosevelt as Wartime Statesman* (Princeton, 1991), 169.

54 Gilbert, *Road to Victory*, 992–3, 1055, 1065, 1095; K.G. Ross, 'The Moscow Conference of October 1944 (Tolstoy)', in W. Deakin, E. Barker, and J. Chadwick, eds, *British Political and Military Strategy in Central, Eastern and Southern Europe in 1944* (London, 1988), 73– 6; J.M. Siracusa, 'The Meaning of Tolstoy: Churchill, Stalin and the Balkans, Moscow, October 1944', *Diplomatic History*, 3 (1979), 444; P. Holdich, 'A Policy of Percentages? British Policy and the Balkans after the Moscow Conference of October 1944', *International History Review*, 9 (1987), 33, 37, 42. As with the 'arrangement' regarding Greece and Romania in May, no agreement was actually finalised, nor definitions of 'influence' agreed, though the parties in many ways acted as if there was. On the other hand, it has been suggested that Stalin's famous blue tick was a sign of *disagreement*, for red was the colour he used to mark proposals from his subordinates that he agreed with, while he used blue to show that he did not: A.E. Titkov, 'Soyuzniki-soperniki (k istorii antigermanskovo soyuza SSSR's SShA i velikobritaniye v 1941–1945 g.)' in L.N. Nezhinski, ed., *Sovetskaya Vneshnyaia Politika 1917–1945 g. Poiski Novikh Podkhodov* (Moscow, 1992), 298–9. Certainly, the percentages were never discussed officially again. Similiarly, Tsakaloyannis suggests there is no evidence

that Soviet officers in Greece delivered any restraining orders to EAM,
P. Tsakaloyannis, 'The Moscow Puzzle', *Journal of Contemporary History*,
21 (1986), 45–52.

55 WM(43)172ndCA 20 December 1943 CAB65/40; Churchill conversation
with Stalin 1 December 1943 CAB120/113; Lockhart diary 6 January
1944; Eden note to Hull 23 August 1943 FO371/36992/N5060.

56 Cadogan to Churchill 31 March 1943 PREM3/354/8; Stalin's views, it
was said in Cabinet, 'might well be different from those of the Russian
FO' WM(44)11thCA 25 January 1944 CAB65/45.

57 Churchill to Eden 7 January 1944 PREM3/355/7; Gilbert, *Road to Victory*, 648; WM(44)15thCA 4 February 1944 CAB65/45.

58 WM(44)28thCA 6 March 1944 CAB65/45; Colville diary 18 March 1944;
Churchill to Eden 10 July 1944 FO371/43636/R7903; Barker, *Churchill
and Eden*, 278–81.

59 WM(44)108thCA 18 August 1944, 111thCA 28 August 1944 CAB65/47.
The CAS reported the military opinion that the Soviets were overextended
and genuinely unable to relieve the Poles in Warsaw.

60 Charmley, *Churchill*, 579; Jones, *Russia Complex*, 92; Dalton diary 30
August 1944, 6 September 1944; Burridge, *British Labour*, 144–9; Nicolson
diary 4 October 1944; Harvey diary 15 August 1944; Kitchen, *British
Policy*, 228, 231, cf. R. Edmonds, *The Big Three* (London, 1991), 384.

61 WM(44)123rdCA 18 September 1944 CAB65/47.

62 Eden to FO 14 October 1944 CAB120/165; Churchill, *Second World War*
vol. 6, 205; Churchill conversation with Mikolajczyk 14 October 1944,
Documents on Polish-Soviet Relations vol. 2 (London, 1967), 417.

63 WM(44)157thCA 27 November 1944 CAB65/48; N.A. Graebner, 'Yalta,
Potsdam and Beyond: the British and American Perspectives', in Lane
and Temperley, eds, *Grand Alliance*, 227.

64 Churchill to Eden 10 July 1944 FO371/43636/R7903; Churchill to Clark
Kerr 13 March 1944, Churchill to Roosevelt 19 May 1944 FO954/26B;
Churchill to Eden 28 May 1944 FO371/44001/R9078. On repatriation
of Soviet personnel captured with the Germans, a prime opportunity
for a firm stance, Churchill noted, 'I thought we had arranged to send
all the Russians back to Russia', Churchill to FO 28 October 1944 FO371/
40396/U8063.

65 Moran diary 30 October 1944, cf. Normanbrook and Colville comments
in Wheeler-Bennett, *Action This Day*, 28–37, 110; Charmley, *Churchill*,
577–8; Edmonds, *Big Three*, 363–6.

66 Churchill found the Soviets in practice to be more accommodating than
they wanted their allies to expect, in the hopes of gaining concessions,
WM(44)47thCA 11 April 1944 CAB65/46, and suggested to Roosevelt
that the 'Soviet bark may be worse than its bite', 1 April 1944 FO954/26B;
WM(44)63rdCA 11 May 1944 CAB65/46; Gilbert, *Road to Victory*, 754.

67 Eden found Churchill's interventions in foreign policy to be 'romantic
improvisations', and blamed Beaverbrook and Cherwell, Charmley,
Churchill, 605; Lockhart diary 10 November 1944; Eden to Cadogan
5 January 1945 FO954/22B; Churchill to Eden 8 February 1945 FO371/
50826/U1900.

68 Warner to Balfour 25 January 1944 FO800/302; for Churchill's mood

swings, see for instance his comments at WM(44)63rdCA 11 May 1944 compared to those at WM(44)47thCA 11 April 1944 CAB65/46. Churchill noted the Soviet leaders' own swings; after a rude message they often did what had been asked, to Roosevelt 19 May 1944 FO954/26B.

69 For an example of how historians have had to resort to speculation on this, see T.D. Burridge, *Clement Attlee: A Political Biography* (London, 1985), 172–3.

70 Lee, *Churchill Coalition*, 142–3; Sainsbury, 'British', 788; Dalton diary 19 July 1944.

71 Dalton diary 1 November 1943. Attlee did give some support to the two schools argument, Attlee to Churchill 25 August 1943 CAB120/113. Dalton had in 1939 seen the Soviets to have passed from being Communists to Nationalists then Imperialists, diary 18 October 1939.

72 'Notes on Post-War Problems' ud 1944–45 Attlee papers, Churchill College ATLE1/24; Ede diary 10 April 1945, in K. Jeffreys, ed., *Labour and the Wartime Coalition. From the Diaries of James Chuter Ede, 1941–45* (London, 1987).

73 Dalton diary 5 January 1943.

74 Harris, *Attlee*, 213, Burridge, *British Labour*, 169.

75 Attlee minute 26 January 1944 PREM3/197/2; Harris, *Attlee*, 210, 213; Bevin to Cranborne 1 February 1945 Bevin papers, Churchill College BEV3/1; Rothwell, *Britain*, 225–6, 228; Bevin at WM(45)7thCA 22 January 1945 CAB65/51, for a bizarre 'therapeutic trust' suggestion about Lvov.

76 Dalton diary 5 January 1943, 5 May 1944; Pimlott, *Dalton*, 389; J.T. Grantham, 'Hugh Dalton and the International Postwar Settlement: Labour Party Foreign Policy Formulation, 1943–44' *Journal of Contemporary History*, 14 (1979), 715.

77 WM(45)10thCA 26 January 1945 CAB65/51; F. Harbutt, *The Iron Curtain. Churchill. America and the Origins of the Cold War* (New York, 1986), 122–3; Dalton diary 13 July 1944; Burridge, *British Labour*, 149.

78 Jones, *Russia Complex*, 89; Burridge, *Attlee*, 168.

79 CM(47)15th 3 February 1947 CAB128/9; Attlee to Bevin 5 January 1947 FO800/502; Bevin minute 5 March 1948 FO800/452; R. Smith, 'A Climate of Opinion: British Officials and the Development of British Soviet Policy, 1945–7', *International Affairs*, 64 (1988), 646–7; Zametica, 'Three Letters', 90. Even in the changed atmosphere of 1947, in a paper wherein he described the objective of the Soviet leaders as the organisation of World Revolution, Jebb saw them having earlier been groping for a policy of cooperation, which was then impeded by the Atomic Bomb, Jebb paper 'Stocktaking II' 19 March 1947 FO371/67587C/UN2622.

80 R. Smith and J. Zametica, 'The Cold Warrior: Clement Attlee Reconsidered', *International Affairs*, 61 (1985), 248–9.

Chapter 6

1 Gilbert, *Road to Victory*, 1350.

2 Cadogan to Mrs Cadogan 20 February 1945 in Dilks, ed., *Diaries*; Dalton

diary 23 February 1945, 12 March 1945; British Yalta Conference Records 9 February 1945 CAB99/31; Dixon diary 6 February 1945, 13 February 1945, in P. Dixon. ed., *Double Diploma. The Life of Sir Pierson Dixon* (London, 1968); Harvey diary 14 February 1945. Portal wrote, 'U.J. is the goods – sincere, simple and big . . .', Richards, *Portal*, 289.

3 Dalton diary 23 February 1945; Colville diary 23 February 1945; Moran diary 6 February 1945, 9 February 1945, 19 July 1945, 6 September 1945; WM(45)22ndCA 19 February 1945 CAB65/51; Kitchen, *British Policy*, 243, 248, 250–1, 267; Gilbert, *Road to Victory*, 1231, 1254, 1261.

4 Balfour to Warner 16 January 1945, JIC(44)467(O) 18 December 1944 FO371/47860/N3013, N678.

5 Balfour to Warner 30 May 1945 FO371/47862/N6417; Macmillan to FO 21 March 1945 FO371/47941/N3097; F.K. Roberts, *Dealing with Dictators* (London, 1991), 90.

6 Clark Kerr to Warner 21 June 1945 FO371/47862/N6417.

7 Sargent to Churchill 2 May 1945 PREM3/396/12.

8 Roberts to Warner 25 April 1945 FO371/47854/N8096.

9 Kennan paper, 'Russia Seven Years Later' ud September 1944 FO800/302; Yergin, *Shattered Peace*, 78; Russell note 19 June 1945 FO371/47883/N7909.

10 Roberts to Warner 25 April 1945 FO371/47882/N4919.

11 Galsworthy minute 4 July 1945, Brimelow minute 5 July 1945 FO371/47883/N7909; V. Mastny, *Russia's Road to the Cold War. Diplomacy, Warfare and the Politics of Communism, 1941–45* (New York, 1979), 260.

12 Sargent paper, 'Stocktaking after VE Day' 11 July 1945 FO371/50912/U5471; Churchill speech 16 August 1945, Hansard, *Debates*, 413/84.

13 Roberts to Warner 30 April 1945 FO371/47854/N8096; Roberts despatch 24 May 1945 FO371/47923/N6582.

14 Roberts to Warner 25 April 1945 FO371/47882/N4919.

15 Ward minute 11 June 1945 FO371/50826/U4283.

16 Comments on political forecast 5 February 1945 FO371/50774/U1080.

17 PHP(45)29(O) 'Security of the British Empire' 29 June 1945 CAB81/46.

18 Sargent paper 11 July 1945 FO371/50912/U5471.

19 Lockhart memorandum 11 April 1945 FO371/47860/N4102.

20 N. Dept draft of section 7 of Harvey to Peterson 4 July 1945 FO371/50826/U4283; Dixon draft of paper 'Questions at issue with the Soviet Government' 17 May 1945 FO371/48192/R9256.

21 Roberts to Harvey 24 July 1945 FO371/50826/U5786.

22 Cadogan minute 11 July 1945 FO371/50912/U5471; see Overy, *Russia's War*, 237–40.

23 JIC(44)467(O) 18 December 1944 FO371/47860/N678, and see COS(45)175th 12 July 1945, JP(45)170(F) 11 July 1945 CAB79/36.

24 Churchill minute 5 March 1945 FO954/23; Churchill to Roosevelt 8 March 1945, W. Kimball, ed., *Churchill and Roosevelt. Their Complete Correspondence*, vol. 3 (Princeton, 1984) 547; Nicolson diary 27 February 1945; FO to Halifax 28 May 1945 FO371/48192/R9256; Kitchen, *British Policy*, 254–5.

25 Stewart minute 23 April 1945 FO371/48192/R7333.

26 FO paper 20 July 1945 FO371/47964/N10036; Eden to Churchill 24 March

1945 FO954/26C; Sargent minute 2 June 1945 FO371/47882/N6141.

27 Williams minute 28 April 1945 FO371/48192/R7333; Boswall to FO 29 June 1945 FO371/48219/R11159; Kitchen, *British Policy*, 255–7; McLynn, *Maclean*, 203; Churchill told the Commons on 18 January 1945 that an understanding had been reached with Stalin on joint wartime policy, Hansard, *Debates*, 407/398–9.

28 Warner note on Lockhart memorandum 11 April 1945 FO371/47860/N4102; Sargent memorandum 'Policy Towards the Soviet Union' 2 April 1945 FO371/47881/N4281.

29 Galsworthy minute 4 July 1945, Stewart minute 12 July 1945 FO371/47883/N7909.

30 Sargent paper, 'Stocktaking' revise 31 July 1945 FO371/50912/U5471.

31 Sargent memorandum 13 March 1945 FO371/48192/R7333.

32 Roberts to Harvey 24 July 1945 FO371/50826/U5786; Roberts despatch 24 May 1945 FO371/47923/N6582.

33 Clark Kerr to FO 7 June 1945, Stewart minute 9 June 1945 FO371/48192/R9818.

34 Sargent paper, 'Stocktaking' revise 31 July 1945 FO371/50912/U5471.

35 Cranborne to Eden 26 March 1945, Eden to Cranborne 28 March 1945 FO954/22B; Eden to Churchill 24 March 1945 FO954/26C.

36 W. Miscamble, 'Anthony Eden and the Truman–Molotov Conversations, April 1945' *Diplomatic History* 2 (1978), 169–76.

37 Eden to Churchill 17 July 1945 FO954/26C.

38 Clark Kerr to FO 6 April 1945 FO371/47881/N3745.

39 FO to Clark Kerr 8 April 1945 FO371/47881/N3745.

40 Roberts to Warner 30 June 1945, Warner minute 17 July 1945 FO371/47855/N9416.

41 Clark Kerr despatch 27 March 1945 FO371/47941/N3934.

42 Clark Kerr despatch 10 July 1945 FO371/47883/N8674.

43 Clark Kerr despatch 27 March 1945 FO371/47941/N3934.

44 Roberts to FO 21 April 1945 FO371/48928/R7704; Lockhart memorandum 11 April 1945 FO371/47860/N4102.

45 Clark Kerr despatch 27 March 1945 FO371/47941/N3934.

46 Roberts to Warner 25 April 1945 FO371/47882/N4919, 24 May 1945 FO371/47923/N6582.

47 Sargent memorandum 13 March 1945 FO371/48192/R7333.

48 Lockhart diary 1 April 1945.

49 Lockhart diary 18 March 1945, 31 March 1945; Lockhart's views reflected those of the Czechs; Benes was at this time also advocating plain and honest speaking, Lockhart diary 17 February 1945, 6 April 1945.

50 Lockhart diary 1 April 1945, memorandum 11 April 1945 FO371/47860/N4102.

51 Sargent papers 2 April 1945 FO371/47881/N4281, 17 April 1945 FO371/48192/R2956.

52 O'Malley to Sargent 22 May 1945, Sargent minute 31 May 1945 FO371/47882/N6645.

53 Sargent paper 11 July 1945: Jebb thought 'crude bargains' could not be avoided – and Britain after all wanted to keep the Soviets from meddling in France, Belgium and Holland, minute 20 July 1945 FO371/50912/U5471.

54   Wilson minute 18 April 1945 FO371/47853/N4044.
55   Howard minute 30 April 1945 FO371/48192/R7333.
56   Churchill to Roosevelt 5 April 1945 FO954/26C.
57   Churchill to Roosevelt 8 April 1945, Churchill to Truman 12 May 1945 FO954/26C.
58   Churchill conversation with TUC delegation 16 March 1945 FO371/47881/N3039.
59   Churchill to Truman 12 May 1945 FO954/26C.
60   Gilbert, *Road to Victory*, 1306, 1330.
61   Gilbert, *Road to Victory*, 1329, 1332, 1350.
62   Gilbert, *Road to Victory*, 1276, 1280, 1303; Churchill to Roosevelt 5 April 1945 FO954/26C; Churchill to Eden 4 May 1945 FO954/20; Admiral Cunningham noted that Churchill was now optimistically placing great faith in the bomb, and that he thought Soviet knowledge of the bomb's existence would make them more humble, M. Gilbert, *Never Despair* (London, 1988), 90; also Brooke diary 23 July 1945.
63   Gilbert, *Never Despair*, 75.
64   Gilbert, *Road to Victory*, 1350.
65   Churchill conversation with Gusev 18 May 1945 PREM3/396/12.
66   Eden diary 17 July 1945, R. Rhodes James, *Anthony Eden* (London, 1987), 307; Gilbert, *Never Despair*, 75.
67   Gilbert, *Road to Victory*, 1349; W. Kimball, *Forged in War. Roosevelt, Churchill, and the Second World War* (New York, 1997), 322.
68   Kitchen, *British Policy*, 262.
69   PHP(45)29(O) 29 June 1945 CAB81/46.
70   COS(45)116th 3 May 1945, JIC(45)163(O) 'Relations with the Russians' 23 May 1945, COS(45)134th 23 May 1945 CAB79/33; Sargent minute 17 May 1945, Eden to Churchill 1 June 1945 FO371/48192/R9256, R9257; cf. Kimball, *Juggler*, 173–6, 181–2.
71   Lockhart diary 6 April 1945.
72   D. Cameron Watt points out the difference between seeing the Soviets as difficult and seeing them as impossible, an important distinction that those who see any sign of disagreement as a proto-Cold War attitude tend to miss, 'Britain, the United States and the Opening of the Cold War', in R. Ovendale, ed., *The Foreign Policy of the British Labour Governments 1945–51* (Leicester, 1984), 50.

Chapter 7

1   Overy, *Russia's War*, 202–5, 272, 348, 389–91; B.F. Smith, *The War's Long Shadow. The Second World War and its Aftermath. China, Russia, Britain, America* (New York, 1986), 93, 95–6.
2   Thurston (Moscow) to Hull 20 March 1942, Atherton memo 9 December 1942 *FRUS1942*:III, 421, 205; Harriman to Roosevelt 5 July 1943 *FRUS1943*:III, 581n; memo by Division of Far Eastern Affairs 17 August 1943 *FR Washington & Quebec*, 627; Harriman to Hull 29 September 1944 RG59 711.61/9–2444.
3   Berle to Welles 3 April 1942, Welles to Berle 4 April 1942 RG59 741.61/

981–2; Standley to Hull 10 March 1943 *FRUS1943*:III, 510; Durbrow memo 3 February 1944, Stettinius memo 8 November 1944 *FRUS1944*:IV, 816, 1025; Hull to Roosevelt 17 June 1944, Roosevelt to Churchill 22 June 1944 *FRUS1944*:V, 124–5.

4 Welles memo 16 March 1943 *FRUS1943*:III, 22, and comments 25 June 1942 RG59 733.61/57; Hamilton to Hull 8 August 1944 *FRUS1944*:II, 347; Kekich memo 27 November 1944 RG59 741.6011/11–2744.

5 J. Kent, 'The British Empire and the Origins of the Cold War, 1944–49', in Deighton, ed., *Britain*, 166–7.

6 WP(42)516 8 November 1942 CAB66/30; Duff Cooper to Eden 30 May 1944 FO371/40696/U5407; Achilles memo of British attitudes to the USA and USSR 3 April 1943 RG59 740.0011/29067; Ross, 'Foreign Office Attitudes', 532, 538; A. Resis, review of Kitchen, *British Policy* in *Slavic Review* 47 (1988), 743.

7 A. Bullock, introduction to Rzheshevsky, *War and Diplomacy*, xix.

8 R. Overy, *Why the Allies Won* (London, 1995), 3, 254.

9 The wartime, as opposed to Cold War, mindset is illustrated in Strang's minute: 'It is better that Russia should dominate Eastern Europe than that Germany should dominate Western Europe. Nor would the domination of Eastern Europe by Russia be as easy as all that. And however strong Russia may become she is unlikely ever to be so grim a menace to us as Germany could be again within a few years...' 29 May 1943 FO371/35261/U2011.

10 D. Dilks, 'British Political Aims in Central, Eastern and Southern Europe, 1944', in Deakin, Barker and Chadwick, eds, *British Political*, 23–5.

11 Eden to Churchill 5 January 1942 FO371/32874/N108; Eden conversation with Roosevelt, Welles memorandum 16 March 1943 *FRUS1943*:III, 22. Kimball ascribes a similar sentiment to Roosevelt, *Juggler*, 183.

12 Clark Kerr despatch 31 August 1944 FO371/43336/N5598.

13 On 21 September 1943 Churchill said in the House of Commons: 'without the close, cordial and lasting association between Soviet Russia and the other great Allies, we might find ourselves at the end of the war only to have entered upon a period of deepening confusion', Hansard, *Debates*, 392/100.

14 Titkov, 'Soyuzniki-soperniki', 310–11. Titkov suggests the PHPS papers sent on by Maclean had the effect of a bombshell in Moscow at the end of 1944. Philby also fed such suspicions, Andrew and Gordievsky, *KGB*, 239.

15 Roberts to Warner 30 June 1945 FO371/47855/N9416.

Bibliography

Primary sources

1. Official documents

a) At the Public Record Office, Kew, London

ADM199	Naval Missions
ADM223	Naval Intelligence Division
AIR8	Chief of the Air Staff Papers
AIR40	Air Intelligence
AIR46	Air Missions
CAB21/1614	Cabinet Offices; UNO/Western Bloc papers
CAB65	War Cabinet Minutes
CAB66	War Cabinet Memoranda
CAB69	Defence Committee (Operations) Minutes
CAB79	Chiefs of Staff Committee Minutes
CAB80	Chiefs of Staff Committee Memoranda
CAB81	Joint Intelligence Committee Papers and Memoranda, Post Hostilities Planning Staff Minutes and Memoranda
CAB84	Joint Planning Staff Minutes and Memoranda
CAB87/2	Cabinet Committee on Reconstruction Problems 1942
CAB98/18	Committee on Communist Activities
CAB99	Papers from International Conferences
CAB118	Lord President Files (Attlee)
CAB119	Joint Planning Staff: various papers, including Military Sub-Committee
CAB120	Cabinet Secretariat
CAB122	British Joint Staff Mission, Washington
CAB127	Private Office Papers; Cripps, Ismay, Bridges
FO181	Moscow/Kuibyshev Embassy
FO371	Political Departments; General Correspondence
FO418	FO Confidential Print: Russia and Soviet Union to 1941
FO490	FO Confidential Print: Soviet Union 1942–45
FO800	Private Papers: Clark Kerr, Halifax, Sargent
FO954	Avon Papers
FO837	Ministry of Economic Warfare
FO898	Political Warfare Executive
HS4	Special Operations Executive: USSR Section
INF1	Ministry of Information: Home Policy Committee, Soviet Relations Division, Home Intelligence Reports
PREM3	Prime Minister Papers: Operational Papers
PREM4	Prime Minister Papers: Confidential Papers
T188	Leith-Ross Papers
WO178	War Diaries, Military Missions

WO202	Military Missions: Russian Liaison Group
WO204	Allied Forces Headquarters
WO208	Directorate of Military Intelligence
WO216	Chief of the Imperial General Staff Papers

b) At US National Archives, College Park, Maryland

Record Group 59, State Department Papers
  711 USA–USSR Relations
  740 European War, 1939–45
  741 Anglo-Soviet Relations
  761 Anglo-American-Soviet Relations
  861 USSR – Internal Affairs

2. Private papers

Alanbrooke (Imperial War Museum and Liddell Hart Centre)
A.V. Alexander (Churchill College)
Archer (Imperial War Museum)
Attlee (Churchill College)
Avon (Birmingham University)
Balfour of Inchrye (House of Lords)
Beaverbrook (House of Lords)
Bevin (Churchill College)
Brabazon of Tara (RAF Museum)
Dalton (British Library of Political and Economic Science)
Davidson (Liddell Hart Centre)
Gammell (Imperial War Museum)
Gedye (Imperial War Museum)
P.J. Grigg (Churchill College)
Hankey (Churchill College)
Harriman (Library of Congress)
Harvey (British Library)
Inverchapel (Bodleian Library)
Ismay (Liddell Hart Centre)
Knatchbull-Hugessen (Churchill College)
Liddell Hart (Liddell Hart Centre)
Lyttelton (Churchill College)
Margesson (Churchill College)
Martel (Imperial War Museum)
Mason-Macfarlane (Imperial War Museum)
Page Croft (Churchill College)
Sinclair (Churchill College)

3. Published collections

British Documents of Foreign Affairs: Reports and Papers from the FO Confidential Print Part II Series A The Soviet Union 1919–39
Foreign Relations of the United States, 1940–45 (Washington DC, 1957–69)

W. Kimball, ed., *Churchill and Roosevelt: the Complete Correspondence*, 3 vols (Princeton, 1984)

A. Polonsky, ed., *The Great Powers and the Polish Question, 1941–45* (London, 1976)

K.G. Ross, *The Foreign Office and the Kremlin* (Cambridge, 1984)

O.A. Rzheshevsky, *War and Diplomacy. The Making of the Grand Alliance. From Stalin's Archives* (trans. T. Sorokina, Amsterdam, 1996)

4. Published diaries

B. Bond, ed., *Chief of Staff. The Diaries of Lieutenant-General Sir Henry Pownall* (London, 1974)

A. Bryant, ed., *Turn of the Tide* (London, 1957)

A. Bryant, ed., *Triumph in the West* (London, 1959)

J. Colville, *The Fringes of Power. Downing Street Diaries*, 2 vols (London, 1985)

D. Dilks, ed., *The Diaries of Sir Alexander Cadogan, 1938–46* (London, 1971)

P. Dixon, ed., *Double Diploma. The Life of Sir Pierson Dixon* (London, 1968)

J. Harvey, ed., *The Diplomatic Diaries of Oliver Harvey* (London, 1970)

J. Harvey, ed., *The War Diaries of Oliver Harvey* (London, 1978)

K. Jeffreys, ed., *Labour and the Wartime Coalition. From the Diary of James Chuter Ede, 1941–45* (London, 1987)

H. Macmillan, *War Diaries. The Mediterranean, 1943–45* (London, 1984)

Lord Moran, *Winston Churchill. The Struggle for Survival 1940–65* (London, 1966)

N. Nicolson, ed., *Harold Nicolson. Diaries and Letters*, vol. 2 1939–45 (London, 1967)

B. Pimlott, ed., *The Political Diary of Hugh Dalton 1918–40, 1945–60* (London, 1986)

B. Pimlott, ed., *The Second World War Diary of Hugh Dalton, 1940–45* (London, 1986)

R. Rhodes James, ed., *'Chips': The Diaries of Sir Henry Channon* (London, 1967)

K. Young, ed., *The Diaries of Sir Robert Bruce Lockhart 1939–65* (London, 1980)

5. Memoirs and autobiographies

Lord Attlee, *As It Happened* (London, 1964)

Lord Attlee, *Granada Historical Records Interview* (Manchester, 1965)

Lord Avon, *The Reckoning* (London, 1965)

H. Balfour, *Wings over Westminster* (London, 1973)

J. Balfour, *Not Too Correct an Aureole* (Salisbury, 1983)

T. Barman, *Diplomatic Correspondent* (London, 1968)

E. Berthoud, *An Unexpected Life* (Tiptree, 1980)

A. Birse, *Memoirs of an Interpreter* (London, 1967)

R. Bruce Lockhart, *Comes the Reckoning* (London, 1947)

R.A. Butler, *The Art of the Possible* (London, 1971)

R.A. Butler, *The Art of Memory* (London, 1982)

W.S. Churchill, *The Second World War*, 6 vols (London, 1948–54)

Lord Cunningham, *A Sailor's Odyssey: The Autobiography of Admiral of the Fleet Viscount Cunningham of Hyndhope* (London, 1951)

H. Dalton, *The Fateful Years: Memoirs 1931–45* (London, 1957)

J.R. Deane, *The Strange Alliance. The Story of Our Efforts at Wartime Co-operation with Russia* (London, 1947)

M. Djilas, *Conversations with Stalin* (New York, 1962)

D. Farrer, *G for God Almighty* (London, 1969)

Lord Gladwyn, *The Memoirs of Lord Gladwyn* (London, 1972)

L. Gourlay, ed., *The Beaverbrook I Knew* (London, 1984)

P.J. Grigg, *Prejudice and Judgement* (London, 1948)

Lord Halifax, *Fulness of Days* (London, 1957)

A. Harriman and E. Abel, *Special Envoy to Churchill and Stalin* (London, 1976)

Lord Ismay, *Memoirs of General the Lord Ismay* (London, 1960)

J. Kennedy, *The Business of War* (London, 1957)

I. Kirkpatrick, *The Inner Circle* (London, 1959)

J. Leasor, *War at the Top. The Experiences of General Sir Leslie Hollis* (London, 1959)

F. Maclean, *Eastern Approaches* (London, 1949)

H. Macmillan, *The Blast of War* (London, 1967)

I. Maisky, *Memoirs of a Soviet Ambassador* (London, 1967)

G. Martel, *An Outspoken Soldier* (London, 1949)

H. Morrison, *Autobiography* (London, 1960)

G. Pawle, *The War and Colonel Warden* (London, 1963)

F.K. Roberts, *Dealing with Dictators* (London, 1991)

W. Strang, *Home and Abroad* (London, 1956)

K.W.D. Strong, *Intelligence at the Top: The Recollections of an Intelligence Officer* (London, 1968)

Lord Tedder, *With Prejudice: The War Memoirs of Marshal of the Air Force Lord Tedder* (London, 1966)

G.M. Thomson, *Vote of Censure* (London, 1968)

F. Williams, *A Prime Minister Remembers: The War and Post-War Memoirs of the Rt Hon Earl Attlee* (London, 1961)

J. Wheeler-Bennett, ed., *Action this Day. Working with Churchill* (London, 1968)

Secondary sources

1. Biographies

S. Aster, *Anthony Eden* (London, 1976)

R. Barclay, *Ernest Bevin and the Foreign Office* (London, 1975)

Lord Birkenhead, *Halifax* (London, 1965)

A. Bullock, *The Life and Times of Ernest Bevin vol. 2, Minister of Labour* (London, 1967)

A. Bullock, *Ernest Bevin Foreign Secretary* (London, 1983)

T.D. Burridge, *Clement Attlee: A Political Biography* (London, 1985)

E. Butler, *Mason Mac* (London, 1972)

D. Carlton, *Anthony Eden* (London, 1982)

J. Charmley, *Churchill. The End of Glory* (London, 1993)

A. Chisholm and M. Davie, *Beaverbrook. A Life* (London, 1992)

R. Churchill, *The Rise and Fall of Sir Anthony Eden* (London, 1959)

C. Cooke, *The Life of Richard Stafford Cripps* (London, 1957)

P. Cosgrave, *R.A. Butler: An English Life* (London, 1981)

B. Donoghue and W. Jones, *Herbert Morrison, Portrait of a Politician* (London, 1973)

E. Estorick, *Stafford Cripps. A Biography* (London, 1949)

K. Feiling, *The Life of Neville Chamberlain* (London, 1970)

D. Fraser, *Alanbrooke* (London, 1982)

M. Gilbert, *Winston S. Churchill*, vol. 5 1922–39 (London, 1976)

M. Gilbert, *Finest Hour. Winston S. Churchill 1939–41* (London, 1983)

M. Gilbert, *Road to Victory* (London, 1986)

M. Gilbert, *Never Despair* (London, 1988)

D. Gillies, *Radical Diplomat. The Life of Archibald Clark Kerr, Lord Inverchapel, 1882–1951* (London, 1999)

K. Harris, *Attlee* (London, 1982)

P. Howarth, *Intelligence Chief Extraordinary. The Life of the Ninth Duke of Portland* (London, 1986)

G. MacDermott, *The Eden Legacy and the Decline of British Diplomacy* (London, 1969)

I. Macleod, *Neville Chamberlain* (London, 1961)

F. McLynn, *Fitzroy Maclean* (London, 1992)

B. Pimlott, *Hugh Dalton* (London, 1985)

R. Rhodes James, *Anthony Eden* (London, 1987)

E. Radzinsky, *Stalin* (London, 1996)

D. Richards, *Lord Portal of Hungerford* (London, 1977)

C. Richardson, *From Churchill's Secret Circle to the BBC. The Biography of Lieutenant-General Sir Ian Jacob* (London, 1991)

A.J.P. Taylor, *Beaverbrook* (London, 1972)

A.J.P. Taylor et al., *Churchill. Four Faces and the Man* (London, 1979)

D. Volkogonov, *Stalin, Triumph and Tragedy* (ed. & trans. H. Shukman, London, 1991)

F. Williams, *Ernest Bevin* (London, 1952)

R. Wingate, *Lord Ismay* (London, 1970)

2. Monographs and General Historical Studies

T.H. Anderson, *The United States, Great Britain and the Cold War, 1944–47* (Columbia, Missouri, 1981)

L. Aronsen and M. Kitchen, *The Origins of the Cold War in Comparative Perspective* (London, 1988)

M. Balfour, *Propaganda in War, 1939–45: Organizations, Policies and Politics in Britain and Germany* (London, 1979)

J. Barber and M. Harrison, *The Soviet Home Front 1941–1945. A Social and Economic History of the USSR in World War II* (Harlow, 1991)

E. Barker, *The British between the Superpowers* (London, 1983)

E. Barker, *British Policy in South-East Europe in the Second World War* (London, 1976)

E. Barker, *Churchill and Eden at War* (London, 1978)

J.E. Beaumont, *Comrades in Arms* (London, 1980)

P.M.H. Bell, *John Bull and the Bear. British Public Opinion, Foreign Policy and the Soviet Union, 1941–45* (London, 1990)

N. Bethell, *The Last Secret* (London, 1974)

C. G. Bolté, *The Soviet Question in British Politics* (New York, 1989)

A. Boyle, *Climate of Treason* (revised edition, London, 1980)

T.D. Burridge, *British Labour and Hitler's War* (London, 1976)

D. Caute, *The Fellow-Travellers* (London, 1973)

J. Charmley, *Churchill's Grand Alliance* (London, 1996)

W. and Z. Coates, *The History of Anglo-Soviet Relations, 1917–1950*, 2 vols (London, 1943 and 1958)

R. Deacon, *The British Connection* (London, 1979)

W. Deakin, E. Barker and J. Chadwick, eds, *British Political and Military Strategy in Central, Eastern and Southern Europe in 1944* (London, 1988)

A. Deighton, ed., *Britain and the First Cold War* (London, 1990)

D. Dilks, ed., *Retreat from Power: Studies in Britain's Foreign Policy in the Twentieth Century*, vol. 2 (London, 1981)

R. Douglas, *From War to Cold War, 1942–48* (London, 1981)

R. Edmonds, *The Big Three* (London, 1991)

J. Erickson, *The Soviet High Command. A Military-Political History, 1918–41* (London, 1962)

J. Erickson and D. Dilks, eds, *Barbarossa. The Axis and the Allies* (Edinburgh, 1994)

H. Feis, *Churchill, Roosevelt, Stalin: The War They Waged and the Peace They Sought* (Princeton, 1957)

A. Glees, *The Secrets of the Service: British Intelligence and Communist Subversion, 1939–51* (London, 1987)

J. Golley, *Hurricanes over Murmansk* (London, 1987)

M.R. Gordon, *Conflict and Consensus in Labour's Foreign Policy, 1914–65* (Stanford, 1969)

G. Gorodetsky, *Stafford Cripps Mission to Moscow 1940–42* (Cambridge, 1984)

E. Grigg, *British Foreign Policy* (London, 1944)

F. Harbutt, *The Iron Curtain; Churchill, America and the Origins of the Cold War* (New York, 1986)

F.H. Hinsley et al., *The History of British Intelligence in World War Two*, 5 vols (1979–90)

M. Howard, *The Mediterranean Strategy in the Second World War* (London, 1968)

W. Jones, *The Russia Complex* (Manchester, 1977)

G. Kacewicz, *Great Britain, The Soviet Union and the Polish Government in Exile* (The Hague, 1979)

C. Keeble, *Britain and the Soviet Union, 1917–1989* (London, 1990)

C. Kennedy-Pipe, *Stalin's Cold War. Soviet Strategies in Europe, 1943–1956* (Manchester, 1995)

L. Kettenacker and W. Mommsen, eds, *The Fascist Challenge and the Policy of Appeasement* (London, 1983)

W.F. Kimball, *Forged in War. Roosevelt, Churchill and the Second World War* (New York, 1997)

W.F. Kimball, *The Juggler. Franklin Roosevelt as Wartime Statesman* (Princeton, 1991)

M. Kitchen, *British Policy Towards the Soviet Union During the Second World War* (London, 1986)

A. Lane and H. Temperley, eds, *The Rise and Fall of the Grand Alliance* (Basingstoke, 1995)

J.M. Lee, *The Churchill Coalition* (London, 1980)

J.M. Lewis, *Changing Direction: British Military Planning for Post-war Strategic Defence 1942–47* (London, 1988)

S.J. Linz, ed., *The Impact of World War II on the Soviet Union* (New Jersey, 1985)

I. McLaine, *Ministry of Morale: Home Front Morale and the Ministry of Information in World War II* (London, 1979)

W.H. McNeill, *America, Britain and Russia: Their Cooperation and Conflict, 1941–46* (London, 1953)

V. Mastny, *The Cold War and Soviet Insecurity. The Stalin Years* (New York, 1996)

V. Mastny, *Russia's Road to the Cold War. Diplomacy, Warfare and the Politics of Communism, 1941–45* (New York, 1979)

S.M. Miner, *Between Churchill and Stalin* (Chapel Hill, 1988)

F.S. Northedge and A. Wells, *Britain and Soviet Communism. The Impact of A Revolution* (London, 1982)

R.J. Overy, *Russia's War. Blood upon the Snow* (New York, 1997)

R.J. Overy, *Why the Allies Won* (London, 1995)

K. Pilarski, ed., *Soviet–US Relations, 1933–45* (Moscow, 1989)

C. Porter and M. Jones, *Moscow in World War II* (London, 1987)

V. Rothwell, *Britain and the Cold War, 1941–47* (London, 1982)

K. Sainsbury, *Churchill and Roosevelt at War: the War they Fought and the Peace they Hoped to Make* (London, 1994)

K. Sainsbury, *The Turning Point. Roosevelt, Stalin, Churchill and Chiang Kai-Shek, 1943 – the Moscow, Cairo and Tehran Conferences* (Oxford, 1985)

C.S. Samra, *India and Anglo-Soviet Relations* (New York, 1959)

T. Sharp, *The Wartime Alliance and the Zonal Division of Germany* (London, 1975)

V.A. Sipols, *The Road to Great Victory, 1941–45* (Moscow, 1985)

B.F. Smith, *Sharing Secrets with Stalin. How the Allies Traded Intelligence, 1941–1945* (Kansas, 1996)

N. Tolstoy, *Stalin's Secret War* (London, 1983)

N. Tolstoy, *Victims of Yalta* (London, 1977)

D. Cameron Watt, *Personalities and Policies* (London, 1965)

A. Werth, *Russia at War 1941–45* (New York, 1964)

P. Winterton, *Report on Russia* (London, 1945)

N. Wood, *Communism and British Intellectuals* (London, 1959)

E.L. Woodward, *British Foreign Policy in World War Two*, 5 vols (1970–76)

D. Yergin, *Shattered Peace. The Origins of the Cold War and the National Security State* (Boston, 1977)

K. Young, *Beaverbrook and Churchill. A Study in Friendship and Politics* (London, 1966)

J. Zametica, ed., *British Officials and Foreign Policy, 1945–50* (Leicester, 1990)

V. Zubok and C. Pleshakov, *Inside the Kremlin's Cold War. From Stalin to Khrushchev* (Harvard, 1996)